LITERATURE ⊞
Uses of the Imagination

The suggestions of reviewers have aided us in our final preparation of materials for this book. We gratefully acknowledge the critical assistance of:

James Ackerman
Indiana University
Bloomington, Indiana

Melvin Merzon
Oak Park High School
Oak Park, Michigan

Rita Smith
Newport Senior High School
Bellevue, Washington

Georg von Tiesenhausen
Huntsville High School
Huntsville, Alabama

ALVIN A. LEE

Professor of English
McMaster University
Hamilton, Ontario, Canada

HOPE ARNOTT LEE

Formerly, teacher, grades 7–12
Dundas, Ontario, Canada

The Garden and the Wilderness

Supervisory Editor
NORTHROP FRYE

University Professor
University of Toronto

General Editor
W. T. JEWKES

Professor of English
The Pennsylvania State University

HARCOURT BRACE JOVANOVICH, INC.

New York   Chicago   San Francisco   Atlanta   Dallas

ISBN 0-15-333510-6

ACKNOWLEDGMENTS: *For permission to reprint copyrighted material, grateful acknowledgment is made to the following sources:*

Cambridge University Press: Excerpts from Genesis, Exodus, Numbers, and Deuteronomy from *The New English Bible,* copyright © The Delegates of the Oxford University Press and the Syndics of the Cambridge University Press 1961, 1970.

William Childress: "The Dreamer" by William Childress from *Harper's Magazine,* March 1966, copyright 1966, by Minneapolis Star and Tribune Co., Inc.

The Devin-Adair Company: "The Fairy Goose" from *The Stories of Liam O'Flaherty,* copyright 1956 by The Devin-Adair Company.

The Dial Press, Inc.: "My Dungeon Shook" from *The Fire Next Time* by James Baldwin, copyright © 1962, 1963 by James Baldwin.

Norma Millay Ellis, Literary Executor: "The Broken Dike, The Levee Washed Away" from *Collected Poems* by Edna St. Vincent Millay, Harper & Row, copyright 1934, 1962 by Edna St. Vincent Millay and Norma Millay Ellis.

Farrar, Straus & Giroux, Inc.: "The Strong Ones" from *A Day of Pleasure* by Isaac Bashevis Singer, copyright © 1963, 1965, 1966, 1969 by Isaac Bashevis Singer.

Funk & Wagnalls Publishing Company, Inc.: Excerpt from *Indian Masks & Myths of the West* by Joseph H. Wherry (retitled: "Why Coyote Always Howls"), copyright © 1969 by Joseph H. Wherry.

Harcourt Brace Jovanovich, Inc.: "Between Worlds" from *Good Morning, America* by Carl Sandburg, copyright, 1928, 1956, by Carl Sandburg.

David Higham Associates, Ltd.: "The History of the Flood" from *The Bluefly in His Head* by John Heath-Stubbs, published by Oxford University Press.

Holt, Rinehart and Winston, Inc.: "The Draft Horse" from *The Poetry of Robert Frost* edited by Edward Connery Lathem, copyright © 1962 by Robert Frost; copyright © 1969 by Holt, Rinehart and Winston, Inc.

The illustrations on pages xvi–1, 46–47, 152–153, 212–213, and 248–249 are by Corita Kent.

COVER: "The Equatorial Jungle" (detail) by Henri Rousseau, Chester Dale Collection, National Gallery of Art, Washington, D. C.

Contents

My Brother's Keeper?

2   The Flood and the Dawn of History

The Windows of the Sky Were Opened

God Spoke to Noah

While the Earth Lasts

3   Father of a Multitude

Promise

4   Joseph, That Dreamer

5 To Set the People Free

Introduction

The Bible is a book that tells a story. Unlike other books we read, either inside or outside the classroom, the Old and New Testaments tell a complete story of man, beginning with the Creation of the world and concluding with a revelation of the end of the world. The Jewish Bible consists of what Jewish people themselves call simply the Bible or Scripture. It includes the Law, the Prophets, and the Writings. The Christian Bible consists of the Jewish Bible (the Old Testament) plus the New Testament. Each group's Bible ends with a vision of doomsday and the coming of a Messiah, that is, a savior or deliverer.

In the Old and New Testaments, we have the story of man, Adam, and the story of a people, Israel. In the New Testament, Jesus is called a second Adam, and is believed by his followers to be the Messiah whose coming was prophesied in the Old Testament. Christian biblical writers thus continue the story begun in the earlier parts of the Bible and see man (Adam) and the people chosen of God (Israel) as rescued by Jesus from the wilderness in which they have been lost. Jewish readers see the Old Testament account of the Exodus from Egypt and the return from captivity in Babylon as the great divine acts of rescue. In addition, they look to the coming of their Messiah at some future time.

The shape of the Bible stretches from the beginning to the end of time. In its first book, Genesis, we read of a man created in the image of God. He is placed in a garden which includes a tree of life and a flowing river. Hundreds of pages later, in the last book, Revelation, we read again of that same river and that same tree. Adam and Eve, we recall, were banished from their garden, Eden, for disobeying God's command, yet the writer of Revelation sees the river and tree of Eden as symbols of the Creator's triumph over all evil in the universe. Now, at the end of the story, whoever wishes may drink freely of the water of life. The leaves of the tree are for the healing of the nations of the world.

Adam and Eve stand for all human beings. Each reader of the Bible is invited to take part in a metaphor, to see himself or herself as Adam or Eve. The Bible addresses us as exiles from our original home, the garden of Eden. The human longing for a better world than the one we inhabit is presented in the Bible as a homesick urge to get back to the

Promised Land or to enter the New Jerusalem of heaven. As we read the Bible, then, we identify ourselves as individuals with Adam and Eve, or as groups with the people of Israel. In so doing, we learn something more of who we are and of what it means to be human.

This great story has within it many complex parts—fragments of history, law codes, moral systems, stories, poems, prophecies, philosophies, visions, wise sayings, letters—but the main structure or outline is simple. It can be seen as a completed circle which first moves downward from the garden of Eden into the wilderness of human history, and then slowly and painfully back to the starting point, as man proceeds toward Eden restored or the New Jerusalem.

The Bible offers its readers an experience of the most complete account of man's life that exists in western civilization. Its imaginative structure has shaped the world we live in: our literature and art, many of our laws and moral beliefs, some of our sense of scientific cause and effect, and three of our great religions, Judaism, Christianity, and Islam.

The book you are about to read is not the Bible but an anthology of selected biblical writings combined with nonbiblical literary selections. The study of literature is concerned primarily with the human imagination as it is expressed in such writings, and as it reaches out to something inside each one of you. The many nonbiblical pieces of literature will help you, here and now, to sense the immediate power and importance of the Bible as literature for our own time and place in history. Remember this book is prepared for you as students of literature, not as students of history or religion. The Bible has enormous importance historically and as a sacred book, but it is also literature, with a central place in any serious study of the works of the human imagination. We hope that in years to come you will be stimulated to move from this volume and its companions to the Bible itself, and that some of you will even study the ancient languages of Hebrew and Greek as paths to the rich absorbing writings found there.

A. A. L.
H. A. L.

The Garden and the Wilderness

1 : Creation and Fall

corita

ALL THAT HE HAD MADE

The Creation of the World

In the beginning of creation, when God made heaven and earth, the earth was without form and void, with darkness over the face of the abyss, and a mighty wind that swept over the surface of the waters. God said, "Let there be light," and there was light; and God saw that the light was good, and he separated light from darkness. He called the light day, and the darkness night. So evening came, and morning came, the first day.

God said, "Let there be a vault between the waters, to separate water from water." So God made the vault, and separated the water under the vault from the water above it, and so it was; and God called the vault heaven. Evening came, and morning came, a second day.

God said, "Let the waters under heaven be gathered into one place, so that dry land may appear"; and so it was. God called the dry land earth, and the gathering of the waters he called seas; and God saw that it was good. Then God said, "Let the earth produce fresh growth, let there be on the earth plants bearing seed, fruit trees bearing fruit each with seed according to its kind." So it was; the earth yielded fresh growth, plants bearing seed according to their kind and trees bearing fruit each with seed according to its kind; and God saw that it was good. Evening came, and morning came, a third day.

God said, "Let there be lights in the vault of heaven to separate day from night, and let them serve as signs both for festivals and for seasons and years. Let them also shine in the vault of heaven to give light on earth." So it was; God made the two great lights, the greater to govern the day and the lesser to govern the night; and with them he made the stars. God put these lights in the vault of heaven to give light on earth, to govern day and night, and to separate light from darkness; and God saw that it was good. Evening came, and morning came, a fourth day.

God said, "Let the waters teem with countless living creatures, and let birds fly above the earth across the vault of heaven." God then created the great sea monsters and all living creatures that move and swarm in the waters, according to their kind, and every kind of bird; and God saw that it was good. So he blessed them and said, "Be fruitful and increase, fill the waters of the seas; and let the birds increase on land." Evening came, and morning came, a fifth day.

God said, "Let the earth bring forth living creatures, according to their kind: cattle, reptiles, and wild animals, all according to their kind." So it was; God made wild animals, cattle, and all reptiles, each according to its kind; and he saw that it was good. Then God said, "Let us make man in our image and likeness to rule the fish in the sea, the birds of heaven, the cattle, all wild animals on earth, and all reptiles that crawl upon the earth." So God created man in his own image; in the image of God he created him; male and female he created them. God blessed them and said to them, "Be fruitful and increase, fill the earth and subdue it, rule over the fish in the sea, the birds of heaven, and every living thing that moves upon the earth." God also said, "I give you all plants that bear seed everywhere on earth, and every tree bearing fruit which yields seed: they shall be yours for food. All green plants I give for food to the wild animals, to all the birds of heaven, and to all reptiles on earth, every living creature." So it was; and God saw all that he had made, and it was very good. Evening came, and morning came, a sixth day.

Thus heaven and earth were completed with all their mighty throng. On the sixth day God completed all the work he had been doing, and on the seventh day he ceased from all his work. God blessed the seventh day and made it holy, because on that day he ceased from all the work he had set himself to do.

This is the story of the making of heaven and earth when they were created.

GENESIS 1; 2:1–4

In what way do we pattern our time so that it imitates the creation story?

What actions described in this story are still happening?

He's Got the Whole World in His Hand

1. He's got the whole_____ world in his hand, He's got the
2. He's got the wind and the rain in his hand, He's got the
3. He's got the gamb-ling man in his hand, He's got the

1. great big world in his hand. He's got the
2. stars and the moon in his hand. He's got the
3. ly - ing man in his hand. He's got the

1. whole _____ world in his hand, He's got the whole world in his hand.
2. wind and the rain in his hand, He's got the whole world in his hand.
3. crap - shoot - in' man in his hand, He's got the whole world in his hand.

4. He's got the little bits of babies in his hand,
He's got the little bits of babies in his hand,
He's got the little bits of babies in his hand,
He's got the whole world in his hand.

5. He's got you and me, brother, in his hand,
   He's got you and me, sister, in his hand,
   He's got you and me, brother, in his hand,
   He's got the whole world in his hand.

6. Well, he's got everybody in his hand,
   He's got everybody in his hand,
   He's got everybody here right in his hand,
   He's got the whole world in his hand.

In what way does this song reflect the biblical creation story?

Try adding additional verses to the song so that it relates even more closely to the biblical account, for example, "He's got the dark and the light in His hand" or "He's got the cattle and the snakes . . ."

Why is the substitution of a baby for a man appropriate for this song?

How does this song make it apparent that the events of the Bible can be thought of as being outside history (that is, always happening)?

The Days

Issuing from the Word
The seven days came,
Each in its own place,
Its own name.
And the first long days
A hard and rocky spring,
Inhuman burgeoning,
And nothing there for claw or hand,
Vast loneliness ere loneliness began,
Where the blank seasons in their journeying
Saw water at play with water and sand with sand.

The waters stirred
And from the doors were cast
Wild lights and shadows on the formless face
Of the flood of chaos, vast
Lengthening and dwindling image of earth and heaven.
The forest's green shadow
Softly over the water driven,
As if the earth's green wonder, endless meadow
Floated and sank within its own green light.
In water and night
Sudden appeared the lion's violent head,
Raging and burning in its watery cave.
The stallion's tread
Soundlessly fell on the flood, and the animals poured
Onward, flowing across the flowing wave.
Then on the waters fell
The shadow of man, and earth and the heavens scrawled
With names, as if each pebble and leaf would tell
The tale untellable. And the Lord called
The seventh day forth and the glory of the Lord.

And now we see in the sun
The mountains standing clear in the third day
(Where they shall always stay)
And thence a river run,
Threading, clear cord of water, all to all:
The wooded hill and the cattle in the meadow,
The tall wave breaking on the high sea wall,
The people at evening walking,
The crescent shadow
Of the light-built bridge, the hunter stalking
The flying quarry, each in a different morning,
The fish in the billow's heart, the man with the net,
The hungry swords crossed in the cross of warning,
The lion set
High on the banner, leaping into the sky,
The seasons playing
Their game of sun and moon and east and west,
The animal watching man and bird go by,
The women praying
For the passing of this fragmentary day
Into the day where all are gathered together,
Things and their names, in the storm's and the lightning's nest,
The seventh great day and the clear eternal weather.

EDWIN MUIR

What is the "fragmentary day" that the poet describes?

What, in contrast, is the "seventh day" for Muir?

The Earth So Fine

Upon what base was fixed the lathe wherein
He turned this globe and riggaled it so trim?
Who blew the bellows of his furnace vast?
Or held the mold wherein the world was cast?
Who laid its cornerstone? Or whose command?
Where stand the pillars upon which it stands?
Who laced and filleted the earth so fine
With rivers like green ribbons smaragdine?
Who made the seas its selvedge, and it locks
Like a quilt ball within a silver box?
Who spread its canopy? Or curtains spun?
Who in this bowling alley bowled the sun?
Who made it always when it rises, set:
To go at once both down and up to get?
Who the curtain rods made for this tapestry?
Who hung the twinkling lanthorns in the sky?
Who? who did this? or who is he? Why, know
It's only Might Almighty this did do.
His hand hath made this noble work which stands
His glorious handiwork not made by hands.

EDWARD TAYLOR

When Edward Taylor wrote this poem about the Creation, he used images from the world he was familiar with—colonial New England. The *lathe* here is a potter's lathe, or wheel, a revolving circular disc. To *wriggle* it is to give the completing touches. *Smaragdine* is an old word referring to green gems like the emerald. *Selvedge* is the border of a fabric which keeps it from being unraveled. Now that you are more familiar with the tools and instruments of the craftsmen of Taylor's colonial period, look back at the poem to discover images which suggest that the poet sees God as a blacksmith, an architect, a tailor. Are there other vocations suggested for God in this poem?

Psalm 8

O Lord our Lord,
How excellent is thy name in all the earth!
Who hast set thy glory above the heavens.
Out of the mouth of babes and sucklings hast thou ordained strength
Because of thine enemies,
That thou mightest still the enemy and the avenger.
When I consider thy heavens, the work of thy fingers,
The moon and the stars, which thou hast ordained;
What is man, that thou art mindful of him?
And the son of man, that thou visitest him?
For thou hast made him a little lower than the angels,
And hast crowned him with glory and honor.
Thou madest him to have dominion over the works of thy hands;
Thou hast put all things under his feet:
All sheep and oxen,
Yea, and the beasts of the field;
The fowl of the air, and the fish of the sea,
And whatsoever passeth through the paths of the seas.
O Lord our Lord,
How excellent is thy name in all the earth!

Make a diagram of the Creation as it is described in this psalm, beginning with the Lord at the top, then the heavens, and so on down the scale. What is special about the location of man in this diagram? Does his place in the Creation suggest to you that the psalmist thought man had a special "nature" even though in some way he is part of nature?

———————————

What characteristics of God do the three nonbiblical selections stress?

Imagine yourself as an inhabitant of a planet in a galaxy outside this one. Write a brief account (either prose or poetry) of the creation of your world.

IN EDEN AWAY TO THE EAST

The Garden of Eden

When the Lord God made earth and heaven, there was neither shrub nor plant growing wild upon the earth, because the Lord God had sent no rain on the earth; nor was there any man to till the ground. A flood used to rise out of the earth and water all the surface of the ground. Then the Lord God formed a man from the dust of the ground and breathed into his nostrils the breath of life. Thus the man became a living creature. Then the Lord God planted a garden in Eden away to the east, and there he put the man whom he had formed. The Lord God made trees spring from the ground, all trees pleasant to look at and good for food; and in the middle of the garden he set the tree of life and the tree of the knowledge of good and evil.

There was a river flowing from Eden to water the garden, and when it left the garden it branched into four streams. The name of the first is Pishon; that is the river which encircles all the land of Havilah, where the gold is. The gold of that land is good; bdellium and cornelians are also to be found there. The name of the second river is Gihon; this is the one which encircles all the land of Cush. The name of the third is Tigris; this is the river which runs east of Asshur. The fourth river is the Euphrates.

The Lord God took the man and put him in the garden of Eden to till it and care for it. He told the man, "You may eat from every tree in the garden, but not from the tree of the knowledge of good and evil; for on the day that you eat from it, you will certainly die." Then the Lord God said, "It is not good for the man to be alone. I will provide a partner for him." So God formed out of the ground all the wild animals and all the birds of heaven. He brought them to the man to see what he would call them, and whatever the man called each living creature, that was its name. Thus the man gave names to all cattle, to the birds of heaven, and to every wild animal; but for the man himself no partner had yet been found. And so the Lord God put the man into a trance, and while he slept, he took one of his ribs and closed the flesh over the place. The Lord God then built up the rib, which he had taken out of the man, into a woman. He brought her to the man, and the man said:

> "Now this, at last—
> bone from my bones,
> flesh from my flesh!—
> this shall be called woman,
> for from man was this taken."

That is why a man leaves his father and mother and is united to his wife, and the two become one flesh. Now they were both naked, the man and his wife, but they had no feeling of shame toward one another.

GENESIS 2 : 5–25

The Hebrew word *Adam* means "a man" and is related to the word *adamah,* "ground, soil." The word for woman is *ishshah,* which means "from man."

What kind of world has God created for Adam and Eve in the garden of Eden? What human desires are fulfilled there?

According to this story, man is formed from the dust of the earth and the breath of life given him by God. What does this suggest about human nature?

Why, on the day that man eats from the tree of the knowledge of good and evil, will he certainly die? What does this suggest to you about human nature?

The Tyger

Tyger! Tyger! burning bright
In the forests of the night,
What immortal hand or eye
Could frame thy fearful symmetry?

In what distant deeps or skies
Burnt the fire of thine eyes?
On what wings dare he aspire?
What the hand dare seize the fire?

And what shoulder, & what art,
Could twist the sinews of thy heart?
And when thy heart began to beat,
What dread hand? & what dread feet?

What the hammer? what the chain?
In what furnace was thy brain?
What the anvil? what dread grasp
Dare its deadly terrors clasp?

When the stars threw down their spears,
And water'd heaven with their tears,
Did he smile his work to see?
Did he who made the Lamb make thee?

Tyger! Tyger! burning bright
In the forests of the night,
What immortal hand or eye,
Dare frame thy fearful symmetry?

WILLIAM BLAKE

Why do you think the speaker asks, about the tiger, "Did he who made the Lamb make thee?" What is suggested about the range of God's creation?

Morning Has Broken

ELEANOR FARJEON, CAT STEVENS

1. (4.) Morn - ing has bro - ken like the first morn - ing,
2. Sweet the rain's new fall, sun - lit from heav - en,
3. Mine is the sun - light, Mine is the morn - ing,

1. Black - bird has spo - ken like the first bird.
2. Like the first dew - fall on the first grass.
3. Born of the one light E - den saw play.

1. Praise for the sing - ing, Praise for the morn - ing,
2. Praise for the sweet - ness of the wet gar - den,
3. Praise with e - la - tion, Praise ev - 'ry morn - ing,

1. Praise for them spring - ing fresh from the world.
2. Sprung in com - plete - ness where his feet pass.
3. God's re - cre - a - tion of the new day.

What is the connection between the biblical account of Creation and the "recreation" this song celebrates?

In Eden Away to the East 13

Fern Hill

Now as I was young and easy under the apple boughs
About the lilting house and happy as the grass was green,
    The night above the dingle starry,
        Time let me hail and climb
    Golden in the heydays of his eyes,
And honored among wagons I was prince of the apple towns
And once below a time I lordly had the trees and leaves
        Trail with daisies and barley
    Down the rivers of the windfall light.

And as I was green and carefree, famous among the barns
About the happy yard and singing as the farm was home,
    In the sun that is young once only,
        Time let me play and be
    Golden in the mercy of his means,
And green and golden I was huntsman and herdsman, the calves
Sang to my horn, the foxes on the hills barked clear and cold,
        And the sabbath rang slowly
    In the pebbles of the holy streams.

All the sun long it was running, it was lovely, the hay-
Fields high as the house, the tunes from the chimneys, it was air
    And playing, lovely and watery
        And fire green as grass.
    And nightly under the simple stars
As I rode to sleep the owls were bearing the farm away,
All the moon long I heard, blessed among stables, the nightjars
        Flying with the ricks, and horses
            Flashing into the dark

And then to awake, and the farm, like a wanderer white
With the dew, come back, the cock on his shoulder: it was all
    Shining, it was Adam and maiden,
        The sky gathered again
    And the sun grew round that very day.

So it must have been after the birth of the simple light
In the first, spinning place, the spellbound horses walking warm
      Out of the whinnying green stable
        On to the fields of praise.

And honored among foxes and pheasants by the gay house
Under the new-made clouds and happy as the heart was long
      In the sun born over and over,
        I ran my heedless ways,
      My wishes raced through the house-high hay
And nothing I cared, at my sky blue trades, that time allows
In all his tuneful turning so few and such morning songs
      Before the children green and golden
        Follow him out of grace.

Nothing I cared, in the lamb white days, that time would take me
Up to the swallow-thronged loft by the shadow of my hand,
      In the moon that is always rising,
        Nor that riding to sleep
      I should hear him fly with the high fields
And wake to the farm forever fled from the childless land.
Oh as I was young and easy in the mercy of his means,
      Time held me green and dying
      Though I sang in my chains like the sea.

DYLAN THOMAS

This is a poem about time, although the actual duration of the activities described in it is brief. From the moment when "Time let me play and be /
Golden" to the end of the poem when "Time held me green and dying" the
speaker undergoes an important development. Could you say that he is not
growing up but growing "down"?

Find the biblical echoes in the imagery (description based on the five senses)
of "Fern Hill." Why would writers equate youth with Adam and Eve in the
garden of Eden?

Between Worlds

And he said to himself
in a sunken morning moon
between two pines,
between lost gold and lingering green:

I believe I will count up my worlds.
There seem to me to be three.
There is a world I came from which is Number One.
There is a world I am in now, which is Number Two.
There is a world I go to next, which is Number Three.

There was the seed pouch, the place I lay dark in, nursed and shaped
  in a warm, red, wet cuddling place; if I tugged at a latchstring
  or doubled a dimpled fist or twitched a leg or a foot, only the
  Mother knew.

There is the place I am in now, where I look back and
  look ahead, and dream and wonder.

There is the next place —
And he took a look out of a window
at a sunken morning moon
between two pines,
between lost gold and lingering green.

CARL SANDBURG

The speaker looks at "lost gold and lingering green." What do you think
the gold stands for? If the green is lingering, what do you think it will give
way to when it finally passes?

In memory of
Miſs Eunice Dean da
of Mr. Simeon Dean,
& Tamesin his wife
who died March 1 80
In her 24th Year

from Psalm 19

The heavens tell out the glory of God,
The vault of heaven reveals his handiwork.
One day speaks to another,
Night with night shares its knowledge,
And this without speech or language or sound of any voice.
Their music goes out through all the earth,
Their words reach to the end of the world.
In them a tent is fixed for the sun,
Who comes out like a bridegroom from his wedding canopy,
Rejoicing like a strong man to run his race.
His rising is at one end of the heavens,
His circuit touches their farthest ends;
And nothing is hidden from his heat.

The psalmist identifies the days and nights as people who speak and sing to each other about the glory of God. What does the psalmist compare the sun to? When a writer identifies one thing with a different thing, he uses a metaphor. When he makes a comparison using *like* or *as*, he uses a simile. Can you rewrite the description of the sun here so that you use metaphors instead of similes?

————————————

Can you list metaphors and similes used by the poets in this second phase to describe a state of innocence?

Which of the six selections in this phase say something about immortality (eternal life)? Do any of them talk about human mortality? How, exactly?

WE SHALL DIE

The Fall of Man

The serpent was more crafty than any wild creature that the Lord God had made. He said to the woman, "Is it true that God has forbidden you to eat from any tree in the garden?" The woman answered the serpent, "We may eat the fruit of any tree in the garden, except for the tree in the middle of the garden; God has forbidden us either to eat or to touch the fruit of that; if we do, we shall die." The serpent said, "Of course you will not die. God knows that as soon as you eat it, your eyes will be opened and you will be like gods knowing both good and evil." When the woman saw that the fruit of the tree was good to eat, and that it was pleasing to the eye and tempting to contemplate, she took some and ate it. She also gave her husband some and he ate it. Then the eyes of both of them were opened and they discovered that they were naked; so they stitched fig leaves together and made themselves loincloths.

The man and his wife heard the sound of the Lord God walking in the garden at the time of the evening breeze and hid from the Lord God among the trees of the garden. But the Lord God called to the man and said to him, "Where are you?" He replied, "I heard the sound as you were walking in the garden, and I was afraid because I was naked, and I hid myself." God answered, "Who told you that you were naked? Have you eaten from the tree which I forbade you?" The man said, "The woman you gave me for a companion, she gave me fruit from the tree and I ate it." Then the Lord God said to the woman, "What is this that you have done?" The woman said, "The serpent tricked me, and I ate." Then the Lord God said to the serpent:

> "Because you have done this you are accursed
>   more than all cattle and all wild creatures.
>   On your belly you shall crawl, and dust you shall eat
>   all the days of your life.
>   I will put enmity between you and the woman,

between your brood and hers.
They shall strike at your head,
and you shall strike at their heel."

To the woman he said:

"I will increase your labor and your groaning,
and in labor you shall bear children.
You shall be eager for your husband,
and he shall be your master."

And to the man he said:

"Because you have listened to your wife
and have eaten from the tree which I forbade you,
accursed shall be the ground on your account.
With labor you shall win your food from it
all the days of your life.
It will grow thorns and thistles for you,
none but wild plants for you to eat.
You shall gain your bread by the sweat of your brow
until you return to the ground;
for from it you were taken.
Dust you are, to dust you shall return."

The man called his wife Eve because she was the mother of all who live. The Lord God made tunics of skins for Adam and his wife and clothed them. He said, "The man has become like one of us, knowing good and evil; what if he now reaches out his hand and takes fruit from the tree of life also, eats it and lives for ever?" So the Lord God drove him out of the garden of Eden to till the ground from which he had been taken. He cast him out, and to the east of the garden of Eden he stationed the cherubim and a sword whirling and flashing to guard the way to the tree of life.

GENESIS 3

What indication is there in this story that the writer thinks of God as merciful even at the same time that he sees him as a severe judge?

A.D. 2267

Once on the gritty moon (burnt earth hung far
In the black, rhinestone sky — lopsided star),
Two gadgets, with great fishbowls for a head,
Feet clubbed, hips loaded, shoulders bent. She said,
"Fantasies haunt me. A green garden. Two
Lovers aglow in flesh. The pools so blue!"
He whirrs with masculine pity, "Can't forget
Old superstitions? The earth-legend yet?"

JOHN FREDERICK NIMS

How does this poem look backward and forward at the same time?

How does it show that man has "fallen" up?

Green Gulch

We stood in a wide flat field at sunset. For the life of me I can remember no other children before them. I must have run away and been playing by myself until I had wandered to the edge of the town. They were older than I and knew where they came from and how to get back. I joined them.

They were not going home. They were going to a place called Green Gulch. They came from some other part of town, and their clothes were rough, their eyes worldly and sly. I think, looking back, that it must have been a little like a child following goblins home to their hill at nightfall, but nobody threatened me. Besides, I was very small and did not know the way home, so I followed them.

Presently we came to some rocks. The place was well named. It was a huge pool in a sandstone basin, green and dark with the evening over it and the trees leaning secretly inward above the water. When you looked down, you saw the sky. I remember that place as it was when we came there. I remember the quiet and the green ferns touching the green water. I remember we played there, innocently at first.

But someone found the spirit of the place, a huge old turtle, asleep in the ferns. He was the last lord of the green water before the town poured over it. I saw his end. They pounded him to death with stones on the other side of the pool while I looked on in stupefied horror. I had never seen death before.

Suddenly, as I stood there small and uncertain and frightened, a grimy, splattered gnome who had been stooping over the turtle stood up with a rock in his hand. He looked at me, and around that little group some curious evil impulse passed like a wave. I felt it and drew back. I was alone there. They were not human.

I do not know who threw the first stone, who splashed water over my suit, who struck me first, or even who finally, among that ring of vicious faces, put me on my feet, dragged me to the roadside, pointed and said, roughly, "There's your road, kid, follow the street lamps. They'll take you home."

They stood in a little group watching me, nervous now, ashamed a little at the ferocious pack impulse toward the outsider that had swept over them.

I never forgot that moment.

I went because I had to, down that road with the wind moving in the fields. I went slowly from one spot of light to another and in between I thought the things a child thinks, so that I did not stop at any house nor ask anyone to help me when I came to the lighted streets.

I had discovered evil. It was a monstrous and corroding knowledge. It could not be told to adults because it was the evil of childhood in which no one believes. I was alone with it in the dark.

LOREN EISELEY

What experience of the author's convinces him of the evil of childhood? Why do you think no one believes in it? Do you? Why or why not?

Why does the author describe the knowledge of evil as "monstrous"? What animal in the biblical account of the Fall represents evil in a "monstrous" way?

The Sick Rose

O Rose, thou art sick!
The invisible worm,
That flies in the night,
In the howling storm,
Has found out thy bed
Of crimson joy:
And his dark secret love
Does thy life destroy.

WILLIAM BLAKE

Here the poet talks of a rose that is destroyed by a worm. What could the rose be a symbol of? Could you say that the boy in "Green Gulch" also discovered the worm that destroys the rose?

Here are some other words that have been used as symbols so far in this book: lamb, tiger, garden, green, gold, serpent, dust, thorns, thistles, goblins, dark. Can you tell what each would symbolize? Do they separate into images that you could list under the headings *garden* and *wilderness?*

Why Coyote
Always Howls

Coyote saw a rattlesnake go into a hole one day. Dancing around the hole, Coyote called all of the people to come and observe.

"A beautiful bird is hiding in the hole," Coyote said. "If you want to see the bird, you must dance as I do."

The chief's daughter danced close to the hole and the rattlesnake struck her on the ankle. When the maiden cried out in pain, Coyote growled, "Your dancing is all wrong."

In a few hours the maiden died from the venom. "Coyote," said the grieving chief, "my daughter must live again."

This is how Coyote had planned to bring Death to the world. "No," he said, "if people always live forever, there will be too many people and not enough acorns and other food."

"You, Coyote, are to blame for my daughter's death," the chief retorted. Secretly he plotted revenge. When the dead maiden was dressed in her finest clothes, she was cremated with much ceremony.

Several days later Coyote's lovely daughter died. The chief had had her poisoned. Now it was the trickster Coyote's turn to mourn and he howled all night. The next day he came to the chief.

"My daughter must live again," Coyote cried. "Let it be so."

"No," said the angry chief. "When my daughter died because of your mischief, you said it was best to let dead people remain dead to prevent the world having too many people."

"Yes, you are right," admitted Coyote. "We must dress my daughter and cremate her as we did your daughter."

The people had another funeral pyre and Coyote mourned and howled every night. It is for this reason that Death came to the world and that Coyote always howls.

POMO INDIAN

What is the origin of death in this story? in Genesis?

Old Adam

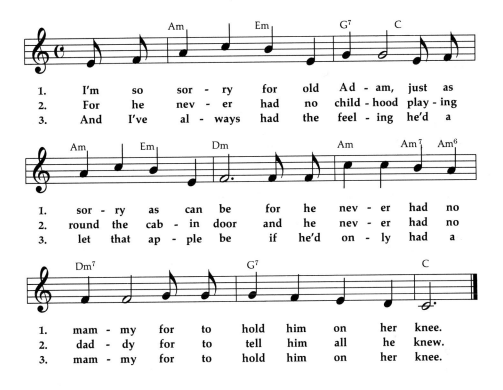

1. I'm so sor - ry for old Ad - am, just as
2. For he nev - er had no child - hood play - ing
3. And I've al - ways had the feel - ing he'd a

1. sor - ry as can be for he nev - er had no
2. round the cab - in door and he nev - er had no
3. let that ap - ple be if he'd on - ly had a

1. mam - my for to hold him on her knee.
2. dad - dy for to tell him all he knew.
3. mam - my for to hold him on her knee.

According to this song, you who sing it have had experiences that Adam lacked. What are they? What does the song suggest about Adam's (and our) fate if he'd had these experiences?

In what way is every baby a new Adam?

_____

How do selections in this third phase, "We Shall Die," illustrate the connection between time and death?

MY BROTHER'S KEEPER?

The First Murder

The man lay with his wife Eve, and she conceived and gave birth to Cain. She said, "With the help of the Lord I have brought a man into being." Afterward she had another child, his brother Abel. Abel was a shepherd and Cain a tiller of the soil. The day came when Cain brought some of the produce of the soil as a gift to the Lord; and Abel brought some of the first-born of his flock, the fat portions of them. The Lord received Abel and his gift with favor; but Cain and his gift he did not receive. Cain was very angry and his face fell. Then the Lord said to Cain, "Why are you so angry and cast down?

> If you do well, you are accepted;
> if not, sin is a demon crouching at the door.
> It shall be eager for you, and you will be mastered by it."

Cain said to his brother Abel, "Let us go into the open country." While they were there, Cain attacked his brother Abel and murdered him. Then the Lord said to Cain, "Where is your brother Abel?" Cain answered, "I do not know. Am I my brother's keeper?" The Lord said, "What have you done? Hark! your brother's blood that has been shed is crying out to me from the ground. Now you are accursed, and banished from the ground which has opened its mouth wide to receive your brother's blood, which you have shed. When you till the ground, it will no longer yield you its wealth. You shall be a vagrant and a wanderer on earth." Cain said to the Lord, "My punishment is heavier than I can bear; thou hast driven me today from the ground, and I must hide myself from thy presence. I shall be a vagrant and a wanderer on earth, and anyone who meets me can kill me." The Lord answered him, "No: if anyone kills Cain, Cain shall be avenged sevenfold." So the Lord put a mark on Cain, in order that anyone meeting him should not kill him. Then Cain went out from the Lord's presence and settled in the land of Nod to the east of Eden.

GENESIS 4 : 1–16

Is it fitting that the first murderer should become a wanderer in a wasteland? If so, why?

How is Cain's reply to God after the murder similar to Adam's reply after the eating of the fruit in the garden of Eden?

Note the metaphor God uses to describe sin. Why might the writer have him describe sin in this way?

How are the boys in "Green Gulch" like Cain?

The Land of Nod

Cain since first he fled
Is endless bound to run
Under a scorching sun
That burns a baneful red,

Or hunt among cold rocks
And stiffened marble streams.
Only in Abel's dreams
The crushing wheel unlocks.

For Abel's sake, the dead
Shepherd dear to God,
Cain in the Land of Nod
Covers his dreadful head.

Where Abel, cheek on hand,
Sleeps his silver night,
An arky moon makes bright
Calm sheepfolds, quiet land;

And while his brother's keeper
Lies so near God's heart,
There shall no judgment fall to part
Sleeper from sleeper.

JAY MACPHERSON

The Land of Nod, besides being the place that Cain settled, is traditionally
thought of as the place we go to when we sleep. Who are the two sleepers of
the last line? Why can they not be parted? What contrast is drawn between
the landscape Cain sleeps in and the landscape of Abel's dream?

The Marking of Trees

Up and down the valley
this smear of red paint
on the branch of a tree
or a drooping trunk
spells death:

           as if a plague
were about in the land
and a solitary hand
with a brush and a can
could stop it:

           as if we couldn't
bear to see live on
this same rot that spreads
even faster in ourselves.

RAYMOND SOUSTER

Why are the trees being marked? What does their marking suggest to the
poet about the condition of all humanity? In what way are we all "marked"?

A Poison Tree

I was angry with my friend:
I told my wrath, my wrath did end.
I was angry with my foe:
I told it not, my wrath did grow.

And I water'd it in fears,
Night and morning with my tears;
And I sunnèd it with smiles,
And with soft deceitful wiles.

And it grew both day and night,
Till it bore an apple bright;
And my foe beheld it shine,
And he knew that it was mine,

And into my garden stole
When the night had veil'd the pole:
In the morning glad I see
My foe outstretch'd beneath the tree.

WILLIAM BLAKE

What distinguishes the poet's behavior toward his friend from his treatment of his enemy in the first stanza of this poem? What metaphorical image does Blake use to illustrate the obsessive quality of his hatred? How has he made use of biblical symbolism to enrich his main image?

The Hero's Kitchen

A seal of holiness descends
    Upon the kitchen floor;
Mrs. Belaney and her friends
    Knit and discuss the war.
Mrs. Belaney has a son
    —Had, I should say, perhaps—
Who deeds of gallantry has done,
    Him and some other chaps.

Into his hand the Seraphim
    Gave the destructive sword,
Beckoning as they did in him
    Creation's restless lord.
Fire and blood became his trade;
    Gentle and clumsy one
At home he was, but on parade
    Creation's restless son.

Mrs. Belaney feels the wall
    Rustle with angel wings;
Tears of a sacred nature fall
    Into the knitting things.
Then begins tea, and cakes and pies
    Muffle the ladies' chat;
Out of the shadows angel eyes
    Watch the encroaching fat.

GEORGE JOHNSTON

What biblical figure does Mrs. Belaney's son become identified with? Why?
What are the seraphim and the angels doing in this poem? (We have already
met creatures like the seraphim, the cherubim, at the end of "The Fall of
Man.") How is Mrs. Belaney closer to her son's world than she realizes?

My Dungeon Shook

Dear James:

I have begun this letter five times and torn it up five times. I keep seeing your face, which is also the face of your father and my brother. Like him, you are tough, dark, vulnerable, moody—with a very definite tendency to sound truculent because you want no one to think you are soft. You may be like your grandfather in this, I don't know, but certainly both you and your father resemble him very much physically. Well, he is dead, he never saw you, and he had a terrible life; he was defeated long before he died because, at the bottom of his heart, he really believed what white people said about him. This is one of the reasons that he became so holy. I am sure that your father has told you something about all that. Neither you nor your father exhibit any tendency toward holiness: you really *are* of another era, part of what happened when the Negro left the land and came into what the late E. Franklin Frazier called "the cities of destruction." You can only be destroyed by believing that you really are what the white world calls a *nigger*. I tell you this because I love you, and please don't you ever forget it.

I have known both of you all your lives, have carried your Daddy in my arms and on my shoulders, kissed and spanked him and watched him learn to walk. I don't know if you've known anybody from that far back; if you've loved anybody that long, first as an infant, then as a child, then as a man, you gain a strange perspective on time and human pain and effort. Other people cannot see what I see whenever I look into your father's face, for behind your father's face as it is today are all those other faces which were his. Let him laugh and I see a cellar your father does not remember and a house he does not remember and I hear in his present laughter his laughter as a child. Let him curse and I remember him falling down the cellar steps, and howling, and I remember, with pain, his tears, which my hand or your grandmother's so easily wiped away. But no one's hand can wipe away those tears he sheds invisibly today, which one hears in his laughter and in his speech and in his songs. I know what the world has done to my brother and how narrowly he has survived it. And I know, which is much worse,

were born into a society which spelled out with brutal clarity, and in as many ways as possible, that you were a worthless human being. You were not expected to aspire to excellence: you were expected to make peace with mediocrity. Wherever you have turned, James, in your short time on this earth, you have been told where you could go and what you could do (and *how* you could do it) and where you could live and whom you could marry. I know your countrymen do not agree with me about this, and I hear them saying, "You exaggerate." They do not know Harlem, and I do. So do you. Take no one's word for anything, including mine—but trust your experience. Know whence you came. If you know whence you came, there is really no limit to where you can go. The details and symbols of your life have been deliberately constructed to make you believe what white people say about you. Please try to remember that what they believe, as well as what they do and cause you to endure, does not testify to your inferiority but to their inhumanity and fear. Please try to be clear, dear James, through the storm which rages about your youthful head today, about the reality which lies behind the words *acceptance* and *integration.* There is no reason for you to try to become like white people and there is no basis whatever for their impertinent assumption that *they* must accept *you.* The really terrible thing, old buddy, is that *you* must accept *them.* And I mean that very seriously. You must accept them and accept them with love. For these innocent people have no other hope. They are, in effect, still trapped in a history which they do not understand; and until they understand it, they cannot be released from it. They have had to believe for many years, and for innumerable reasons, that black men are inferior to white men. Many of them, indeed, know better, but, as you will discover, people find it very difficult to act on what they know. To act is to be committed, and to be committed is to be in danger. In this case, the danger, in the minds of most white Americans, is the loss of their identity. Try to imagine how you would feel if you woke up one morning to find the sun shining and all the stars aflame. You would be frightened because it is out of the order of nature. Any upheaval in the universe is terrifying because it so profoundly attacks one's sense of one's own reality. Well, the black man has functioned in the white man's world as a fixed star, as an immovable pillar: and as he moves out of his place, heaven and earth are shaken to their foundations. You, don't be afraid. I said that it was intended that you should perish in the ghetto, perish by never being allowed to go behind the white man's definitions, by never being allowed to spell your proper name. You have, and many of us have, defeated this intention; and, by a terrible law, a terrible paradox, those innocents who believed that your imprisonment made them safe are losing their grasp of reality. But these men are your brothers — your lost, younger brothers. And if the word *integration* means anything, this is what it means: that we, with love, shall force our brothers to see themselves as they are, to cease fleeing from reality and begin to change it. For this is your home, my friend, do not be driven from it; great men have done great things here, and will again, and we can make America what America must become. It will be hard, James, but you come from sturdy, peasant stock, men who picked cotton and dammed rivers and built railroads, and, in the teeth of the most terrifying odds, achieved an unassailable and monumental dignity. You come from a long line of great poets, some of the greatest poets since Homer. One of them said, *The very time I thought I was lost, My dungeon shook and my chains fell off.*

You know, and I know, that the country is celebrating one hundred years of freedom one hundred years too soon. We cannot be free until they are free. God bless you, James, and Godspeed.

Your uncle,
James [BALDWIN]

Does the one thing that can destroy the nephew have a connection with the demon crouching by Cain's door? Who are the two actual brothers in this essay? Who are the two symbolic ones?

Baldwin says white men are "trapped in a history." In what way do all the selections in this phase illustrate the trap of history (that is, time)?

Try categorizing some of the figures in this chapter as one of three types, Adam in Eden, Adam outside Eden, Cain. What of the female figures?

Look back over the chapter at the vegetable imagery and divide it into two groups, one to connect with the tree of life and the other to connect with the tree of death (i.e., of the knowledge of good and evil). How do these two groups relate to the title of this book, *The Garden and the Wilderness?* What does the garden symbolize? What does the wilderness symbolize?

SING UNTO THE LORD A NEW SONG

Sing unto the Lord a new song:
Sing unto the Lord, all the earth.
Sing unto the Lord, bless his name;
Show forth his salvation from day to day.
Declare his glory among the heathen, his wonders
    among all people.
For the Lord is great, and greatly to be praised:
He is to be feared above all gods.
For all the gods of the nations are idols:
    but the Lord made the heavens.
Honor and majesty are before him:
    strength and beauty are in his sanctuary.
Give unto the Lord, O ye kindreds of the people,
    give unto the Lord glory and strength.
Give unto the Lord the glory due unto his name:
    bring an offering and come into his courts.
O worship the Lord in the beauty of his holiness:
Fear before him, all the earth.
Say among the heathen that the Lord reigneth:
The world also shall be established that it shall not
    be moved:
He shall judge the people righteously.
Let the heavens rejoice, and let the earth be glad;
Let the sea roar, and the fulness thereof.
Let the field be joyful and all that is therein;
Then shall all the trees of the wood rejoice before the
    Lord:
For he cometh, for he cometh to judge the earth:
He shall judge the world with righteousness,
    and the people with his truth.

PSALM 96

The biblical and nonbiblical pieces of literature you
have been reading present the story line of the first
four chapters of Genesis. You have probably noticed
what a rich source of inspiration the Bible has been
for later writers, and you would be quite right in

assuming that the writers represented here are a very small minority of those who have used the Bible in their writings. Why has the Bible had such an enormous influence on the creating of works of literature? Could the story the Bible tells suggest an answer? Despite the differences among the stories that men tell, there are similar story patterns that cross the boundaries separating times, places, and languages. In this sense the Bible has many similarities to later literature, even to that of our day. But at the same time the Bible is unique. Because its story is so ancient and so complete, it has a special imaginative authority of its own.

The Bible is central to the study of western literature. Its characters, narratives, events, and images have been constantly used by later writers. The connections between the biblical selections in this volume and the nonbiblical ones often are pointed out to you, and your own insights will reveal others. When writers consciously build such connections into their work, we can assume that the Bible has special significance for them. We must study such connections if we are to understand fully what the writers tried to say.

Even within the Bible itself many connections may be found. It took a thousand years or more of writing, rewriting, editing, and collecting to get the Bible into the written form we know today; and the materials which were written down in the earliest period of biblical writing (about 1000 B.C.) had existed for centuries in memorized story form. The work of many different authors is found in the Bible, and the later writers were strongly influenced by the earlier ones. They knew the Bible well, and even as they added new materials they commented on the older writings.

One kind of biblical literature which shows these connections effectively is the psalm. A psalm is a song accompanied by stringed instruments; reading a psalm is similar to reading the text of an old folk

tune. You must imagine the psalm as being sung to understand the feelings it expresses. We have selected certain of these songs because their images and themes connect with other biblical literature.

Psalm 96, for example, evokes the central theme of this chapter, "Creation and Fall." The song is a "new song," and it sings about how "the Lord made the heavens." The singers celebrate their idea of creation when all things were new. But they also say that God is more "to be feared" than idols, and warn that he will "judge the earth." This suggests that there has been a fall from perfection: there would be no reason to judge a world which had remained innocent. You may wish to compare the narrative of creation and fall with this psalm to see how the events are described in different ways. The same comparison could be done with other narratives and psalms in this book.

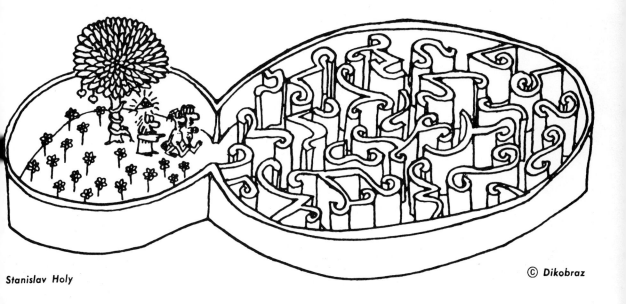

Stanislav Holy

If we think about the period of time covered by Psalm 96, we catch a glimpse of the way the biblical writers thought about time itself. The psalm sings about how the Lord "made the heavens," reigns now, and shall judge the earth. It encompasses the entire span of time from beginning to end. Israel thought of time, and of all reality, in terms of the Lord: time began with his act of creation and will close with the establishment of his kingdom of justice. The Bible reflects this. Its literature recalls the very remote past, illuminates the present, and offers a vision of the future. James Baldwin handles time in much the same way in his letter to his nephew (page 36). His view of his nephew's situation causes him, too, to speak about the distant past and the unforeseeable future. He attempts to explain the black man's situation by placing it within the broadest perspective. A reader who knows something of the biblical narrative can understand better the argument Baldwin makes in his letter.

The biblical narrative begins with the creation of a perfect world and tells of Adam's (man's) fall from

innocence into experience. It is in this fallen world that death and murder become possible. Other cultures also have narratives which tell of creation and fall, or the coming of death (the Indian story about Coyote, for example). We have, then, in this first chapter, a narrative which ends with the first murder. At the same time we have works of literature which suggest the overall narrative pattern of the whole Bible, from creation to doomsday.

The poems in the first chapter reveal a pattern that you will see frequently throughout the book. Blake speaks about a tiger, and contrasts it with a lamb. The folk spiritual "He's Got the Whole World in His Hand" sings about gambling, lying, and crapshooting men at the same time as it sings about "little bits of babies." Dylan Thomas speaks of things as green, golden, carefree, happy, young, lovely, and blessed; but he also tells of following time "out of grace," and talks about shadows, the childless land, and dying. In describing the rose, Blake seems uninterested in the traditional beauties, joys, and warm emotions it ordinarily suggests; instead he mentions sickness and invisible night worms. In "The Hero's Kitchen," one side of the two-edged pattern tells about holiness, deeds of gallantry, angel wings, and tears of a sacred nature. The other side is about war, the destructive sword, fire and blood, and encroaching fat. In all of these poems there is a pattern of opposites which shift back and forth in a rhythm, now one predominating, now another.

A pattern that is closely similar is present also in the biblical selections. And so it becomes clear that the Bible is more than a continuous narrative, moving from event to event in time. It is also an expression of patterns of imagery. The pattern in the first chapter might be called the pattern of the garden and the wilderness, or inside Eden and outside Eden. We might also say that it is the pattern of our dream world as opposed to our world of experience. It is such a basic pattern that you will find it repeated throughout this book. In fact, you will find it almost everywhere you look—on television, in the movies, and even (if you want to study them at all) in your own daydreams.

This recurring pattern of good and evil, light and dark, garden and wilderness, innocence and experience, inside and outside Eden, is an important key to the study of literature. It is a pattern basic to man's imagination. The images which make up the pattern, and the stories and poems which contain the images, are what literature is all about. They are the realities of literature. They cannot be scientifically proven or tested like the realities of science; they are not "out there" in the world around us. They are all in your head. You cannot study literature with a telescope or a microscope: you can only study it with that combination of reason and emotion we call the imagination.

Literature, then, is a record of what men think. Its realities are inside men's minds. They are inside your own mind, as well as inside the minds of the authors who wrote the Bible and the rest of literature. In order to understand these realities, you must go into your own mind, and let it expand by bringing it into touch with what other men have written. The more you read, the deeper you will be able to go inside your own thoughts. You will find that much of what other men have written down is already there, waiting to be awakened. As you read this book, discovering what others have thought, echoes will stir inside you, as though somehow you already know what those earlier writers knew, but never saw it until now. Perhaps you will find that you, too, are in a garden and also in a wilderness, and that your own life, all along, has been going on inside and outside Eden. When you, like the psalmist, juggle past, present, and future together in your head, you will be able to live in that long ago garden, your immediate "fragmentary day," and the desired "eternal weather" to come, all at the same time.

2 : The Flood
and the Dawn of History

THE WINDOWS OF THE SKY
WERE OPENED

To Destroy Every Living Creature

When the Lord saw that man had done much evil on earth and that his thoughts and inclinations were always evil, he was sorry that he had made man on earth, and he was grieved at heart. He said, "This race of men whom I have created, I will wipe them off the face of the earth—man and beast, reptiles and birds. I am sorry that I ever made them." But Noah had won the Lord's favor.

This is the story of Noah. Noah was a righteous man, the one blameless man of his time; he walked with God. He had three sons, Shem, Ham, and Japheth. Now God saw that the whole world was corrupt and full of violence. In his sight the world had become corrupted, for all men had lived corrupt lives on earth. God said to Noah, "The loathsomeness of all mankind has become plain to me, for through them the earth is full of violence. I intend to destroy them, and the earth with them. Make yourself an ark with ribs of cypress; cover it with reeds and coat it inside and out with pitch. This is to be its plan: the length of the ark shall be three hundred cubits, its breadth fifty cubits, and its height thirty cubits. You shall make a roof for the ark, giving it a fall of one cubit when complete; and put a door in the side of the ark, and build three decks, upper, middle, and lower. I intend to bring the waters of the flood over the earth to destroy every human being under heaven that has the spirit of life; everything on earth shall perish. But with you I will make a covenant, and you shall go into the ark, you and your sons, your wife and your sons' wives with you. And you shall bring living creatures of every kind into the ark to keep them alive with you, two of each kind, a male and a female; two of every kind of bird, beast, and reptile, shall come to you to be kept alive. See that you take and store every kind of food that can be eaten; this shall be food for you and for them." Exactly as God had commanded him, so Noah did.

GENESIS 6 : 5–22

How can the men of Noah's time be said also to have "eaten from the tree of the knowledge of good and evil"? What is the punishment for having done this? Does this punishment seem to you more severe than Adam and Eve's? If so, why? What characteristic of God is emphasized in this selection? What quotations support your view?

What echoes of the creation story in Chapter One can you find in this biblical episode?

Electrical Storm

(for Arna and Alberta)

God's angry with the world again,
the grey neglected ones would say;
He don't like ugly.
Have mercy, Lord, they prayed,
seeing the lightning's
Mene Mene Tekel,
hearing the preaching thunder's deep
Upharsin.
They hunched up, contracting in corners
away from windows and the dog;
huddled under Jehovah's oldtime wrath,
trusting, afraid.

I huddled too, when a boy,
mindful of things they'd told me
God was bound to make me answer for.
But later I was colleged (as they said)
and learned it was not celestial ire
(Beware the infidels, my son)
but pressure systems,
colliding massive energies
that make a storm.
Well for us. . . .

Last night we drove
through suddenly warring weather.
Wind and lightning havocked,
berserked in wires, trees.
Fallen lines we could not see at first
lay in the yard when we reached home.
The hedge was burning in the rain.

Who knows but what
we might have crossed another sill,
had not our neighbors' warning
kept us from our door?
Who knows if it was heavenly design
or chance
(or knows if there's a difference, after all)
that brought us and our neighbors through—
though others died—
the archetypal dangers of the night?

I know what those
cowering true believers would have said.

ROBERT HAYDEN

In a story about the prophet Daniel further on in the Bible the words *mene* (to number), *tekel* (to weigh), and *upharsin* (to divide) mysteriously appear on the wall of King Belshazzar's palace in Babylon. Daniel interprets the words to mean that Belshazzar is weighed in the balance and found wanting. His kingdom is to be divided and given to the Medes and Persians.

How is the lightning seen by the speaker of "Electrical Storm" as a kind of prophetic handwriting? What two "explanations" can be given for the survival of the speaker and his family while others were killed by the storm?

The Everlasting Covenant

When the waters had increased over the earth for a hundred and fifty days, God thought of Noah and all the wild animals and the cattle with him in the ark, and he made a wind pass over the earth, and the waters began to subside. The springs of the abyss were stopped up, and so were the windows of the sky; the downpour from the skies was checked. The water gradually receded from the earth, and by the end of a hundred and fifty days it had disappeared. On the seventeenth day of the seventh month the ark grounded on a mountain in Ararat. The water continued to recede until the tenth month, and on the first day of the tenth month the tops of the mountains could be seen.

After forty days Noah opened the trap door that he had made in the ark, and released a raven to see whether the water had subsided, but the bird continued flying to and fro until the water on the earth had dried up. Noah waited for seven days, and then he released a dove from the ark to see whether the water on the earth had subsided further. But the dove found no place where she could settle, and so she came back to him in the ark, because there was water over the whole surface of the earth. Noah stretched out his hand, caught her and took her into the ark. He waited another seven days and again released the dove from the ark. She came back to him toward evening with a newly plucked olive leaf in her beak. Then Noah knew for certain that the water on the earth had subsided still further. He waited yet another seven days and released the dove, but she never came back. And so it came about that, on the first day of the first month of his six hundred and first year, the water had dried up on the earth, and Noah removed the hatch and looked out of the ark. The surface of the ground was dry.

By the twenty-seventh day of the second month the whole earth was dry. And God said to Noah, "Come out of the ark, you and your wife, your sons and their wives. Bring out every living creature that is with you, live things of every kind, bird and beast and every reptile that moves on the ground, and let them swarm over the earth and be fruitful and increase there." So Noah came out with his sons, his wife, and his sons' wives. Every wild animal, all cattle, every bird, and every reptile that moves on the ground, came out of the ark by families. Then Noah built an altar to the Lord. He took ritually clean beasts and birds of every kind, and offered whole-offerings on the altar. When the Lord smelt the soothing odor, he said within himself, "Never again will I curse the ground because of man, however evil his inclinations may be from his youth upward. I will never again kill every living creature, as I have just done.

> While the earth lasts
> seedtime and harvest, cold and heat,
> summer and winter, day and night,
> shall never cease."

God blessed Noah and his sons and said to them, "Be fruitful and increase, and fill the earth. The fear and dread of you shall fall upon all wild animals on earth, on all birds of heaven, on everything that moves upon the ground and all fish in the sea; they are given into your hands. Every creature that lives and moves shall be food for you; I give you them all, as once I gave you all green plants. But you must not eat the flesh with the life, which is the blood, still in it. And further, for your lifeblood I will demand satisfaction; from every animal I will require it, and from a man also I will require satisfaction for the death of his fellow man.

> He that sheds the blood of a man,
> for that man his blood shall be shed;
> for in the image of God
> has God made man.

But you must be fruitful and increase, swarm throughout the earth and rule over it."

God spoke to Noah and to his sons with him: "I now make my covenant with you and with your descendants after you, and with every living creature that is with you, all birds and cattle, all the wild animals with you on earth, all that have come out of the ark. I will make my covenant with you: never again shall all living creatures be destroyed by the waters of the flood, never again shall there be a flood to lay waste the earth."

God said, "This is the sign of the covenant which I establish between myself and you and every living creature with you, to endless generations:

My bow I set in the cloud,
sign of the covenant
between myself and earth.
When I cloud the sky over the earth,
the bow shall be seen in the cloud.

Then will I remember the covenant which I have made between myself
and you and living things of every kind. Never again shall the waters
become a flood to destroy all living creatures. The bow shall be in the
cloud; when I see it, it will remind me of the everlasting covenant between God and living things on earth of every kind." God said to Noah,
"This is the sign of the covenant which I make between myself and all
that lives on earth."

The sons of Noah who came out of the ark were Shem, Ham, and
Japheth; Ham was the father of Canaan. These three were the sons of
Noah, and their descendants spread over the whole earth.

Noah, a man of the soil, began the planting of vineyards. He drank
some of the wine, became drunk and lay naked inside his tent. When
Ham, father of Canaan, saw his father naked, he told his two brothers
outside. So Shem and Japheth took a cloak, put it on their shoulders and
walked backwards, and so covered their father's naked body; their faces
were turned the other way, so that they did not see their father naked.
When Noah woke from his drunken sleep, he learned what his youngest son had done to him, and said:

"Cursed be Canaan,
slave of slaves
shall he be to his brothers."

And he continued:

"Bless, O Lord,
the tents of Shem;
may Canaan be his slave.
May God extend Japheth's bounds,
let him dwell in the tents of Shem,
may Canaan be their slave."

After the flood Noah lived for three hundred and fifty years, and he was
nine hundred and fifty years old when he died.

GENESIS 7:24; 8; 9

Why is it appropriate that an altar be built on a mountaintop?

What is the covenant (promise) that God makes with Noah? One of the nameless black poets, whom Baldwin refers to in his essay in Chapter One, wrote:

> "God gave Noah the rainbow sign
> No more water, the fire next time."

In the complete biblical story, which ends with the Last Judgment, the final destruction of the world is by fire. Twice now we have read how God has saved life from the waters. What symbolism, then, do you think could be attached to water and fire respectively?

When did Adam and Eve show the same feelings as Noah in this episode? What do the two stories suggest about human nature?

Noah

When old Noah stared across the floods,
Sky and water melted into one
Looking glass of shifting tides and sun.

Mountaintops were few: the ship was foul:
All the morn old Noah marveled greatly
At this weltering world that shone so stately,
Drowning deep the rivers and the plains.
Through the stillness came a rippling breeze;
Noah sighed, remembering the green trees.

Clear along the morning stooped a bird—
Lit beside him with a blossomed sprig.
Earth was saved; and Noah danced a jig.

SIEGFRIED SASSOON

Noah stared, marveled, sighed, and danced. Why in each case?

What aspect of "old" Noah's character is revealed by his ability to jig?

The Broken Dike,
The Levee Washed Away

The broken dike, the levee washed away,
The good fields flooded and the cattle drowned,
Estranged and treacherous all the faithful ground,
And nothing left but floating disarray
Of tree and home uprooted — was this the day
Man dropped upon his shadow without a sound
And died, having labored well and having found
His burden heavier than a quilt of clay?
No, no. I saw him when the sun had set
In water, leaning on his single oar
Above his garden faintly glimmering yet . . .
There bulked the plow, here washed the updrifted weeds . . .
And scull across his roof and make for shore,
With twisted face and pocket full of seeds.

EDNA ST. VINCENT MILLAY

How do the "twisted face" and the "pocket full of seeds" in the last line
of this poem suggest that Edna St. Vincent Millay sees man as both Adam
and Noah?

The History of the Flood

Bang Bang Bang
Said the nails in the Ark.

It's getting rather dark
Said the nails in the Ark.

For the rain is coming down
Said the nails in the Ark.

And you're all like to drown
Said the nails in the Ark.

Dark and black as sin
Said the nails in the Ark.

So won't you all come in
Said the nails in the Ark.

But only two by two
Said the nails in the Ark.

So they come in two by two,
The elephant, the kangaroo,
And the gnu,
And the little tiny shrew.

Then the birds
Flocked in like wingèd words:
Two racket-tailed motmots, two macaws,
Two nuthatches and two
Little bright robins.

And the reptiles: the gila monster, the slow-worm,
The green mamba, the cottonmouth, and the alligator—
All squirmed in;

And after a very lengthy walk,
Two giant Galapagos tortoises.

And the insects in their hierarchies:
A queen ant, a king ant, a queen wasp, a king wasp,
A queen bee, a king bee,
And all the beetles, bugs and mosquitoes,
Cascaded in like glittering, murmurous jewels.

But the fish had their wish;
For the rain came down.
People began to drown:
The wicked, the rich—
They gasped out bubbles of pure gold,
Which exhalations
Rose to the constellations.

So for forty days and forty nights
They were on the waste of waters
In those cramped quarters.
It was very dark, damp and lonely.
There was nothing to see, but only
The rain which continued to drop.
It did not stop.

So Noah sent forth a Raven. The raven said "Kark!
I will not go back to the ark."
The raven was footloose,
He fed on the bodies of the rich—
Rich with vitamins and goo.
They had become bloated,
And everywhere they floated.
The raven's heart was black,

He did not come back.
It was not a nice thing to do:
Which is why the raven is a token of wrath,
And creaks like a rusty gate
When he crosses your path; and Fate
Will grant you no luck that day:

The raven is fey:
You were meant to have a scare.
Fortunately in England
The raven is rather rare.

Then Noah sent forth a dove
She did not want to rove.
She longed for her love—
The other turtle dove—
(For her no other dove!)
She brought back a twig from an olive tree.
There is no more beautiful tree
Anywhere on the earth,
Even when it comes to birth
From six weeks under the sea.

She did not want to rove.
She wanted to take her rest,
And to build herself a nest
All in the olive grove.
She wanted to make love.
She thought that was the best.

The dove was not a rover;
So they knew that the rain was over.
Noah and his wife got out
(They had become rather stout)
And Japhet, Ham, and Shem.
(The same could be said of them.)
They looked up at the sky.
The earth was becoming dry.

Then the animals came ashore—
There were more of them than before:
There were two dogs and a litter of puppies;
There were a tom-cat and two tib-cats
And two litters of kittens—cats
Do not obey regulations;
And, as you might expect,
A quantity of rabbits.

God put a rainbow in the sky.
They wondered what it was for.
There had never been a rainbow before.
The rainbow was a sign;
It looked like a neon sign—
Seven colors arched in the skies:
What should it publicize?
They looked up with wondering eyes.

It advertises Mercy
Said the nails in the Ark.

Mercy Mercy Mercy
Said the nails in the Ark.

Our God is merciful
Said the nails in the Ark.

Merciful and gracious
Bang Bang Bang Bang.

JOHN HEATH-STUBBS

How has the character of God changed in this phase, "The Windows of the Sky Were Opened"?

Do the people in "Electrical Storm" (page 50) believe that God meant to keep his promise never again to destroy the world by flood? Why do you think people fear that God will continue to punish them?

GOD SPOKE TO NOAH

Noah

ANDRÉ OBEY
Translated by ARTHUR WILMURT

Characters

NOAH	ADA
MAMMA	SELLA
SHEM	NAOMI
HAM	A MAN
JAPHETH	

THE ANIMALS: *Bear, Cow, Elephant, Lamb, Lion, etc.*

SCENE I

A glade. The Ark is at the right, only the poop deck showing, with a ladder to the ground. NOAH *is taking measurements and singing a little song. He scratches his head and goes over the measurements again. Then he calls.*

NOAH (*softly*). Lord . . . (*louder*) Lord . . . (*very loud*) Lord! . . . Yes, Lord, it's me. Extremely sorry to bother You again, but . . . What's that? Yes, I know You've other things to think of, but after I've once shoved off, won't it be a little late? . . . Oh, no, Lord, no, no, no. . . . No, Lord, please don't think that. . . . Oh, but naturally, of course, I trust You! You could tell me to set sail on a plank— a branch—on just a cabbage leaf. . . . Yes, You could even tell me to put out to sea with nothing but my loincloth, even without my loincloth—completely— (*He has gone down on his knees, but he gets up immediately.*) Yes, yes, Lord, I beg Your pardon. I know Your time is precious. Well, this is all I wanted to ask You : Should I make a rudder ? I say, a rudder. . . . No, no, Lord. R for Robert ; U for Una ; D for . . . that's it, a rudder. Good . . . very good, I never thought of that. Of course, winds, currents, tides . . . what was that, Lord ? Storms ? Oh, and while You're there just one other little thing. . . . Are You listening, Lord ? (*To the audience*) Gone !! . . . He's in a bad temper. . . . Well, you can't blame Him ; He has so much to think of. All right ; no rudder. (*He considers the Ark.*) Tides, currents, winds. (*He imitates the winds.*) Psch ! . . . Psch ! . . . Storms. (*He imitates the tempests.*) Vloum ! Be da Bloum ! Oh, that's going to be (*he makes a quick movement*) simply . . . magnificent !! . . . No, no, Lord, I'm not afraid. I know that You'll be with me. I was only trying to imagine. . . . Oh, Lord, while You're there I'd like just to ask . . . (*to the audience*) Che ! Gone again. You see how careful you have to be. (*He laughs.*) He was listening all the time. (*He goes to the Ark.*) Storms ! . . . I think I'll just put a few more nails in down here. (*He hammers and sings.*)

> When the boat goes well, all goes well.
> When all goes well, the boat goes well.

(*He admires his work.*) And when I think that a year ago I couldn't hammer a nail without hitting my thumb. That's pretty good, if I do say so myself. (*He climbs aboard the Ark and stands there like a captain.*) Larboard and starboard ! . . . Cast off the hawsers ! . . . Close the portholes ! . . . 'Ware shoals ! . . . Wait till the squall's over ! . . . Now I'm ready, completely ready, absolutely ready ! I'm ready. (*He cries to heaven.*) I am ready ! (*Then quietly*) Well, I should like to know how all this business is going to begin. (*He looks all around, at the trees, the bushes, and the sky.*) Magnificent weather—oppressively hot and no sign of a cloud. Well, that part of the program is His lookout.

(*Enter the* BEAR)

Well ! . . . What does *he* want ? (*The* BEAR *moves toward the Ark.*) Just a minute, there ! (*The* BEAR *makes a pass at the Ark.*)

(*Frightened*) Stop that. (*Pulls up ladder. The* BEAR *stops.*) Sit down !

Good. (*The* BEAR *sits.*) Lie down. (*The* BEAR *lies down on its back and waves its legs gently.*) There's a good doggie.

(*Enter the* LION)

What the devil! (*The* LION *puts its paw on the Ark.*) None of that, you! . . . Lie down. (*The* LION *lies down beside the* BEAR.) Fine! . . . Splendid! . . . Now what do they want? Besides, why don't they fight? (*To the animals*) Hey! Why aren't you fighting? Come on, there. Boo! Woof! (*The* BEAR *and the* LION *get up and sniff at each other sociably.*) Whoever heard of wild animals behaving like that?

(*Enter the* MONKEY)

Another one! . . . It's a zoo. . . . Sit down, monkey, sit down. Now, look here, my pets, here have I been working every day for a whole year and not one of you has ever shown me the tip of his nose before. Are you out to make trouble for me now that I've finished my work? Come, you can't mean that, surely. (*He thinks it over.*) Unless . . . Oh! But that makes all the difference. Lord! Lord! (*Between his teeth*) Not there as usual.

(*Enter the* ELEPHANT)

Get back there, Jumbo! No pushing out of turn. (*The* ELEPHANT *salutes him.*) Good morning, old fellow. Now, if I understand you rightly, you want to come on board, eh?

(*The animals move forward.*)

Stop! I didn't say you could! . . . Well. All right, I'll let you come aboard. Yes, I don't see what I can. . . . No, I don't see anything against it. (*He sighs deeply.*) So the time has come! All right. Up with you!

(*Enter the* COW, *gamboling*)

Gently there, gently . . . (*He taps the* COW *on the rump.*) Wait a minute. Don't I know you? Aren't you that old cow from Mordecai's herd? (*The* COW *moos gaily.*) Bless my soul! (*With feeling*)

And He picked on you! . . . (*To the* BEAR) Well, my friend, will you make up your mind?

(*The* BEAR *sniffs the ground, but doesn't advance.*)

What's the matter, old boy? (NOAH *puts on his spectacles and leans over the spot where the bear is sniffing.*) What? Afraid of that insect? An ant! Ha, ha, ha! A bear afraid of an ant. Ha, ha, ha! (*But suddenly he strikes his brow.*) Oh! but what a fool I am! Why it's not an ant, it's *the* ant! It got here first, and I never saw it. Lord! What marvels there are on the threshold of this new life. It will take a stout heart, a steady hand, and a clear eye! I think my heart is right, but my eyes are dim . . . my hands are trembling . . . my feet are heavy. . . . Ah, well, if You've chosen me, perhaps it's because I am, like her — the least wicked of the herd. Come, all aboard. Make yourselves at home.

(*The animals go into the Ark.*)

Straight ahead, across the deck! Down the stairway to the left. You'll find your cabins ready. They may look like cages, but they'll be open always. (*He turns toward the forest.*) Come on, all of you! Hurry, you lazybones, you slow-coaches, creepy crawlers; you who travel in herds and you who walk alone — mustangs, mastadons, jabberwocks and unicorns, cloven hoofs and crumpled horns! Hurry! Everyone! Everyone! (*He catches his breath.*) Ah, ha! Here come the wolf and the lamb, side by side.

(*The* WOLF *and the* LAMB *enter and go into the Ark.*)

Here are the frog and the bull . . . the fox and the crow . . . and the birds! What are they waiting for? Come, my little ones. Come! Come!

(*The singing of the birds begins.*)

Look. The hare and the tortoise! Come on. Come on. Hurrah! The hare wins! Things are getting back to normal! Ah, this will be the golden age!

(*A great concert of birds.* NOAH *falls on his knees. A pause. Then the* TIGER *enters behind* NOAH. *He goes to* NOAH *and taps him on the shoulder. The birds are suddenly still.*)

(*Terrified*) Ooooo! (*He rises to flee.*) I know you wouldn't hurt me; it's just the surprise, you know. I'm not a bit afraid. . . . (*His teeth are chattering.*) I'm not afraid a bit. It's not me. It's just that my feet have gone cold! It'll soon pass. Wait a minute! They are still cold.

(*The* TIGER *creeps toward him.*)

Perhaps, if I do this. . . . (*He turns his back and covers his ears.*) Go on, get aboard! Hurry up.

(*The* TIGER, *with one bound, leaps aboard the Ark.*)

Are you still there?

(*Roaring from the Ark*)

Good! (NOAH *turns around and wipes his brow.*) Phew!

(*Off-stage is heard the voice of a boy. It is* JAPHETH.)

JAPHETH. Whoo-hoo! Father!
NOAH. Ah, here come the children. . . . Whoo-hoo!
JAPHETH (*nearer*). Whoo-hoo!
NOAH. Whoo-hoo!
VOICE OF SHEM. Look here, Japheth. We agreed; no running. Stick to the rules, or I won't play.
JAPHETH (*entering up right. He is seventeen*). I'm not running. Morning, Dad! (*He goes to* NOAH *in great strides.*)
SHEM (*entering up left. He is twenty-one*). You are running! Isn't he, Father?
JAPHETH (*throws himself into* NOAH'S *arms*). Home! I told you my way was shorter.
SHEM. If you're going to run the whole way. . . . Hello, Father.
NOAH (*embracing them both*). Good morning, children. You both win; Japheth got here first, but he cheated a little. Well, my big sons,

did you have much difficulty finding where I was?

JAPHETH. Hoho, Dad! So this is where you've been coming every day.
Come on, tell us about it.

NOAH. Just a minute.

(*Enter* HAM *left. He is nineteen.*)

SHEM *and* JAPHETH. We beat you!

HAM. All right, all right.

SHEM *and* JAPHETH. We won!

HAM. All right!(*He goes to* NOAH.) Good morning, Father.

NOAH (*embracing him*). Hello, Ham, my boy. (*To the three of them*) Where
is your mother?

HAM. She's coming.

NOAH. One of you might have waited for her.

(HAM *wanders over to the Ark.*)

JAPHETH. She didn't want us to. She said she'd get along better alone.
Then she can puff as much as she likes.

NOAH. You can both go back some of the way and meet her.

SHEM (*lying on the ground*). Aw, Father, it's so hot.

JAPHETH. Come on, we'll take it slowly.

SHEM (*getting up*). Oh, what a bore!

(*They go toward the left.*)

JAPHETH (*pointing to the Ark*). New house?

NOAH. Ssshh!

JAPHETH. It's nice.

NOAH. Isn't it?

(SHEM *and* JAPHETH *go out down left.* HAM *is examining the Ark, his
hands behind his back.* NOAH *goes to him and takes his arm.*)

Well, son, what do you think of it?

HAM. That?

NOAH. Why, yes.

HAM. What is it?

NOAH. Can't you guess? Is it such a funny shape?

HAM. Hm! It's hard to say. Come on, Father, what is it exactly?

NOAH. It's . . . well, it's made of cypress. It's all cypress. And it's . . . it's coated with pitch, inside and out.

HAM. Like a boat?

NOAH. Like a . . . yes. Hm! And it's three hundred cubits long and fifty cubits wide and thirty cubits high . . . .

HAM. But that's ten times too big for us.

NOAH. It's . . . yes, it's pretty big. But does it . . . look like *anything*?

HAM. It's not bad . . . not bad, but why the devil build a house like a boat?

NOAH. Ah! It does look like a . . . ?

HAM. Exactly.

NOAH. Listen. (*His tone changes.*) Who knows what will happen? Suppose there was a great flood. . . .

HAM (*laughing*). Here?

NOAH. A . . . tidal wave. . . .

HAM. In this part of the world?

NOAH. A deluge . . .

(*A noise is heard off-stage.*)

(*To* HAM) Ssshh!

(*Enter* SHEM *and* JAPHETH, *carrying their* MOTHER *on their crossed arms and singing : "Here is Mamma. Look at Mamma. See who is bringing in darling Mamma."*)

| SHEM and JAPHETH. | Here is Mamma. Look at Mamma. See who is bringing in darling Mamma. |

(NOAH *begins to laugh.* SHEM *and* JAPHETH *seat* MAMMA *on the grass and dance around her.*)

HAM. Oh, don't make such a row!

NOAH. Good morning, old lady, good morning! (*He kisses her.*)

MAMMA (*panting*). Phew! Phew!

NOAH. Tired, eh?

MAMMA. It's so terribly hot. (*To* JAPHETH) Oh, did you lock the door carefully?

JAPHETH. Why . . . er . . . yes.

MAMMA. You didn't at all.

JAPHETH. I did, but . . . I think I left the key in the lock.

MAMMA. We must get it out at once. Run back to the house——

JAPHETH. Oh, I say look here ! . . .

MAMMA. Go on, run !

NOAH. No, you stay here ! (*To* MAMMA) I'm sorry, Mother, but it's no use getting the key.

MAMMA. No use ! . . . What, with neighbors like ours ?

NOAH. Well . . . I had a nice little speech in my head explaining everything, but now I don't know quite how to tell you. . . . My dear wife, my darling children, we're never going back to our house. . . . There !

(*A short pause*)

THE THREE BOYS. What ?

MAMMA. For months I've felt that there was something worrying you. Why don't you tell me about it ? You know I always understand.

HAM. Father always did like a mystery.

NOAH. Don't be so silly.

HAM. All right, but you must admit that we might have been consulted. People don't build houses out in the middle of a forest miles from everybody, and everything. Why, just to get provisions it'll take two hours, there and back.

NOAH. Be quiet.

HAM. Suppose Mother forgets the bread . . . and that has been known to happen. . . .

NOAH (*laughing bitterly*). Bread ! Ha, ha, ha ! bread . . .

HAM. We'll need it, won't we ? Aren't we going to eat any more ?

NOAH. Be quiet, do you hear ? Quiet !

MAMMA. Now stop it, both of you, stop it ! All right, dear, we're not going home any more. That's that. You've told us the worst, I suppose.

JAPHETH. And I don't see that it's so terrible. This house looks much nicer than the old one. Doesn't it, Shem ?

SHEM (*practically asleep*). Hmmmm ?

JAPHETH. You see, he isn't losing any sleep over it.

(JAPHETH *and* MAMMA *have a good laugh.*)

NOAH. How sweet of you! How sweet of you both to take it like this.

MAMMA. We are very fond of you, that's all. It isn't hard to be fond of someone like you. Now finish your story and we'll go and see our new house.

NOAH (*in a low voice*). It isn't a house.

JAPHETH and MAMMA. What?

JAPHETH (*nudging* SHEM). Listen to this, you.

NOAH. It's not a house.

SHEM. What is it?

NOAH. It's a ship.

MAMMA and THE BOYS. A what?

NOAH. A ship.

JAPHETH. Splendid!

HAM. Nonsense!

SHEM (*sitting up*). Honest Injun?

MAMMA. A ship!

JAPHETH. Didn't I tell you? Shem, what did I tell you? It's a boat.

SHEM. Can we go on board?

NOAH. Not without me. Admire it from here.

HAM. That's right. Wait.

(*The two boys go behind the Ark.*)

SHEM. What shall we call it?

MAMMA. A ship. . . .

HAM. What on earth for?

NOAH. Well . . . er . . . for going sailing.

HAM. Sailing! But on what?

NOAH. God will provide, my son.

HAM. Oh, come now, Father. Let's be serious!

NOAH. We're going sailing. Yes . . . we're going on a little trip.

MAMMA. But you hate trips.

NOAH. Oh, no, no! One can change one's mind sometimes, you know. We'll be nice and quiet, all by ourselves. We won't see another soul. People are pretty unbearable nowadays, don't you think? Wicked! Coarse! Hateful! A bit of solitude with nothing but sea and sky will do us a world of good, it will give us new ideas. And when we get back . . . (*in a low voice*) when we get back. . . .

HAM. But, my dear Father, here we are living in the middle of such a terrible drought that we've almost forgotten what water's like, hundreds of miles from the sea, with every stream and river as dry as a bone, and you, who've been a farmer all your life, suddenly choose this moment to want to be a sailor.

NOAH. No, it isn't that, a bit. I don't feel that at all.

MAMMA (*tenderly*). Tell us, Noah. There's something on your mind, I'm sure. Tell us about it.

HAM. Yes, for heaven's sake, tell us.

VOICE OF JAPHETH (*off-stage*). Why, this is wonderful!

VOICE OF SHEM. You bet it is. This is great!

NOAH. Come on, let's go and join them. (*He helps* MAMMA *to her feet.*) It will do us good to hear them laugh.

HAM. But Father . . .

JAPHETH (*appears right, beaming*). Papa! What's that gadget with the rope . . . !

NOAH. Gadget? Rope! Which one? There are plenty of gadgets and ropes.

JAPHETH. The one with the two pulleys in front: a big one and a little one, for lifting machinery.

NOAH. Ah, yes.

JAPHETH. Well, it's a stroke of genius! Come and see it, Ham.

HAM. All right! What's the hurry?

JAPHETH. You're a genius, Father.

SHEM (*appearing*). Japheth, come and see the sliding panel. Father, you're an ace! Mother, your husband's an ace!

MAMMA. I don't doubt it for a minute.

JAPHETH. But, Father, how did you ever invent it?

NOAH. I'll tell you. Have you ever noticed that when a woodcutter wants to lift a tree trunk . . . the way he rolls up his rope . . .

(*They go out up right.*)

HAM (*following them*). Crazy!

(*Their voices die away.*)

(*Enter from back three girls:* ADA, SELLA, *and* NAOMI.)

ADA. Come, girls, follow the cat. Don't lose it. I feel we must follow the cat.

SELLA. And *I* think it's getting us lost. We've never been so far into the forest.

NAOMI. Besides, we've lost it.

ADA. Then we must look for it. We've got to find it. Hunt for it, sisters, hunt for it! (*She calls.*) Kitty! Kitty!

SELLA
NAOMI
} Kitty, Kitty, Kitty!

(*They make the little lip-noise that calls cats.*)

ADA. There it is. Look at its little white tail sliding through the grass. Come on, come on!

NAOMI. I can't go any further. It's so hot!

(*They see the Ark.*)

ADA. Look! A woodcutter's house.

SELLA. Huh. What a funny-looking house.

NAOMI. Ada, I'm afraid you've led us into some kind of danger.

ADA. We must go into that house.

SELLA (*frightened*). Oh, no!

NAOMI. No, no!

SELLA. Please, let's go back!

NAOMI. Yes! Yes, let's try to find the road back to the village.

(*Mrs. Noah's voice off-stage: "Kitty, Kitty."*)

ADA. Be quiet. Listen.

VOICE OF MAMMA. Oh, look! The cat! Noah! Noah! Look at the cat!

JAPHETH. Kitty!

NOAH. Kitty!

SHEM. Well, if it isn't dear old Kitty!

ADA. What did I tell you? (*She calls.*) Mrs. Noah!

THE THREE GIRLS. Mrs. Noah!

(MAMMA *enters up right.*)

MAMMA. What's this? You here, my pretties? (*She calls off-stage.*) Shem! Ham! Japheth! Come and see your friends. (*To the girls*) What brought you here?

ADA (*wrapping her arms about* MAMMA's *neck*). Oh, Mrs. Noah. Dear Mrs. Noah!

MAMMA. There, there. What's the matter?

SELLA. She's been excited all morning.

(*The three boys enter down right.*)

NAOMI. Yes. She couldn't stay still. She burst into tears for no reason at all.

SELLA. She never stopped talking about you.

NAOMI. She wanted to go to your house. She wanted to see you. She insisted on seeing you.

ADA. Dear Mrs. Noah! (*To her sisters*) We've just escaped a great danger.

NOAH (*enters above Ark*). How do you know, little one?

ADA. I . . . I feel it. (*She goes and kneels before* NOAH.) I'm *sure* of it.

(NOAH *lifts her up, gazes at her, presses her to him, and raises his eyes to heaven. A short silence*)

THE THREE BOYS (*in a low voice, but joyously*). Good morning!

NAOMI and SELLA. Good morning!

JAPHETH. Are you sailing with us?

SELLA and NAOMI. What?

SHEM. You know, you'd make pretty little cabin boys.

SELLA and NAOMI. Pretty . . . *what?*

HAM. If we have to draw lots to see who's to be eaten, I hope the lot falls on Naomi. She's so nice and brown. I'll take a wing, please.

(MAMMA *and the boys laugh.*)

NAOMI. What are you talking about? (*More laughter*)

NOAH (*coming back to earth*). Yes, you have indeed escaped a great danger. (*A pause; then joyously*) Why on earth didn't I think of it before? We have three lovely neighbors. . . . Orphans, if you please. They share our life with us. We say our prayers together. We talk across the fence. And I—I forgot all about them! Now, isn't it lucky that. . . . but how did you happen to meet the cat?

ADA. She was over in your house . . . .

MAMMA. Oh, you've been to our house?

ADA. Yes.

SELLA. Yes. Do you know there were a lot of people waiting outside.

NOAH. Aha.

NAOMI. Oh, yes, a whole crowd. Men and women and children from the village. And some men from other villages, too. And they were all whispering and waving their arms.

NOAH. Ah! We were just in time! . . . Go on.

SELLA. All of a sudden Ada cried out, "Come with me."

NAOMI. She took each of us by the hand and led us out of doors.

SELLA. We went through the crowd—

NAOMI. We found ourselves at your gate.

ADA. I pulled away a man who was listening at the door. I went in—

MAMMA. Japheth, the key!

ADA. Nobody was there.

SELLA. Except the cat.

ADA. Except the cat. She rubbed herself against my legs and meowed enough to break your heart.

MAMMA. Poor Kitty!

ADA. We came out again . . . .

SELLA. That is, we wanted to get out, but the crowd was so thick—

NAOMI. It was like a wall of faces across the door . . . .

JAPHETH. Meow!

SELLA. She arched her back—

NAOMI. She spat like mad—

ADA. And the crowd backed away.

(*The three boys laugh.*)

ADA. So we went through. We followed the cat and she led us into the forest.

THE BOYS. Ah!

SELLA. Every now and then she turned around to see if we were following.

THE BOYS. Oh!

NAOMI. We lost her!

THE BOYS. Och!

ADA. We found her again!

THE BOYS. Whee!

ADA, SELLA, and NAOMI. And here we are!

THE BOYS. Hurray!

(*General embraces*)

HAM (*to* NOAH). Now, are you going to explain?

NOAH (*his voice vibrating*). Yes!

ALL. Ah!

NOAH. I'll tell you everything. It's a great secret, a terrible secret. It has been vexing my heart and preying on my mind for months . . . for a whole year . . . I had no right to trouble you with it before. But now . . . today . . .

JAPHETH. Sshh!

NOAH. Eh!

JAPHETH (*in a low voice*). Someone's hiding just over there!

ALL. Where?

JAPHETH. Sshh! There. (*He points off left.*) In the bushes.

(*Something whistles over the stage.*)

THE THREE BOYS. An arrow!

NOAH. Women to the back!

(MAMMA *and the girls retreat toward the Ark.*)

(*Another whistling*)

THE BOYS. Another!

NOAH. To the ship!

(*All move toward the Ark. A shout offstage. Then a* MAN, *a sort of hunter, with a savage face, runs in from the left, stops short, plants himself firmly, points a spear at* NOAH.)

THE MAN. Stop! . . . Stop! . . . Stop! (*To the girls who are moving up ladder*) Well, you fillies, are you deaf? One move and I skewer the old boy to the wall.

JAPHETH (*trying to drag his brothers*). Come on! Let's go for him!

MAMMA. Don't move.

MAN (*to* JAPHETH). If you are looking for trouble, cocky . . .

NOAH. Steady, Japheth, steady. He'll kill you.

MAN. You bet I will!

MAMMA *and* THE CHILDREN. Scoundrel! Ruffian!

NOAH. Silence.

(*Mutterings from the youngsters*)

Now, that's enough! (*To the* MAN) Don't keep on waving that thing about. Your arm will get tired.

MAN. I seen you. I seen you! You sorcerer. Talking to the animals. Pinching a cow from Mordecai. Playing with bears and lions and tigers, not to mention elephants. I seen you! The whole village is going to know. I'll tell them. Sorcerer! Sorcerer!

THE THREE BOYS. Stop it!

MAN. It's none of your business. All you've got to do is keep your mouth shut. What's more, the animals are in there! (*He points to the Ark.*) I've seen 'em coming. That's where they are . . . in there!

(MAMMA *and the youngsters laugh. The* MAN *rushes to the Ark and beats on it with his fist. Roaring from the animals*)

MAMMA and THE YOUNGSTERS (*frightened*). Oh!

MAN. Hahaha! Who's laughing now? Ah, he looks gentle enough, but he's up to plenty of tricks behind your back! He's bad. He never could make anything with his hands before that. (*Pointing to the Ark*) He's a menace to the whole country.

MAMMA. Be quiet!

MAN. Listen, I'll tell you something. This drought that's been roasting us for three months, that nobody's never seen nothing like before, that'll knock us all dead with our mouths open this winter . . . that's him. He done it! He's the one that done it.

NOAH. Are you sure you're quite all right in the head?

MAN. You done it! There! We all got together! We took a vote. And we all voted alike — unanimous — that it's all your fault.

NOAH. Oh, well, in that case . . .

MAN. Listen! I represent the community, so to speak. The head man says to me, "Watch that old bird," he says. "He acts stupid, but he knows all the tricks." Everything that's gone wrong . . . he started it.

MAMMA. Oh, Noah, if they think that, that's terrible!

NOAH. Ssshh! Ssshh!

MAN. I seen you! You look up in the air like this. (*He imitates* NOAH *praying.*) And straight away it gets hotter, and hotter. I seen you doing your abracadabra. And then the sky opens like an oven door, and the oven is white hot, and the ground where I was lying was like a gridiron.

YOUNGSTERS (*in a low voice*). Oh!

MAN. All right, now you got to pay for it. Yes, you've got to come with me. But I don't need the whole issue. The head'll do. (*He leaps toward* NOAH.)

(MAMMA *and the girls scream. The boys line up in front of* NOAH.)

NOAH. You wretched creature! (*He steps in front of them all and smiles. A pause*) This drought (*He half turns toward his family.*) . . . He hoped it would make them see; that they'd say to themselves, "It must be. It's a judgment from heaven." I told them so myself, in every possible way. They laughed in my face. They spat on me. They threw stones at me.

MAMMA and THE YOUNGSTERS. Yes.

NOAH. Didn't I tell them often enough?

MAMMA and THE YOUNGSTERS. Oh, yes.

NOAH. I told them again and again, didn't I?

MAMMA and THE YOUNGSTERS. Oh yes, yes, yes.

NOAH (*turning toward the* MAN). Fool! To think they're all like you. Idle, greedy, thieving, wicked!

(MAN *sneers.*)

And on top of that, sneering and sniggering at everything!

MAN. Aw, you old fool. You old idiot.

NOAH (*walking up to him*). Tell me, my friend, can you swim?

MAN. What?

NOAH. I asked if you could swim.

MAN. Aw, come on! None of your tricks with me. I know you.

NOAH. Once and for all, yes or no. Can you swim?

MAN. Of course.

NOAH. Can you swim for a long time?

MAN. You bet!

NOAH. You'll have to swim a long time . . . so long that it might be better if you couldn't swim at all. Then it would be over sooner.

MAN. Over?

NOAH. Yes, over. That's what I said—finished.

MAN. What's going to be finished?

NOAH. Everything! You. Your friends. Your relations. The village. All the villages. This forest. All the forests, all the animals, all human beings in the water! Under the water! With your sins like stones around your neck.

MAN (*bending double*). Hahahahaha!

NOAH (*bending double, too*). Hahahahahaha!

MAN. Hahahahahaha!

NOAH. It's going to rain. Rain! You hear what I say? . . . *rain!*

(*The* MAN, *the children, and* MAMMA *raise their eyes to the sky.*)

MAN. Hahahahahaha!

HAM (*to* SHEM, *under his breath*). Has father got a touch of the sun? There's not a cloud in the sky!

NOAH. Such rain as has never been before. Pouring, drenching, spouting rain. Water swirling, water roaring—hurricanes sweeping madly across the sky—tattered clouds streaming out like great black flags ripped by lightning. Fish will play in the trees. On the tops of mountains, where there were soaring eagles, there will be ravening sharks. And the bodies of the drowned with arms outstretched, rolling over and over, down and down and down. He told me.

MAN. Who?

NOAH. God.

MAN. Who's that?

NOAH. God!

MAN. Oh, of course!

NOAH (*louder*). God.

MAN. Try again.

NOAH (*very loud*). Almighty God!

(MAMMA *and the children drop to their knees.*)

MAN. Hahahaha! (*He stutters with glee.*) God! . . . Almighty God be . . . (*He stops short. His hands go to his forehead.*)

(*The light dims.*)

NOAH. Splash! Did you feel that, my friend? You felt the first drop! Right on your forehead? Between the eyes, as straight as a die. A perfect shot. (*Savagely*)

(MAMMA *and the children rise trembling.*)

MAN. Oh, you think so? Well, it was a bird—a sparrow.
NOAH. And that?

(*The* MAN'S *hand goes to the back of his neck.*)

I suppose that was a nightingale? And that?

(*The* MAN'S *hand covers his eyes.*)

A robin, maybe?

(*The* MAN *stretches out his hands and quickly draws them in again.*)

And those. A brace of pigeons?
MAMMA and THE CHILDREN. Oh!
NOAH. Dance, my friend, dance!

(*And the* MAN *dances as if he were trying to avoid a cloud of arrows.*)

Shoot, O Lord! Strike this vile target, pierce it through and
through!
MAMMA and THE CHILDREN (*every hand extended*). It's raining, raining,
raining!

(*Pantomime of the children seeking the rain with every gesture around
the* MAN *whose every gesture dodges the rain. The light is growing dim.*)

NOAH. Pierce the wicked eyes! The prying nose. Those ears. Seal up
those lips and silence that blaspheming tongue. Pierce the hands
that were never raised to You! The feet that strayed! The glutton's
belly and his heart, O God, split that accursed heart. Shoot, King
of Archers, shoot!

(*The* MAN *sinks down, still warding off the rain with both hands.*)

MAN. Help! Help! It's burning . . . .

(*The light grows dimmer.*)

MAMMA (*her hands stretched to the rain*). It's cool, cool like the evening breeze.

THE CHILDREN (*their hands outstretched*). Like the evening breeze.

MAMMA. Like the blue of the sky.

THE CHILDREN. Like the blue of the sky.

MAMMA. Like the laughter of angels.

THE CHILDREN. The laughter of angels. . . .

THE MAN (*on his knees*). Help me! Help me! Help me! Help me!

(*Thunder rolls.*)

NOAH. All aboard! Into the Ark, my good crew! Heavy weather tonight! Up into our home! Into the ship of God! You first, Mother, then you, Ada! now Sella! Naomi! Shem! Ham! Japheth! And we must sing, my children, come! All together, sing!

(*A clap of thunder*)

(*The chorus is singing in unison.* NOAH *goes up last. The storm rages. It is completely dark.*)

(*The singing spreads through the Ark.*)

SCENE II

In the cabin of the Ark. It is a sort of hut, placed well downstage, in the center. The light is concentrated on its interior, which is open on the down-stage side; above, on the bridge of the Ark, there is rain-soaked darkness. When the curtain rises, MAMMA *and the three girls are seen, mending and darning in silence.*

MAMMA (*holding up a pair of trousers*). There, that's done. Oh! What a lot of work! I never saw so many holes . . . six weeks. It's disgraceful the way Noah gets through things.

ADA. He has to work so hard.

MAMMA. Yes, poor dear, what a time he has. Six weeks of storms and hurricanes and bad luck! Oh, these dreadful days.

SELLA. And these dreadful nights!

NAOMI. And still it goes on.

ADA. Oh, well, it isn't as bad as it was.

NAOMI. Listen to the rain.

ADA. The rain's nothing compared to the wind.

SELLA. What I hate the most is the thunder. Lying there in my bed, it sounds as if cartloads of empty barrels were going to tumble down on top of me.

MAMMA. Yes, and the lightning. Do you remember that night when there was so much lightning it was like broad daylight ? Ada's right though, things aren't as bad as they were.

NAOMI. Just listen to the rain.

(*Silence except for the drumming of the rain. An animal begins to howl in the hold.*)

ADA. The lion's worried about something.

NAOMI. That's not the lion.

ADA. Isn't it ?

NAOMI. I'd say it was the tiger.

SELLA. It isn't either of them ; it's the panther. Isn't it, Mrs. Noah ?

MAMMA. *I* don't know, dears. All I can tell you is that it isn't the cat. Apart from the cat they all sound alike to me.

(*Laughter*)

ADA. Oh, Mrs. Noah, you're sweet.

(SHEM *comes in from the rear.*)

SHEM. Hello everybody. . . . It seems to be raining a bit.

(*Pause*)

MAMMA. Where are your brothers ?

SHEM. Arguing. Exchanging ideas on the situation in general.

MAMMA. And Father ?

SHEM. He's taking a reckoning.

MAMMA. Taking a reckoning ?

SHEM. That means he's trying to find out where we are.

MAMMA. What do you mean, where we are ?

SHEM. What part of the world we're drifting over now.

MAMMA. Drifting ? . . . Do you mean the boat is moving ?

SHEM. Moving ! We're tearing along.

MAMMA. What ?

SHEM. Didn't you realize that ?

MAMMA. I hadn't the slightest idea ! (*Pause*) I . . . I thought we were floating just above our house. Yes . . . I thought all we did each day was rise a little higher above the house. . . . And — when it was all over — we'd just sink back home again.

SHEM. Oh, no. We must be at least six hundred miles away from home.

NAOMI. Really ?

SHEM. Do I look as if I were joking ?

SELLA. Six hundred miles !

SHEM. About ! Approximately . . . .

(*Silence. A howl from the hold*)

MAMMA. Then — then — we're right out at sea.

SHEM. You're quite right, Mother.

MAMMA. Good gracious me ! (*She gets up.*)

SHEM. What difference does that make ?

MAMMA. Then, down there, underneath us — is the sea ?

SHEM. Underneath us, all around us, as far as the eye can reach — all over the world.

MAMMA. And it's — it's waves that make the boat move ?

SHEM. Yes, Mother, it's the salt sea waves.

MAMMA. What ? Then all this water everywhere . . . is . . . *salt* water ?

SHEM. I wouldn't like to swear to it. I've never tasted it, you know.

MAMMA. Is it . . . is it very deep ?

SHEM. Incredibly deep, so Father says.

(*Silence. The beast howls. The three girls begin to cry.*)

MAMMA. Now, now, children, you mustn't take it like this. At your age, you ought to see the bright side of things.

ADA. I know, but this great big ocean . . .

NAOMI. This rain —

SELLA. So much water !

MAMMA. Yes, but look at me. I always used to be afraid of water, that during the rainy season — Noah will tell you — I didn't dare step over a puddle. And here I am in the middle of a puddle so big it hasn't any edges.

(*Laughter*)

All right then. We'll talk and laugh and work and stop worrying about it all.

(*They go back to their sewing. Vocies are heard off-stage.*)

JAPHETH'S VOICE. No, you're wrong. You're all wrong.
HAM'S VOICE. Oh, go on, it's clear as daylight.
JAPHETH'S VOICE. I say you're wrong, do you hear?
HAM'S VOICE. And I tell you I'm not.

(HAM *and* JAPHETH *come in at the back.*)

HAM. Well, well, how's the mothers' meeting?
MAMMA. Now, Ham! Where are your manners?
HAM. Waterlogged. Like everything else. (*To* JAPHETH) It's amazing how obstinate you can be.
JAPHETH. I'm not a bit obstinate. I just understand things clearly, that's all.
HAM. Oh, do you?
JAPHETH. Yes, I do.
SHEM and THE WOMEN. Oy, stop it.
HAM. You *see* the hand of God?
JAPHETH. No, I don't see it, but I can feel it. That's the same thing.
HAM. You idiot!
JAPHETH. What did you call me?
THE WOMEN. Quiet! That's enough!
SHEM. If anyone's an idiot, here, I'm the one. Allow me to present the idiot who does all the work while all the loafers stand about and chatter.
HAM. All right, all right.
SHEM. No, it's not all right. I've been minding those animals for a fortnight now, grooming them, feeding them, and putting them to bed! You don't know what that's like.
HAM. I've done it as well.
SHEM. You did once.

HAM. That was enough to find out what it's like. (*Laughter*)

SHEM (*laughing*). Lord what a cheek! (*To* HAM) You've an awful cheek, you old blackamoor.

NAOMI. I think it rather suits him.

HAM (*laughing too*). It isn't cheek at all. I'm just sensible, that's all. If something bores me, I don't do it. If it amuses me, I jolly well see that no one else does it.

JAPHETH. If everyone were like you . . .

HAM. I know young shaver, but everyone isn't like me.

MAMMA. Your conceit doesn't seem to have got waterlogged . . . like everything else. (*Laughter*)

(NOAH *appears at the back ; there is silence.*)

NOAH. Go on. Go on. (*He comes down.*) Enjoying yourselves, are you?

MAMMA. Yes, Noah. We were having a little laugh.

NOAH. Good, good. I like you laughing, it shows that everything is all right.

HAM. Otherwise you might be beginning to doubt it, mightn't you?

NOAH (*sharply*). Might I? How about you?

HAM. Oh, so far as I'm concerned . . .

NOAH (*imitating him*). I know, I know . . . you have your own pet little ideas about the world, haven't you?

HAM. Well, perhaps I have.

NOAH. I know you have.

HAM. Now look here, Father, just one little question . . .

NOAH. I'm only interested in big questions. (*He goes upstage.*)

MAMMA (*going to him*). What is it, Noah? Is something the matter?

NOAH. No, let me alone, let me alone.

MAMMA. I—I won't; we must share everything, good and bad; tell us what it is.

NOAH. Perhaps I should have called you—no, no, I think I was right not to call you. Oh, children, children! Such a terrible half-hour I have just been through—only a little while ago—just now, at twilight— just as it was getting dark, the last people on earth—well, I saw them die, that's all, yes, imagine—I had to watch them die—those few poor wretches, huddled together on the top of a mountain, there they were, that last pathetic little handful of living beings, and I watched them sinking into the water, one by one. Such a queer collection too—men and women and some children—a dog (or a wolf, it may have been, it was too far off for me to see distinctly)—and a bear—I'm sure it was ; there were some birds too, big white ones, but they flew away as soon as—oh, well, well, the wind was driving us along in their direction, and they must have been able to see us quite clearly, but they never made a sign. They must have understood, you see. And I felt—oh ! if only I could stop the ship and not go sailing quietly by staring at them. But what could I do ? We drifted on and passed them, quite close by—so slowly—so terribly slowly—oh, children ! Children !

HAM. Father, you ought to have—

NOAH. Child, don't you see—there was nothing that I could do. They never made a sound, just went into the water. Of course, they knew they could have waited on that mountain the whole night long, crying for help—no, into the water, without a word.

ALL. Oh !

NOAH. Do you know what happened then ? They started to swim. Oh ! That seemed to me—it seemed so—to watch them swimming like that—in water twenty thousand fathoms deep—quietly, carefully, as if there was still hope—can you imagine it ! They swam as if they had hope ! Long before that, the animals, the bear and the other one, had given up and gone under, in spite of their instinct to preserve themselves. But men keep on swimming—men are still swimming over this dreadful waste of water. Oh ! I hope, I only hope He saw it from up there. I hope He saw it too, that was something for Him to see !—And now they're dead.

(*Silence*)

MAMMA. And we're the only people in the world ?

NOAH. I'm afraid so, Mother. I'm afraid we are.

(*Silence*)

ADA. The only ones in the world . . .

NOAH (*gently*). It was bound to happen, you know. The day was bound to come.

NAOMI. All alone, all alone . . . the only ones in the world.

NOAH. Yes, I must say it isn't very cheerful.

SELLA. The only ones . . .

(They fall to crying.)

NOAH. Now, now, little ones, you knew perfectly well that it was going to happen. It was all leading to this. You must have known.

(Silence)

JAPHETH. No, I can't! I simply can't take it in, that's all. The only ones in the world! . . . The only ones? . . . What? . . . Then . . . we'll never see any more people? We're never going to meet anybody again? . . . We'll never . . . never . . .

(He breaks off with a whistle.)

SHEM *(spellbound)*. But all those people we knew . . . all our old crowd, our friends in the village . . . well—it's hard to believe there's no one left. And all the others too . . . the thousands we've never seen, but we knew they existed of course . . . in other villages, in towns, in other countries—all over the world, I mean . . . Pffit? . . . It doesn't seem possible.

MAMMA. Shem, we didn't know many people, really. . . .

SHEM. But all the same, Mother, all the same—*(He stops.)* I don't know why I should suddenly think of the postman.

JAPHETH. Funny, I was thinking of him, too.

SHEM. Remember him, Japheth? With his crooked jaw sticking out and his satchel flopping about on his tummy? He was a character, that postman. *(MAMMA sobs.)* And now! The postman's dead, think of that. Condemned to die because of the rottenness of all the rest of mankind, a shameful death for something he wouldn't even understand.

JAPHETH. I know; it hardly seems possible.

(A pause)

HAM. I'll tell you something that's going to seem even more impossible.

JAPHETH. What?

HAM. Sooner or later something will have to be done about replacing all those dead people.

SHEM. What about it?

HAM. Well, my boy, that's where we come in.

JAPHETH. What?

HAM. Who else is there to do it, except us three—and—our three charm-
ing companions.

THE THREE GIRLS. Oh!

HAM. Well, damn it all! Unless the Lord begins the work of creation all
over again, I don't see how else . . . (*He turns to* NOAH.) Well, Father.
How about it? Any ideas?

ADA (*frightened*). Mr. Noah!

NAOMI. It can't be true?

SELLA. Mr. Noah!

NOAH (*to* HAM). Now then, young man . . . (*He turns to the girls.*) My dear
girls, what on earth's the good of making plans about the future?
Haven't we enough worries and troubles for the moment? . . . Just
be patient. . . . We'll see.

NAOMI. It isn't a matter of making plans; we've got to face the future—
look at it squarely. (*Disgustedly*) Ugh . . . Ha . . . Are we supposed to
turn into wild beasts again . . . to behave like animals?

SELLA. Oh, it's all too horrid. It's degrading, that's what it is, simply
degrading.

ADA (*pleading*). Mr. Noah . . . Mr. Noah . . .

NOAH (*to* HAM). Now perhaps you are satisfied?

NAOMI. Well, three boys like these; just three boys; no one else at all,
but just these three boys . . . (*To her sisters*) Just look at them. . . .
How's that for the world's supply of husbands!

SHEM. I suppose you think we are any better off?

(*The boys all laugh.*)

SELLA (*to* NOAH). And if two of us should want the same one?

NOAH (*never ceasing to smile*). I don't think that will happen.

SELLA and NAOMI. Why not?

NOAH. God wouldn't muddle things like that.

NAOMI. But He doesn't know us. . . . We're—How could He understand
us? We're women!

SELLA. What we want is love, and love must choose for itself. Don't you
understand?

NOAH. No, I can't say I do.

NAOMI. If you could only make one—one perfect man—out of the three
of them! But it can't be done. The tall one is much too skinny, the

short one is far too fat, the middle one is neither one thing nor the other. . . . Oh dear, oh dear, oh dear.

HAM (*coming forward*). Anything more ?

NAOMI. Don't touch me !

HAM. That's just what I'm going to do. (*He takes her by the arm.*)

NAOMI. Don't touch me ! Don't touch me !

HAM. Listen ; you're not going to be the ones to choose ; *we* are. Just get that into your head. (*He laughs.*) Ha, ha ! And to make things easier, how would it be if I chose you straight away, eh ? Come on, Naomi, you're booked.

NOAH. Now, now, there's no need to hurry.

HAM (*to* NAOMI). Now I'm going to kiss you.

NOAH. I say there isn't any hurry.

HAM (*kissing* NAOMI *violently three times*). There ! There ! There !

NAOMI. Oh, you . . . you brute !

NOAH. Now stop it ! . . . Ham, let her alone ! . . . Oh, you've made her cry.

HAM. I know, for joy. (*To* NAOMI) Isn't it ?

NAOMI (*without conviction*). I hate you.

HAM (*to* NOAH). See ? It's joy. Ha, ha, ha.

NOAH. All right, all right, but that's enough. Ham ! Do you hear what I say ? That's enough, do you understand ? Enough. We're all tired, and we've had a hard day. Time for bed now.

SELLA. Bed !

NOAH. Yes, bed, as fast as you can. Things will be better in the morning.

HAM. I don't see what difference the morning's going to make.

NOAH. Well, bless my soul, neither do I ! But that doesn't prevent my living in hopes. Good heavens above, do I have to give you lessons in being young ? Great heavens, you're all living in a miracle ! Here have you been, seeing nothing but wonders for the last six weeks and now you want to know what is going to happen next. Oh, what babies you all are still ! Such babies ! But they're good children, really, Mother, they'll turn out all right, you'll see !

JAPHETH. Why don't you ask Him what's going to happen ?

NOAH. Oh, certainly, that's a fine idea ! I might ask Him the time too, eh ! . . . You have a fine idea of God, you have.

(*He laughs, then the others do, too.*)

JAPHETH. You always tell us He's so simple.

NOAH. Of course He is simple. But that doesn't mean that He's half-witted . . . anyway . . . well, He takes things as they come. Good heavens, we're alive, aren't we ? What more do you want ? Now it's time you hopped into bed. Good night, everybody.

THE CHILDREN. Good night, Father.

(The family swing their hammocks. HAM starts to go out.)

NOAH. Where are you off to ?

HAM. Just going for a stroll.

NOAH. What on earth for ?

HAM. Well, I'm not sleepy.

(He goes out.)

MAMMA *(going to NOAH)*. Good night, Noah.

NOAH. Good night, Mother. *(Then he holds her back and whispers to her.)* Listen, Mother, what do you think about all this ? Do you think . . . *(He breaks off.)* Who is that crying ?

ADA. I am, sir. . . . Please excuse me. . . . I'll try to stop now.

NOAH. My dear child, whatever's the matter ?

ADA. Nothing, sir . . . only this rain . . . this rain.

NOAH. But it will stop some day, Ada, dear.

ADA. Are you quite sure, sir ?

NOAH. Quite sure. You'll see. Sleep, now, go to sleep and dream about the sun.

ADA. I'll try, sir.

NOAH *(to MAMMA)*. Good night, now, Mother. You're all right now, aren't you ?

MAMMA. Of course, Noah. Everything's all right.

NOAH *(imitating her)*. Of course, Noah, of course. Oh, you old darling. . . . Now go on to bed. It must be almost morning.

(MAMMA kisses him and goes to her bed in a corner. A pause. NOAH sits thinking as the rain pours down and the beasts howl below. NOAH talks to himself.)

I thought today would never end. It's seemed so long. One felt it wouldn't go unless one gave it a push. Ouch ! Well, it's over now. Let me see. . . . That makes exactly forty days ! I wonder how many there'll be altogether. Fifty, sixty, eighty ? People are funny, always thinking everything will turn out just as they expect—why, I scolded them just now for trying to look ahead, and here I am doing it myself. Well, I suppose I was right to scold them, but it's not so easy when it comes to yourself. Hullo ! Now who's snoring ? Oh, Mother, bless her heart, and she still says she's never snored in her life. Oh, well, she's tired out, poor thing. They all are, tired and anxious, that's why they squabble and complain. They're good children really, though. Yes, there's nothing wrong with this cargo . . . not even Ham. He wants to seem grown-up, that's why he plays the fool. Oh, it's a fine cargo ! When we get to harbor, and they're all lined up on the quay—I can see it now—a big white quay all shining in the sunlight—and God says to me, "Claim your reward, Noah," then I'll say to him, "Lord, all I want is to parade my flock. Look at them : how fine and strong the people are. And how well the beasts are looking. There isn't a pennyworth of disease or wickedness in the whole world. The men are all laughing, and the animals would be laughing too, if they knew how." And He'll begin to laugh Himself, and He'll laugh so loud He'll knock us all sprawling. Ha, ha.

JAPHETH (*raising his head*). What's the matter ? What's the matter ?

NOAH. Nothing, son, I was laughing, that's all.

JAPHETH. Aren't you going to bed ?

NOAH. Yes, yes, of course . . . go to sleep. (JAPHETH *lies down again and* NOAH *goes on speaking to himself.*) I can laugh if I want to, can't I ? If they won't laugh with me I can laugh just by myself. I don't know why, but I feel as if something good—something gay—were going to happen. I can feel it !

(*An animal howls.*)

They feel it too !

(*More howling*)

Something's up. Something's up ! (*He gets up.*)

(*A cock crows.*)

The cock ? The cock ? But he's never crowed since—

(The cock crows again, waking everyone up. There is much excitement. Above, the day is dawning.)

Quiet, quiet, keep quiet. . . . Something's happening. . . . I'm going to look ; wait for me. . . . Stay here quietly . . . till I look . . .

(He climbs a ladder in a corner, opens a trap-door and goes through it. The children sit motionless in their beds. Again the cock crows. NOAH *appears on deck above the cabin. Quickly the daylight brightens.)*

Why . . . look . . . . It has stopped raining !

(The suns bursts forth.)

My goodness ! The sun's coming out ! *(He leans over the cabin.)* Children ! Children, come here !

(They all rush to the bridge. The cock is crowing at the top of his lungs.)

(Quieting his flock) Sh ! Sh ! Sh ! On tiptoe, everybody. Walk on tiptoe. It's so fresh . . . so young . . . so delicate.

ADA. Look, the deck is steaming.

SELLA. The planks are drying up.

NAOMI. The sea is singing.

MAMMA. The silence . . .

SHEM *(staring at the sun)*. A . . . At . . . tchou !

NOAH. Sh ! . . . Where's Ham ?

JAPHETH. Not here, the silly ass !

NOAH. Ah well, well, well, well. *(Having lined them all up at the back, steps in front of them and cries in a resounding voice.)* For . . . the . . . Lord . . . God ! King of the Earth ! *(He raises his arm.)*

CHORUS. Hurray ! Hurray ! Hurray !

CHORUS OF ANIMALS *(from below)*. Ouahh ! Ouahh ! Ouahh !

(The children laugh.)

NOAH. The Golden Age ! . . . just as I said. *(A pause. He gazes at the sky, the water, the Ark, then turns to the chorus and cries, profoundly joyful.)* Good morning, children !

ALL. Good morning, Father !

NOAH. How are you?

ALL. Well!

NOAH. Good!

ALL. And how are *you*?

NOAH. Very well!

ALL. Splendid!

NOAH. Louder!

ALL. Splendid!

NOAH. Louder still!

ALL. Splen-did!

NOAH. That's it! We must breathe, my children, we must breathe. Like this; ha! We must blow away these forty days of darkness, these forty nights of fear. Our lungs are choked with dust and ashes—blow them away—ha!

ALL. Hah!

NOAH. Once again!

ALL. Hah-ah!

NOAH. There, we're washed clean. . . . I feel all new inside. In my breast —(*he taps his chest*)—there are white birds all ready to fly straight from my heart to God! . . . Oh, English is a beautiful language. . . . (*He places himself before them, his voice vibrating.*) Walk, children. Let's walk!

(*They line up and walk in great strides toward the audience.*)

To the south, as you see, we have a view of the ocean.

CHORUS (*interested*). Aha!

NOAH (*walking right*). To the east we have a vast expanse of water, probably salt, of an appearance and character distinctly . . . oceanic.

CHORUS. Well, well!

NOAH (*walking up*). To the north, our prospect opens immediately on to . . . well . . . the sea.

CHORUS. How very convenient!

NOAH. Lastly, to the west we see . . . see and hear . . . the rippling laughter of the waves. (*Toward audience*) To sum up the entire situation: we are on the water.

CHORUS. We're at sea! Ha!

NOAH. Ha!

CHILDREN. Ha! Ha!

JAPHETH. Faster!

(They all walk more quickly.)

NOAH. Don't you think it's marvelous?
CHORUS. Marvelous!
JAPHETH. Faster!

(Again they quicken the pace.)

NOAH. I don't believe Mother can keep up with this.
MAMMA *(panting)*. Yes . . . I can! I'm so . . . so happy.
NOAH. No, no, Mother, you needn't keep in line. Just sit out and give us
   your blessing.
MAMMA *(dropping out)*. Oh, Noah! You're . . . so young . . . .
NOAH. Young! Upon my soul. I'm as old as the world . . . I was born . . .
   this morning.
CHORUS. Come on. Faster, faster!
NOAH. On the sea, beneath the sky, between the two great elements as
   it was in the beginning—
CHORUS *(impatient)*. Come on! Come on! Come on! Come on!
NOAH. I give up. *(He drops out and joins his wife.)* But you go ahead. Go
   on, go on!
THE BOYS. A-Hi! . . . A-Ha! . . . Ah-Yah! Ah-You!
THE GIRLS. You-ou-ou-ou!
NOAH and MAMMA *(sitting on the sidelines beat the measure with their
   hands)*. March! . . . March! . . . March . . . March—march!
CHORUS *(beside itself with joy)*. Ha—ah—ah—ah . . . Ha!

(They drop down in a circle.)

ALL. The sun!!

SCENE III

The deck of the Ark, partially shaded by an awning. The sunlight is intense.
   SHEM, HAM, *and* NAOMI *are leaning over the rail watching the fish that
   swim about the Ark.*

NAOMI. There's a beauty! Look at him!
HAM. Grand!

NAOMI. Look at him diving. He is like a paper lantern on a summer night.

HAM. Yes, he is, isn't he ? Look, there's the female.

NAOMI. Where, where ? . . . Oh, yes, I see her.

SHEM. How do you know it's a female ?

HAM. Because it's not as pretty as the other.

NAOMI (*tenderly*). Oh, you pig !

(*She embraces him.* HAM *turns around ; their lips meet.*)

SHEM. Now you two. There are plenty of dark corners on this boat for that sort of thing.

HAM. What's the matter, don't you like it ?

SHEM. On the contrary, that's just why . . .

NAOMI. Don't you ever kiss Sella ?

SHEM. Why should I ? Hey, look at those fellows going by.

HAM. Whew ! what whoppers ! Look, Naomi, look !

NAOMI. All right ! I'm not blind.

HAM. What sort of fish are they, Shem ?

SHEM. I don't know. Never seen them before.

HAM. But I thought you used to be the finest fisherman in the world !

(*A pause*)

NAOMI. Why do they all swim two by two ?

HAM. Do they ? Oh yes, so they do. . . .

SHEM. I don't know. . . . It is funny . . . Unless it's because . . .
   (*to* HAM) but you'll laugh at me.

HAM. Never mind, go ahead.

SHEM. Well, don't you think they might be . . . well . . . specimens?

HAM. How do you mean ?

SHEM. You know. The sole survivors—

HAM. God's own particular pets, eh ! Ha ha ! That's good.

SHEM. Well, that would explain why there are so many of them, and why they go in pairs, and why they've been following us for weeks.

NAOMI. They can't come into the Ark, so they just keep as close as they can. Ha ha !

SHEM. Well, you find a better explanation, then.

HAM. My dear fellow, we're not expert fishermen ; there must be some natural explanation. Look at that mass of them ! The place is alive ! Well, doesn't that make your mouth water, you old angler, you ?

SHEM. Yes, I must say it does rather.

HAM. Well, what about having a shot?

SHEM. What?

HAM (*casting a line in pantomime*). Tchk.

SHEM. Do you think we could?

HAM. Why not?

NAOMI. Oh, do let's!

HAM. Run and rig up a line, Shem. . . .

SHEM. But Father—

HAM. Oh Father my eye! Is fishing forbidden? Since when?

SHEM. Well, I don't believe he . . .

HAM. Ah, you're always in such a funk!

(SHEM *goes toward the back.*)

Hurry up, will you? Go on—they're just dying to bite.

(SHEM *goes out.*)

I'll burst their little bubble for them.

NAOMI. I knew that you were planning something.

HAM. It isn't the fish that I want to catch. . . .

NAOMI (*secretively*). Isn't it really?

HAM. No, my pretty! It's the old man.

NAOMI. Funny, I thought as much.

(*They laugh.*)

HAM. Ah, here's the fisherman.

(SHEM *returns with his fishline.*)

(*To* SHEM) Quick work! Good . . . come on, come on! Here. (*To*
NAOMI) You go and keep cave, my child, do you hear?

NAOMI. Oh, I wanted to watch. . . .

HAM. I'll call you when the fun begins. Come on, Shem. Look, cast here,
right in the middle of that bunch.

(SHEM *sits down and throws in his line.* HAM *stands near him;* NAOMI
mounts guard upstage. A pause. SHEM *pulls in his line and casts again.*)

SHEM. They don't seem to be hungry.

HAM. Give them time, give them time.

SHEM. Hum!

(*Another pause*)

No, they don't seem to bite ; perhaps we were making too much noise.

HAM. What are we going to do then ?

SHEM. Nothing, just wait.

HAM. Oh, go on, Father—

(*A pause*)

NAOMI. Well ?

SHEM. Nothing doing.

HAM. There ! There ! Surely that's a bite ?

SHEM. No, it's weed.

HAM. Pull in a little and see.

SHEM (*pulling in without result*). Weed !

HAM. I suppose you'll be telling me next there aren't any fish.

SHEM. There are fish all right. They're just not biting, that's all.

HAM. Oh, you and your specimen fish ! They're resisting temptation, I suppose.

SHEM. Joke if you like, I bet I'm right.

HAM. Hahaha !

SHEM. Not so loud, you fool ! (*He turns.*) See anything, Naomi ?

NAOMI. Not a thing. I'll tell you if I do.

SHEM (*to* HAM). Do you know what Father's doing ?

HAM. He's down with the animals. They're all he cares about nowadays. He says he understands them. Do you know he even talks to them ! Ha, ha !

NAOMI. Look out !

(*The two fishermen turn their backs to the rail and pretend to chat innocently.*)

False alarm !

HAM. Good. (*To* SHEM) Come on, my boy ! You're not half trying. There, try for that big one. He's a five-pounder, I bet. Get him by the nose! Quick!

(SHEM *casts the line.*)

Whew! See him jump. He's biting, isn't he? Go on, strike!

SHEM (*striking without catching anything*). They're not biting, I tell you. Even when their noses are bumping against the hook, they change their minds.

HAM. Go on, try again.

SHEM. I've tried enough.

HAM. Ah, come on, Shem, just once more. One more shot.

NAOMI. Look out! Careful!

HAM (*to* SHEM). Stay where you are! Lean over the side. . . . If it's him you can drop the rod into the water.

(ADA *and* SELLA *appear.*)

NAOMI. Oh, it's nobody. Only the girls.

HAM. All right, now Shem, come on. One last try. Give it everything you've got.

NAOMI. I must be in on this.

(*She comes down and leans over* HAM'S *shoulder.* ADA *and* SELLA *move forward whispering.*)

SELLA (*softly to* ADA). Did you hear that? "Nobody! Only the girls."

ADA. Yes, that's what she thinks these days.

SELLA. Always chasing the men.

ADA. We can clean the dishes and wash the clothes, that's all we're good for.

SELLA. All she does is doll herself up.

HAM. Don't whisper like that, kids. It's maddening.

(ADA *and* SELLA *move away a little and continue their whispering.*)

HAM. Well, Shem, how about it, old boy? Things aren't going so well, are they? . . . Well . . .

SHEM. I tell you these fish aren't—

HAM. Oh, shut up! Now go on! Fish!

NAOMI. Oh, you darling, you're so wonderful when you want something! (*She kisses him.*)

ADA and SELLA. Oh!

HAM (*disengaging himself*). Yes, I know. . . . You keep watch, dear, that's all. . . . (*To* SHEM) Now you listen to me. You've got to catch a fish, see? Just one, but I've got to have it.

SELLA. A what?

HAM. Shut up! I want to hook something out of the water alive so that I can see it wriggle and die before my eyes! Is that clear? (*To* SHEM) Now jump to it!

(SHEM *casts again . . . silence.* HAM *follows every movement of the line with burning eyes.*)

(*Softly*) That one's showing some interest. Look, isn't he?

SHEM. Perhaps . . .

HAM. Of course he is! See that he gets a good bite! Careful! One . . . two . . . three . . . strike!

SHEM (*casting in vain*). Blast!

HAM. Damnation! It's no good, no damn good at all. Everything we do, everything we try, it all seems to go wrong. It's all just damn silly nonsense!

(SHEM *throws down the fishpole.* HAM *paces the deck in a rage. He settles down to sleep. The others sigh.* JAPHETH *comes in.*)

JAPHETH (*gaily*). Oh, here you are!

NAOMI (*pointing to* HAM). Sh!

JAPHETH (*softly, coming down*). What's the matter?

NAOMI. He's bored.

JAPHETH. Hm. Hm.

(*He sits down with the others and they talk in low tones.*)

(*To* SHEM) Some of the animals don't seem to me to be very well.

SHEM. Did you tell Father about it?

JAPHETH. I couldn't find him. The old tub still not moving?

HAM. Moving! I believe the blasted thing has taken root. Five months it's been like this!

SELLA. Five months.

HAM. That's what I said. Oh, I've kept count all right. Five months of water, of animals, of each other! Five months of waiting—and, my God, we don't even know what for! I tell you it's driving me crazy! And the old man doesn't do anything—he doesn't do a thing—not a single thing.

JAPHETH. What do you want him to do?

HAM. Anything, I don't care! Anything, so long as it'll tire us out and stop us thinking. It's up to him to say what. I don't care how stupid or useless. Why doesn't he treat us like dirt, trample us under foot?

JAPHETH. You'd be the first to kick.

HAM. Well, and then there'd be some fun, there'd be something to struggle for, something to fight against.

JAPHETH. You can't fight against God.

HAM. Do you mean to say you still—no, you make me tired. Haven't I told you a hundred times—

JAPHETH. Yes, but you haven't convinced me yet.

HAM. Listen, Japheth, Dad's a farmer, isn't he?

JAPHETH. And a jolly good one too—

HAM. Agreed. You probably wouldn't find a better, but still he is only a farmer.

JAPHETH. That's better than being—

NAOMI. Oh, be quiet!

JAPHETH. Who are you talking to?

SHEM. Oh, shut up! Go on, Ham, go on.

HAM. Well, this is what I feel about Father. He's a man of the soil. He understands all about animals and plants and stars and all that sort of thing. He has a sort of instinct for changes of the wind and weather—an amazing instinct—in fact he almost seems to be able to pop in and out according to whether it's going to be wet or fine. He was the only man in the world to foresee that some great catastrophe was going to happen. And so he used his imagination and saved himself and us. But don't you see that all that is only just instinct—it's got nothing to do with miracles. Oh, don't think I'm running him down. On the contrary, it's pretty marvelous. In fact, it's a damn sight more marvelous than calling up God every five minutes for orders. Well, that's what I think, and I don't mind how soon I tell him so.

JAPHETH. If you did it would kill him.

HAM. You can't kill things any more, young feller. That's what you keep on telling us. How about it, all of you, shall I tell him all that? And a bit more too?

(*No one speaks.*)

Don't all speak at once.

SHEM. It's awfully serious, you know. . . . It would put the whole ship in a state of war. And besides . . .

HAM. Well?

SHEM. Well . . . it's no joke.

HAM. All right, my friends, all right! But don't say I didn't warn you.

(*The* BEAR *comes in at the back.*)

HAM. Hullo, what's he up to? (*He goes to the* BEAR.) What do you want, you old fathead?

(*The* BEAR *attempts to flee, but* HAM *bars the way.*)

No, no, stupid. Not that way. Get in front now, go on.

(*The* BEAR *remains frozen with terror.* HAM *whacks him with his belt. The* BEAR *comes forward and stops among the children.*)

Get up!

(*The* BEAR *doesn't move.*)

Get up, I tell you! (HAM *kicks him in the back.*) Will you get up?

(*The* BEAR *sits up.*)

Come on, sit up. Higher. Straighter, hear? More! More! There! Ladies and gentlemen! I have the honor to present the guv'nor's old friend; his favorite pal and confidential adviser. My God! It makes me mad to think of all those fine men and women rotting at the bottom of the sea, while we feed up a brute like this—and all those other beasts down there in the hold. I vote we chuck 'em all overboard. What do you say? And we'll start with you, my lad, do you hear? Well, go on, answer, say something. Chatty, isn't he?

Look at him ; half a ton of stupid speechlessness. He could talk all right if he wanted to, but he's too cunning. They're all the same, animals ; great stupid lumps with cunning little minds. Look at him ! And he hates me. You do hate me, don't you ?

ADA. Oh, don't hurt him, Ham !

HAM. Hurt him ! the old windbag ? Just you wait !

NAOMI. No, Ham, make him dance !

SELLA. Yes, yes, let's have a bear dance.

HAM. Oh, yes ! that's an idea ! (*To the* BEAR) Did you hear that ? All right, get going. One, two ! (*He lashes him with his whip, first one paw, then the other.*) One, two ! One, two !

(*The* BEAR *begins to dance. The children clap their hands and chant a sort of melopoeia as an accompaniment, interrupting it with bursts of laughter. For a while the* BEAR *dances. Then* NOAH *comes in at the back.*)

(*At first the children do not see him, but the moment he reaches them they are abruptly silent. The* BEAR *drops on to all fours and moves away to a corner. As* NOAH *gazes at them the children, excepting* HAM, *lower their heads one by one.*)

NOAH. Not a ripple, not a breath !

(*Meanwhile at the back,* MAMMA *pokes an anxious head out on deck, then comes trotting down. She places herself behind* HAM, *who suddenly takes a step forward.*)

HAM. Father—

NOAH (*firmly*). No.

(*A pause*)

HAM. Look here, Father—

NOAH (*more firmly*). No, I say !

MAMMA (*softly to* HAM). Be quiet, dear, be nice. Don't be tiresome. . . . Father's busy.

(*Pause*)

NAOMI (*simpering*). Excuse me, Mr. Noah, but—

NOAH (*thunderously*). No!

(*He takes a step and the children recoil.*)

Go away.

(*The children mutter, but continue to back up.*)

Not a word! Off with you! Be off! Get below, everybody!

(*The children are now all the way upstage.*)

Who's cabin boy today?

JAPHETH. I am, Father.

NOAH. Send the animals up on deck. It's past their time.

JAPHETH. Yes, Father.

NOAH. No violence, do you hear? No shouting, or swearing, or beating them. Go along.

(*The children go away, with* MAMMA *following them.*)

(*Suddenly tender*) No, you stay here, Mother. You know I wasn't talking to you. . . . Please stay here with me.

MAMMA. I'd better go with them. . . . They want cheering up. (*Her voice is choked.*) It's been a long voyage for them, you know . . . they're not bad, really, Noah. They're not really wicked. . . .

(*She goes away sobbing.*)

(*Then* NOAH, *with a great helpless gesture, sinks down under the awning, facing front. He seems very old and tired. There is a little pause, and then the* LION *appears. He stretches himself and comes down to* NOAH. *The* BEAR *joins him. The two animals lie down at* NOAH'S *feet.*)

NOAH. No, don't lie down. . . . Walk about a bit. . . . You must have some exercise.

(*The animals get up and rest their heads on* NOAH'S *knees.*)

(*Stroking them*) Yes, you're good beasts. . . . But don't worry about me . . . I'm just a little tired, that's all. . . . Go along now.

(*The* LION *moves away a little. The* BEAR *rises up and tries a dance step.*)

No, Bruin, old boy, no, old boy, don't do that . . . on all fours. It's so much better.

(*The* BEAR *obediently drops and goes to join the* LION. *The* TIGER *comes in, followed by the* MONKEY. *They both want to stay near* NOAH.)

Run along. Leave me alone, my friends. . . . Go and play with the others.

(*The four animals sit up in a row, contemplating* NOAH *very sadly.*)

(*Deeply moved*) Leo . . . Sultan . . . Bruin . . . Jacko . . . My friends . . . my friends. . . . (*He weeps.*)

(*The four animals toss their heads in sympathy. Suddenly the* MONKEY *jumps to his feet, calls for attention and begins to dance a hornpipe to amuse* NOAH. *But the* BEAR *trots to him, growling, and pushes him down on all fours with a paw. The* LION *and the* TIGER *approve heartily.*)

My friends ! . . . My friends ! . . .

(*The* COW *comes in, galloping daintily. She nods to* NOAH *in passing.*)

(*Drying his eyes*) Good morning, Daisy, good morning.

(*The* COW *begins to circle the deck, but the* TIGER *bars her way and forces her into line.*)

(*His voice trembling, but growing stronger as he speaks*) It's the children, you see, it's the children. (*The animals nod their heads.*) And then Mother too, she's beginning to give way—she's beginning to fail me. I never knew that to happen before. All this happening at once, you know, it's taken me by surprise. It's worn me out, bowled me over. They all keep asking questions : '' Why this ? Why that ? What now ? What next ? '' Well, I don't know everything, I'm only an old farmer after all. If it was only their natural curiosity . . . because they're young, I mean . . . but it isn't. There's only one thing they're after . . . to catch me out. Oh, my friends, I'm afraid that Ham—

(*The animals growl.*)

Now, now, behave yourselves. . . . Yes, I'm afraid it's Ham that—

(*The animals growl.*)

He's very unkind to you, isn't he ? Well, so he is to me. . . . You've no idea.

(*The animals are growling louder and louder.*)

(*Getting up*) There, there we musn't mind. . . . It's all over. We'll say no more about it.

(*He strokes the animals and they crowd around him.*)

And then there is another thing. . . . But mind this is just between ourselves—between friends, eh ?

(*He looks about to be sure they are alone, then speaks very quietly.*)

God isn't with us any more. . . . Sh ! . . . there !

(*The animals lower their heads brokenly.*)

Well, put yourselves in His place. Try to put yourselves respectfully in His place. Every day, all day long, hearing His existence doubted, even at times when it is most apparent. It was all mankind before, now it's these children. Always asking Him for proofs and miracles; demanding—ah, it's too much—guarantees ! "If you are God, give us something else for dinner. " "If you are God, take away my toothache. " " If there was a God, He wouldn't have let me bang my head coming upstairs this morning. " Yes, my friends, that was what one of the little girls dared to say today. So He's gone off on a holiday, you see. Well, you can't really blame Him, all I can say is it's a wonder He didn't do it long ago. Goodness knows He's had patience enough. Well, He hasn't any more, that's all. After all, He's not a saint, that man. Just think of it, my friends, God! Almighty God! (*The* TIGER *howls.*) Now, now, never mind. He'll come back. He's gone to have a little rest, that's all. He's just shut up shop for two or three weeks. All right, we'll wait till He opens up again.

(*The other animals howl with the* TIGER.)

Sh! Sh! Now—yes, I understand—I know what's the matter. But we mustn't give up.

(*All the animals howl desperately.*)

Steady! Steady! He'll be horrified if He hears you up there! Call— yes. Call out by all means. We'll all call out together if you like, but not in fear, not in anger. Something that may come sweetly to His ears. Lord! Lord! Now once more, and a good one this time—no shadow of doubt or fear, my children. Lord! Lord! Lord! There, that's enough now. Courage now! Quiet, every one of you. There, there. Rest now. I'm tired, my children. Bruin is going to lend me his back, and I'm going to lie down among you, just the same as you. We'll build a great tower of patience in the midst of the waters, and as the oak tree draws down the lightning, His eyes will light upon it. There, there, we must show Him how well we understand that everything must take time in this world. Hark! The birds are singing. . . . They've not sung for a long time. . . . God is not far off, my children. . . .

(*He sleeps.*)

(*The animals lie down, slowly lowering their heads on their paws, and sleep. All is still. A faint sound of wind passes over the stage. The beasts wake up again. The noise of the wind rises again, louder now. The awning begins to flap a little. The animals raise their muzzles to the sky.*)

SCENE IV

The deck of the Ark. A great wind is blowing. As the curtain rises a gale howls over the stage. NOAH *is alone on deck, bursting with delight.*

NOAH. Oh, what a wind! What a wind! Such a fine, splendid wind!

(*A gale*)

The waters are sinking—draining away unseen. . . . And good old Mother Earth, buried all this while, comes heaving back to the light with her face washed all clean and shining—

(*A gale*)

Bravo, wind! Three cheers for the wind! Oh Lord, many thanks for the wind.

(*He sings a sort of triumphal hymn: "Boom, boom, boom!" After a moment* HAM *comes in up right.*)

HAM (*interrupting the song*). Father.
NOAH. Ha, ha!
HAM. Father!
NOAH. Eh? (*He turns.*) Oh, it's you. . . . Pretty fine breeze this, isn't it? How about it, my boy?

(HAM *is silent.*)

Isn't it fine, this wind?
HAM (*coming down*). Fine—if only we make use of it.
NOAH. I am making use of it! Listen! (*He sings.*) Boom—boom—boom! (*He breaks off.*) Ham, be a good boy, sing with me. Just a minute, son. (*He tries to take* HAM's *arm.*)
HAM (*pulling away*). Sorry, I can't keep in tune.
NOAH. Neither can I. What does that matter?
HAM. Well, *I* don't care to make myself ridiculous.
NOAH. Oh, so I'm ridiculous, am I?
HAM. N-no. . . . No! To do you justice you're so utterly yourself, you are miles beyond being ridiculous.

NOAH. It's nice to hear you say that.

HAM. The pleasure's mine. Look here, Father—

NOAH. Come on now, just sing a duet with me, won't you ? It would sound beautiful, I promise you.

(*Gale*)

Oh, just listen to that ! Don't you think it deserves a shout of welcome ? Come on, Ham, join in. (*He takes his arm, shouting.*) Ha, ha ! Ha ! Ha !

HAM (*breaking loose*). Let me alone, will you ? I tell you I can't—I don't want to.

NOAH. All right, all right. Too bad . . . (*He sighs.*) You want to talk to me ?

HAM. I want to ask you something.

NOAH. A favor ?

HAM. Advice.

NOAH. Advice ! You must be joking.

HAM. Well, it's like this : we—we've been—working below. We've— we've been building things.

NOAH. I thought I heard hammering. Sawing, too. . . . Are you pleased with what you've done ?

HAM. I don't think it's bad, but we're not sure it will work. Anyway, we'd like to show it to you. . . .

NOAH. Why yes, with pleasure, come along, let's have a look. What is it ?

HAM. Rigging for the ship.

NOAH. Excellent ! Splendid ! . . . Very good ! What a good idea. Oh, there are lots of things we could do, lots of improvements—I've thought about it often. . . . What kind of rigging ?

HAM. It's a—well, a sort of—mast. Yes, that's what it is, a big mast.

NOAH (*delighted*). A mast ? Really ? . . . Oh yes, yes, excellent ! A big mast. That will be nice. (*He laughs.*) Ha, ha ! . . . How high ?

HAM. About twenty feet.

NOAH. You don't say so ! . . . You took one of those spare tree trunks, I suppose ?

HAM. We should have asked you first.

NOAH. Yes, of course, of course. . . . Twenty feet ! (*He tries to imagine the mast set up.*) Good for you, carpenters ! The old craft is going to look superb !

HAM. We've made a sail, too.

NOAH. Well, I never.

HAM. It's triangular. I cut it out myself. The girls did the sewing, and we used rings off the flour bags for eyelets. The cloth wasn't big enough, so there's a patch in one corner.

NOAH. There's a crew for you ! Sneaking away into corners — and then popping up with all sorts of running gear and suchlike ! Fancy those girls, too ! All those mischievous little fingers scampering over the cloth like busy little ants. Think of that ! No, they're not bad at heart, this crew. They're not wicked. Quite possibly it's me after all, who — Well, let's go down and see this business ! (*He goes toward the back.*)

HAM. And then there's a rudder.

NOAH. Why, you've started a regular shipyard. (*He laughs.*) Ha, ha, ha ! . . . A rudder ! (*He stops short and turns around.*) A rudder ? (*There is silence. He comes back toward* HAM.) A rudder ! . . . (*Again there is silence. Then*) Yes, you are wicked, Ham.

HAM. Now for it ! Just as I expected !

NOAH. I should think you did expect it ! Yes, you did it on purpose, didn't you ? You planned this to bring us face to face — just as we are at this very moment.

HAM. You know, Father, you're not well.

NOAH. You dare to look me in the face and say that ?

HAM (*avoiding his eye*). I tell you, you're ill.

NOAH. My poor boy, you're not even wicked, you're just contemptible.

HAM. Look here, Father !

NOAH (*straight at him, through clenched teeth*). You little wretch !

HAM (*the same*). And you — you old —

NOAH (*shouting*). Be silent !

(*Silence.* MAMMA *appears nervously at the back. She does not dare approach.*)

You coward ! You little coward ! Plotting against me. Behind my back ! Pretending to be working so hard ! . . . a good carpenter . . . with your work bench, and hammer, and saw : using all the things I love so much, just to make a fool of me !

HAM. Oh well, of course if you want to go on drifting about. . . .

NOAH. And so sly he is ! So clever ! Such an eye for catching people out. . . . Ha, ha. A mast ! . . . A big tall mast — set up a beautiful mast ! Take the old man up to the top and show him the pretty little rudder !

HAM. Oh, all this fuss about a rudder . . .

NOAH (*crying out*). Don't you know He's forbidden it?

HAM (*lying*). No . . . I . . . no, I didn't.

NOAH. You didn't know a rudder was forbidden?

HAM. I just said so, didn't I?

NOAH. You didn't know that we must be in His hands? Helpless as featherless birds in His warm gentle hands? You didn't know we must drift like straws in this great wind He's sent? Or that this boat He made me build was to be nothing but a nutshell on His flood? You didn't know that?

(HAM *shrugs his shoulders without replying.*)

Listen to me! Just take that rudder of yours and make kindling of it. Break it into matchwood—into toothpicks if you'd rather. There's no man living can steer the ship of God!

HAM. That remains to be seen.

NOAH. It's been foreseen! And what's more—

(*He turns about and goes upstage.* HAM *starts to follow. Turning back*) Stay where you are!

(*He goes away.* MAMMA *comes down to* HAM.)

MAMMA. What's the matter?

HAM. Bah! A little argument.

MAMMA. What about?

HAM. I'll tell you later . . . just now there's work to do . . . the great game has begun! (*He rubs his hands.*) Ha, ha, ha! This makes me laugh!

MAMMA. You frighten me.

HAM. Go on, Mother. You've got lots of pluck.

MAMMA. Not so much these days.

HAM. I mean it! You're wonderful. Well, just leave everything to me. Just you trust me and don't fuss. (*He goes upstage, stops, and comes back to* MAMMA.) How would you like me to take you to a country where it's warm and mild . . . where the earth is kind, and there's plenty of sunshine . . . where the flowers grow wild, yes, and the vegetables as well? How would you like that, eh?

MAMMA. Oh, my goodness! I'd be so happy.

HAM. All right, just you back me up whatever happens. And you'll have your garden, with a south aspect.

MAMMA. Back you up . . . against Noah ?

HAM. Well, why not ? Can't you understand ? He's not in his right mind any more.

MAMMA. But you won't do him any harm, will you ?

HAM. Leave everything to me. I'll be back soon.

(*He starts out and bumps into* NOAH *coming in.*)

NOAH. Hmph . . . you'd better go and cheer up your friends down there. They seem a bit depressed, I can tell you.

(*He comes downstage, laughing.* HAM *goes away without a word. Joyfully at the sight of* MAMMA) Hullo, Mother ! Oh no, don't run away. Why are you looking so cheerful ?

(MAMMA *doesn't answer.*)

What is it, Mother, won't you tell me ? . . . Well ? Well ?

MAMMA. Why are you always so nasty to Ham ?

NOAH. What's that ? Why am *I*— ? Listen, Mother, you must have made a little mistake. But never mind about that. You just keep out of the argument. Just stay happy and light-hearted, as you've always been.

MAMMA. I'm sorry, Noah, but . . . I can't stand it any longer !

NOAH. Why, what's the matter ?

MAMMA. I can't tell you.

NOAH. Well, please try anyway.

MAMMA. This cold wind . . . this icy water . . . my rheumatism . . . your arguments . . . hardly any sleep at night . . . the memories that break my heart . . . is it going to last much longer, Noah ?

NOAH. Why, it's over, Mother.

MAMMA. Oh, you always say that.

NOAH. What do you mean I " always say that " ? Do you think I'm making fun of you ?

MAMMA. Oh, don't be cross. I only want my house ! My house !

NOAH. You shall have it, Mother, I promise you.

MAMMA. When ?

NOAH. Very soon.

MAMMA. Yes, but when ? When ?

NOAH. Well . . . I don't know when exactly.

MAMMA. There you are ! You can answer all sorts of odd questions no one would dream of asking. But you can never tell us what we want to know.

NOAH. Oh, come now, Mother, that isn't fair.

MAMMA. I want a house. I can't bear living on this boat any longer, like a gypsy in a caravan. I want a house, with little window curtains. I want a kitchen full of copper pots. I want a garden full of flowers.

NOAH. Listen, Mother, as soon as the Ark touches ground —

MAMMA. When, Noah, when?

NOAH. Well . . . you see . . .

MAMMA. And what are you doing to make it touch ground?

NOAH. Doing? . . . why, nothing . . . I . . .

MAMMA. But if you don't do anything, we'll still be drifting round and round the ocean twenty years from now.

NOAH. What do you want me to do? . . . I've asked God a hundred times.

MAMMA. That's it, you plague Him. You said so yourself. And so He's getting His own back by letting us be battered about on this wretched sea.

NOAH. Please, Mother, don't go on. You'll be saying things in a minute that. . . .

MAMMA. You must *do* something, don't you see? Do something practical, like a man.

NOAH. But my dear good woman, what is it you want me to do?

MAMMA. Oh, I don't know; how should I? Couldn't you just ask Ham —

NOAH. What?

MAMMA. He knows! He's capable, he thinks things out. He's a clever boy and he's . . . up to date.

NOAH. Oh, and I'm an old fossil, I suppose!

MAMMA. Oh, no, no, don't you see, you poor dear . . . ? We're a little — you and I, we . . . we date from before the Flood!

NOAH. Oh, but this is too much! This is — this is monstrous!

MAMMA. Of course, if you're going to fly into a temper.

NOAH. Fly! That's just what I am doing! I feel as if I were flying head over heels above the moon with everything below me upside down!

MAMMA. Good-by, Noah. We'll talk it over later when you're serious.

NOAH. But I am serious, I promise you!

MAMMA. Do you think I don't know you? You're dying to laugh.

NOAH. Me, Mother?

MAMMA. Yes, you, Father, you . . . Well, good-by now. Just try to think over what I've been saying.

(*She goes away.*)

NOAH (*after a pause*). Ah, well . . . (*Another pause*) Oh, well . . . (*He sits down on the rail.*) It's too much for me. . . . (*Pause*) What do they want ? . . . What in the world do they want ? . . . When it rained I asked for sun, the sun came. When we were becalmed—I asked for wind ; the wind came. Now I ask for land ; land will come. Well then ? . . . We have everything ! They ought to laugh the whole day long and the whole day long they grumble.

(*A pause. Indistinctly from below the voice of an orator rises, and outbursts of applause.*)

Hmph. . . . A mass meeting in the hold.

(*Cheers*)

Well ! Well ! What are they up to now ?

(*Again the voice is heard.*)

Listen to that ! . . . speeches ! arguments ! discussions ! (*He raises his eyes to heaven, as if waiting for a word from God. Then he drops his head and sighs.*) Oh . . . men . . . men . . . (*Another little pause, then* NOAH *pricks his ears suddenly.*) What's that ? (*He gets up.*) What's that noise ? Eh ! Eh ? What can it be ? Oh !

HAM } Come on—now this time settles it.
JAPHETH } But look here, can't we talk it over quietly ?

NAOMI. Baby ! Baby !

ADA } He's right—he's right !
SHEM } Don't all talk at once.

HAM. Very good, I'll do the talking.

JAPHETH } Of course !
SELLA } You always do.

HAM. I thought we'd made up our minds that all this nonsense had got to stop !

SHEM } All right, all right then.
NAOMI } You know we're all with you.

ADA } Well, I'm—
HAM } Come on !

JAPHETH. But—

HAM. Father! We have decided that—

NOAH. Be quiet—quiet all of you—Something is going on down there! Listen to them all down there and running round mile after mile in that small space . . . as if they felt the earth—as if it made them restless. Listen to them tramping!

CHORUS. Ah!

NOAH. In that tramping you can hear the elephants' great pads . . . the little white paws of Mother's cat, the buffaloes' hooves, the lion's claws, the tiny feet of the fly.

CHORUS. That's true!

NOAH. The earth is coming back. God told me so. I believe it, but I can't be certain. My five senses that I am so proud of—Ha, ha, not one of them senses earth. But they know everything down there. They're all certain, from the greatest to the smallest. Isn't it amazing?

CHORUS. Yes, yes, it's wonderful!

NOAH. Ham, my boy, honestly, don't you think it's amazing?

HAM. Oh, I suppose so.

NOAH. Let yourself go a bit, like the rest of us. Don't be so calculating all the time. Try it: it will do you good. (*He raises his hands to heaven passionately.*) Oh, God!—You are so—absolutely . . . God! Ada, my child, you are the youngest here. Go and fetch the little white-winged creature, the purest and loveliest of all the animals. Go and fetch the dove.

CHORUS. The dove?

NOAH. Yes, the dove.

NAOMI. Hm! Hm!

CHORUS. Sh!

HAM. You'll spoil the effect.

NAOMI. I'm so excited!

CHORUS. Sh!

(ADA *returns with the dove.*)

NOAH. No, no, dear, let it go yourself.

ADA. Oh, I'm not—

NOAH. Just let it go like that, quite easily.

ADA. No, no, Mr. Noah, I daren't.

NOAH. Very well, then, give it to me. (*He takes the bird from* ADA's *hands.*)

ALL. Let it go, let it go!

NOAH. Tell me, children, don't you think a nice little prayer would fit into the picture?

ALL. Later, later!

NOAH (*laughing*). Well, well, what a patient family I've got to be sure. All right, then. . . . One, two, three . . . Go!

ALL. Go!

(*Silence. Every head is thrown back, watching the flight of the dove in three great circles.*)

Good-by! Good-by!

JAPHETH. Look how she's climbing!

SELLA. The wind's carrying her right up to the sky!

ALL. Yes, yes, straight up!

HAM. Straight into God's mouth.

NOAH. Ssh! Ssh!

SHEM. 'Ware below! The wind's knocking her down! She's falling!

ALL. Falling!

JAPHETH. No, no, no! She's up again!

NOAH. Bravo, little one. Look at her! Look how she's climbing! Climbing the snowcaps, higher and higher, into the distant blue. Bravo, my brave little mountaineer!

SELLA. I can't see her any more.

ALL. Neither can we.

HAM. Perhaps God's eaten her.

ALL. No, no, no, no. We won't listen.

ADA. There she is again!

ALL. Where? Where?

ADA. There where I'm pointing. . . . Higher! Much higher! . . . See that cloud like a horse's head? Well, just beyond that!

ALL. Oh yes!

(*For a little time everyone gazes up into space.*)

MAMMA. I can't see her any more. I'm feeling dizzy. There are spots in front of my eyes.

JAPHETH. Now I've lost her myself.

ALL. So have we. We've lost it.

NOAH. She's disappeared.

ALL (*gently*). Oh! . . .

(*Silence. The eyes drop from heaven and meet each other. There is general annoyance and the group breaks up. Somebody coughs anxiously. Someone moves about on tiptoe.* NOAH, *obviously very much moved, goes apart from the others and paces up and down in a dream.* HAM, *moving aside also, watches the others ironically.*)

(*There is a pause. Little groups collect, whispering. The annoyance becomes unbearable. The children, in the center, begin to swing their gaze back and forth from* NOAH, *on the right, to* HAM, *on the left. Again there is a pause filled with taut silence. Then*)

HAM. Well, Father, what now?

NOAH (*from afar*) . . . Eh?

HAM. I said, what now?

NOAH. I don't know what you mean.

HAM. What are we going to do?

NOAH. Well . . . we just wait.

HAM. Ah, we wait? . . . Of course, of course . . . What for?

NOAH. Results.

HAM. I see, I see. . . . In other words we do just what we've always done.

NOAH. Did you expect a miracle?

HAM. Oh, no . . . Good Lord, no! I didn't expect anything. But I did expect that you idiots—(*he points to the children*)—wouldn't let yourselves be fooled by him for the hundredth time.

SHEM. But listen, old boy, you didn't say anything, so we . . . how were we to know?

HAM. He's caught you, my little pets; he's caught you again.

SHEM. He tells us to watch something, well, we watch it, that's all.

HAM. Yes, and you don't see anything, but you're quite happy all the same.

SHEM. You must admit that all that business with the dove was rather fun.

HAM. Killingly funny, I must say.

SHEM. I don't mean that, I mean—

NOAH. Ah, good heavens, are you going to start arguing all over again? Well, go somewhere else to do it.

HAM. I beg your pardon. We've finished arguing. Quite finished! Completely finished! You can take your authority, your absolute power, your divine right—and all the other relics of the past—and make matchwood of them—or toothpicks, if you'd rather.

NOAH (*taking a step toward* HAM). What did you say?

HAM. You heard what I said.

NOAH. Listen to me!

HAM. I won't listen.

NOAH. Be off at once, for the last time. I order you, do you hear?

HAM. I won't!

THE OTHERS. We won't!

NOAH. You young puppy, you're asking for a thrashing, and you needn't think that you're too old for me to give it to you.

HAM. I'll see you damned first!

MAMMA (*throwing herself between them*). Stop!... You're both mad! Don't! Don't! Go away! Please! Stop! (*With all her strength she pushes them apart.*) Lord, isn't the world big enough to hold the pair of you!

HAM. The world, probably, but not this boat... certainly not this boat.

NOAH. Then get off it!

HAM. Why don't you get off it yourself?

NOAH. You young cub!

HAM. Oh, don't get excited. You know I didn't mean that literally. All I want you to do is to give up your command, that's all.

NOAH. Oh, that's all, is it?

HAM. I demand this in the name of every one of us.

NOAH (*to the children*). Is this true?

SHEM. Listen, Father—

NOAH. I asked you, is this true?

SHEM. Well, yes.

THE OTHERS. Yes.

NOAH. Is this true, Mother?

SHEM. Father, you must understand—

NOAH. Be quiet, you!... Is this true?

MAMMA (*very softly*). Yes, Noah... yes, Noah.

(*Silence*)

(NOAH *goes upstage a little, stops for a moment, his back turned. Then he comes back smiling to the children.*)

NOAH. Now, look here, children—don't you think you could make just one more little effort to try again?

HAM. Impossible, out of the question!

NOAH (*to the children*). You know I don't care a bit about my command. Only, over me—good heavens, there's God!

VOVE Ê DILVVIVꟼVADRAGÎTA DIEB SVꟼ TꞂAETQVINDECICVBITIS ALCIOR ꟼ
AQVAS VꟼOᛘS MONTES · CVꟼCÔSꟼꞂAÊTOISCꞂOS VꟼTꞂA ÊMISꟼNOECO
BꞀ

ÆTLLA VENIT AD EV POꞂTꞂÂS RAMVOLIꞂEÊORE ET ITELLEX NOE ꟼCESSAS ÊTÔ DILVVII
PONAMARCVINNVBIB· ETERITSIGNVFEDERIS
TROSIT VꞀ A
AQ E
EOLVVI ꟼ

NOE OPTVLIT HOLOCVSTV PRO PIOLVVIÔ

HAM. Oh, always God.

NOAH. Why, He was talking to me only this morning. You've no idea how kind He is to me. He's changed so much lately—and for the better, you know. Not less tremendous, of course, but nearer, less remote. He joked a bit—at least. He pretended to be joking to hide His real feeling, but I've a pretty keen ear, you know, and I could hear His great voice shaking with emotion at finding us again. So how could you have the heart . . .

HAM. No, no, stop! . . . That's enough. . . . Stop it! Those old tales again! . . . You're as cunning as a serpent. (*He turns to the children.*) Wake up! Wake up! Don't believe him, it's not true. Why, the old man's telling you fairy tales—throwing dust in your eyes. It's nothing! Nothing at all! Come on, are you with me?

THE CHILDREN (*hesitantly*). Yes . . . yes . . .

NOAH. Listen to me!

HAM. Not another word! (*To the children*) We're banded together, comrades! Together! Remember all we've said, all we've agreed together was good, and true, and real! Do you remember?

THE CHILDREN. Yes!

HAM. Remember it all?

THE CHILDREN. Yes! Yes!

HAM (*to* NOAH). We don't believe you any longer. We don't believe the pretty fairy tales that drop from heaven.

THE CHILDREN. No, we don't!

HAM. We only believe in the truth that we know ourselves.

THE CHILDREN. That's right! That's what we believe!

HAM. We want to live! We want excitement and adventure. We want to make discoveries and risk dangers. What's the good of humility and prayer and contemplation—that's all just cowardly laziness. We want to live!

THE CHILDREN. That's what we want!

HAM. Forward! Forward! Set up the mast! Hoist the sail—our fine big sail. We'll catch this wind and head straight for the south, rolling with the ship, singing with the ship, laughing as we know how to laugh!

THE CHILDREN. Hahaha! Come on, come on!

(*They break into chant, and rush away to get the mast and the sail.* MAMMA *remains alone.*)

NOAH. And where do you think you are going, you young fool?

HAM. Somewhere there must be land—cities—people—crowds of people—that never saw your flood! All over the world there are men who won't even believe all this when we tell it.

NOAH. That's not true.

HAM. I know it is!

NOAH. It's not true! It's not true!

HAM. It is true! I feel it! We all feel it! Come on, forward!

THE CHILDREN (*returning*). Forward! Forward!

(*They raise the mast, singing.*)

NOAH. You can't! You can't! It's wicked!

HAM. I'll take the blame.

THE CHILDREN. So will we!

(*The mast rises.*)

NOAH. Stop! Wait! I beg you only to wait until the dove comes back!

HAM and THE CHILDREN (*laughing*). Hahaha! The dove—

NOAH. We must wait for the little creature! That's all I ask. If she doesn't find us here when she comes back—

HAM. She won't come back!

NOAH. Won't come back?

HAM. Of course not, old boy. She's drowned.

(*Laughter from the children*)

HAM (*to the children*). Come on, hurry! We've a long way to go. We must get started before dark.

THE CHILDREN. Aye, aye, Captain!

HAM. Oh, this is going to be a glorious trip!

THE CHILDREN. Hurrah! Hurrah!

(*The sail unfurls.*)

NOAH. Oh, my poor old boat! (*To the children*) Stop! Stop! No! No! Don't trim the sail! Oh! Just a little, please, please—(*He runs to the foot of the mast.*)

HAM. Get back, Father! Back!

NOAH. Think! Think a minute, I beg of you! Don't . . . don't—don't force the Ark of God into the channels of Mankind! It's free! Let it be free!

THE CHILDREN. Keep back! Keep back!

NOAH (*clinging to the mast*). No. You can't do it! You haven't the right! You mustn't do it!

HAM. Look out, Father! . . . Get out of the way!

NOAH. I won't budge! I won't move! I stay here!

HAM. Seize that man and lock him up below!

(SHEM *and* JAPHETH *rush at* NOAH. *Just as they come to grips,* MAMMA *shrieks suddenly.*)

MAMMA. Here it is! Stop! Look! Here it is! Look here!

THE CHILDREN. What? . . . What? . . . What?

MAMMA. The dove. It fell straight from heaven into my hands.

HAM. That's a lie.

MAMMA. I swear it!

HAM. It's a lie!

NOAH (*hitting him with all his strength*). Perhaps you will believe that! Well, come on, who's next?

(*Silence.* MAMMA *goes to* NOAH, *kneels before him, and offers him the dove.*)

NOAH. Now, Mother, come, come . . . get up.

MAMMA. Oh, no, Noah, please let me stay like this. . . . Oh, Noah, I'm not worthy.

NOAH. Now, now . . . (*He lifts her up.*) Ah! . . . Why can't we all be simple-hearted? . . . (*He strokes the dove.*) It wasn't hard, was it, my pet, to do your little bit to help, and now all's well! Look, Mamma, see how well she is . . . warm . . . happy . . . cooing . . . she's cooing here in my hands . . . and look. . . . What has she got in her beak?

(*The children come nearer.*)

A little leaf . . . three little leaves . . . a little green twig!

THE CHILDREN (*very softly*). A little green twig!

NOAH. What's the name of it, Mother? You know all the plants.

MAMMA (*drying her eyes*). It's . . . an . . . olive branch.

NOAH. An olive branch.

THE CHILDREN. An olive branch.

NOAH. The trees are above the water.

THE CHILDREN. Hoo! . . . Hoo! . . . Hoo! . . .

HAM. Above the water?

SHEM and JAPHETH (*slowly*). Above the water!

THE GIRLS (*quickly*). Above the water!

ALL OF THEM (*loudly*). Out of the water! (*They begin to tremble violently.*)
Haa! . . . Hoooo! . . . Out of—the waters! Out of—the waters!
(*More quickly*) Out of the waters! (*They run toward the hold.*) Out of
the waters! Out of the waters!

(*They disappear, screaming. There is a pause.*)

MAMMA. It's happened . . . just as you said it would.

NOAH (*without any joy*). Yes.

MAMMA. Everything's happened just as you said.

NOAH. Yes.

MAMMA. Just as you said.

NOAH. Yes, Mother.

MAMMA. Just as you said . . . just as you said!

NOAH. Please don't, Mother.

(*Below there is an explosion of glee. Shouts, songs, a sound of an
accordion mingle.*)

Ah! Even this moment—they destroy it!

(*Shouting and pounding from the hold.*)

Bunglers! Ruining everything you see; spoiling everything you
touch! Bunglers.

(*A perfect din rises from below.*)

Spoiling joy! Spoiling youth! Spoiling happiness!

(*The din grows louder and louder.*)

Oh Lord, Lord! Old Friend. . . . It's all a failure! Everything's a
failure! Kick the lot of us overboard and say no more about it!

(*He drops his head on* MAMMA'S *hair, sobbing.*)

SCENE V

The top of Mount Ararat. The Ark is to the left. Only the bow is visible, with a ladder to the ground. The animals are grouped in the center of the stage. They take a last look at the Ark, and exit in various directions. NOAH *comes down the ladder, alone and silent. He descends the last rungs slowly, places one foot on the ground, then the other, and kneels. A pause.* MAMMA *enters on the Ark.*

MAMMA. There now. I'm quite ready. I arranged a basket for the cat. She'll be very comfortable. It's like a little house. (*Then she is gloomy.*) But she won't want to stay in it. She scratched me. Then she jumped out of the basket. All the animals have gone wild again and they're making her wild, too. Oh, children, children, what a shame, what a shame.

(*She weeps.* NOAH *gets up and crosses to up right. The* LION *and the* TIGER *howl in the distance.*)

Oh, what a desert place! So cold. So bare! And this horrible smell of stagnant water. Why is it all so cold? Noah! Where are we? Where's the water? Where's the ocean? . . . I'm frightened. Oh, I was getting a basket ready for the cat. . . . Kitty! Kitty! Come here, dear, you're all I have left.

(*She goes back into the Ark.* NOAH *coughs. The* LION *is heard again in the distance. Suddenly all the children throw their bundles to the ground and jump off the Ark.*)

ALL. Ah!
THE BOYS. Aha!
THE GIRLS. Haha!

(*They are all lined up before the Ark.*)

HAM. Ha! Old Earth!
THE BOYS. Good old Earth!
THE GIRLS. Dear old Earth!

JAPHETH (*stepping out of line*). Look! I'm going to walk! Watch me walk! (*He takes a step.*) What am I doing?

ALL. Walking!

JAPHETH (*slapping his chest*). What's this boy doing?

ALL. He's walking!

JAPHETH. Walking where?

ALL. On the ground!

NAOMI (*getting out of line*). Look at me! Look at me! (*She pulls her skirts up to her knees.*)

ADA and SELLA (*copying her*). Look at us.

NAOMI (*tapping the ground*). I'm squelching in the mud.

ADA and SELLA. We're squelching, too.

THE BOYS. Let's all squelch. (*They do so.*)

HAM. It's wet!

JAPHETH. It's cold!

SHEM. But it's warming up under our feet.

THE THREE BOYS. It's soft! It feels so good!

ALL. One, two! One, two!

NAOMI (*with a shrill laugh*). Look! My feet are all black!

ALL. One, two! One, two!

HAM (*getting out of line*). Be quiet!

ALL. One, two!

HAM. Shut up! Shut up! (*Pause*) I want to feel that at last—I'm really *free!*

(*All are silent.*)

(*Stretching*) Nobody. (*Louder*) Anybody here?

(NOAH *coughs.*)

ALL. Sh!

HAM (*shouting*). Ham!... Me!... I... (*He climbs a little hill, center.*) Ham!

NAOMI (*pulling her sisters*). Let's go and look!

ADA and SELLA (*they run upstage*). Let's look at everything.

NAOMI (*glaring at Ark*). Boo! Boo! That old wreck!

ADA. Rotten decks.

SELLA. Rusty nails!

ALL THREE. Boo! Boo! Boo!

(They spit on the Ark.)

HAM *(from his height)*. Ham is on top of his world.
JAPHETH *(climbing up)*. Here comes Japheth.
HAM. No, you don't.
SHEM. Shem's coming too!
HAM. Neither Japheth *nor* Shem! *(Planting himself firmly, he keeps them off with both hands.)*
NAOMI *(upstage)*. We're on a mountain.
SELLA and ADA. A high mountain.

(The three girls separate. SELLA goes down right, ADA up center, NAOMI down left. Meanwhile SHEM and JAPHETH shout and attack the hill from opposite sides.)

HAM *(driving them off)*. No! No! No, you don't.
SHEM and JAPHETH *(slipping)*. Why not?
HAM. I climbed up first. I got here first! I'm the strongest.
SHEM. I'm the oldest.
JAPHETH. Well, I'm the youngest.

(They come to blows. NOAH turns and watches without saying anything.)

ADA. Look at the water! It's streaming down the mountain in little rills.
SELLA. The animals are streaming down after them.
NAOMI. Everything's streaming down. They're all going down.
ADA. There are plains already.
SELLA. There's a jungle, too.
NAOMI. And deserts, too.

(The boys are fighting.)

THE GIRLS *(running toward them)*. No!
JAPHETH *(to HAM)*. Black man! Blackamoor! Nigger!
SHEM *(to JAPHETH)*. Baby! Cissy! Pale face!
HAM *(to SHEM)*. Yellow! Yellow skin! Chink!

(They roll down the hill and start up again. But their wives cling to them.)

God Spoke to Noah **127**

NAOMI. No, no! Why fight over a little lump of rock when the world is
    so wide.
SELLA. The world is all around us.
ADA. There it is! Down there!
THE THREE GIRLS. Down there! Down there!

(*But the boys free themselves and go back to their fight.*)

JAPHETH (*to* SHEM). Chink! Slant-eyes!
HAM (*to* JAPHETH). Paleface! Whitey!
SHEM (*to* HAM). Nigger! Blackamoor!

   (*They roll down the hill again. The girls pick them up and hold them
   fast.*)

NAOMI (*to* HAM). Behind you, Ham! Look behind you. Southward.
    Southward! Look straight into the south. Come. Come, my hunter.
    Follow the lion over the sands to the south!
SELLA (*to* SHEM). To the east! To the east! After the tiger! We'll ride an
    elephant through the jungle, where monkeys chatter as we pass.
    Come, my peasant!
ADA (*to* JAPHETH). Come, my shepherd. Take up your pipes. We'll follow
    the cow and the sheep and the dog into the mists and valleys of the
    west. Come, my shepherd!

(*The three panting boys each turns in his own direction.*)

THE GIRLS. Come!
NAOMI. All life has gone down the mountain.

(*The boys start to follow the girls, then suddenly turn and embrace.*)

THE BOYS. Good-by!
THE GIRLS. Come!

(*They run and gather up their bundles.* NAOMI *struggles up with hers
and* HAM's *and puts them on her head.* SHEM *loads his on his shoulder.*
JAPHETH *and* ADA *put theirs together and carry them between them.*)

THE GIRLS. Well. There.

THE BOYS. There!

(*They all look at the Ark, then at* NOAH. NOAH *is on his knees, up right.*)

ALL. Sshh! (*Softly*) Farewell.

(*They go away,* NAOMI *before* HAM, SHEM *leading* SELLA, JAPHETH *and* ADA *side by side, and disappear down the roads they have chosen.*)

(*A shepherd's pipes are heard. A pause.* NOAH *gets up and turns fearfully to the deserted stage.*)

NOAH. They've all gone down the mountain. . . . Every living thing. What of me, my children? I'm alive! (*He calls.*) Children! Children! You've left someone behind! . . . You've forgotten someone!

(*The pipes grow more distant.*)

It isn't possible. Surely they can feel me willing them to turn their heads. I can't believe that you'll look straight before you, without a thought. You will come back, won't you? You'll come back sometimes at least. In your hearts you cannot really feel content—it isn't possible. You're my flesh and blood. Something still binds you to me like a cord. It must be wrenching at you, straining, pulling you back to your poor old Father. Isn't it? Isn't it? Shem, old chap—Japheth, my child, Ham, Ham, my boy.

(*The pipes stop.*)

Ah! ah! ah! It's all over—I can't hear them any more. Help! Help! I can't follow them, I can't go with them—which way? which way? They've bound me, fenced me round, shut me up in nothing. I'm caught in the midst of nothing. All! Hark, there they are. I can hear them again—their steps, little footsteps in the distance. Ah, tell me I still hold fast the reins of my three splendid teams . . . Shem and Sella . . . Ham and Naomi . . . Japheth and Ada! . . . Steady there, steady. (*He kisses the ground.*) Oh, the reins are slipping—they're stretched to breaking point—they're snapping! Oh, my children, catch up my voice as it flows to you through the earth in three fresh streams. Take one last drink. . . . (*He stops, places his ear to the ground and then gets up. His voice is cold and dead.*) Gone over.

Finished . . . very well! (*He sighs and beats his breast.*) How's the heart inside, then? My blood! The old lungs! You must make plenty of noise and work hard, to keep me company. (*He surveys the scene, laughing despairingly.*) Ah! Ah! Ah! Ah! I think I'll have to raise an echo, a fine, deep echo—so that I and myself can have a bit of a talk! (*He cries.*) Noah! Noah! (*He listens.*) Nothing!

(*Enter the* BEAR *right*)

Well, if it isn't Bruin. This *is* a surprise. D'you know you couldn't have turned up at a better moment! I thought you'd left me, too. . . . Oh, I'm delighted to see you again. . . . I always thought we had a little weakness for one another. (*He goes toward the* BEAR, *who stands up.*) Yes, you understand all sorts of things.

(*The* BEAR *opens his arms.*)

What? Come on then, give us a hug. Good old comrade! (*He goes into the* BEAR's *arms.*) Dear old friend! Oh, I say! He's squeezing hard! . . . Oy, there, you're hugging me so I can't breathe! . . . Here, steady, old man! Oof! . . . You're smothering me! Let go, do you hear? Let go! Heah! High!

(*His voice is muffled in the* BEAR's *fur. Man and beast struggle in silence.*)

NOAH (*throwing back his head*). Help! Help!

(MAMMA *appears on the Ark.*)

NOAH. Help!
MAMMA (*bursting into laughter*). Hahaha!
NOAH. Mother!
MAMMA. Hahaha!

(NOAH *succeeds in getting free, gets his wind and rushes shouting at the* BEAR, *who scampers away.*)

(NOAH *pants and mops his brow.*)

MAMMA. That was funny! That was so funny!

NOAH. It nearly killed me, Mother.

MAMMA. Dancing together like that. A real bear dance. Ha, ha, ha. (*She roars with laughter.*) Tra la la, tra la lee, I kiss you, you kiss me—ha, ha, ha, ha!

NOAH (*raising his eyes to heaven*). There's the vulture already. It will take a lot of courage.

MAMMA (*squatting downstage, her chin in her hands*). Where are the children?

NOAH. They'll be back soon. They've gone to look round a bit now that things are coming back down below. But they'll be back here soon. They'll come back in a few days.

MAMMA. It's very strange that none of our friends have taken the trouble to come and see us.

NOAH. What friends, Mother?

MAMMA. Well, our friends in the village. My personal friends. Of course, nobody liked you. But I had a lot of relations. After a trip like this you'd really think they might have called.

NOAH. But, Mother . . .

MAMMA. What? . . . has that been forbidden, too?

NOAH. No, no!

MAMMA (*getting up*). It's Him up there! . . .

NOAH. No, no. . . . You mustn't say that!

MAMMA. Somebody's got to say it. I'm not afraid to tell Him what I think. I'm not mad, you know. (MAMMA *sobs softly.*)

NOAH. Sit down, Mother. There, there, there. I want you to help me choose a nice place for our new house. You know I'm going to build you a brand new house. There's plenty of wood here. You're going to have that wonderful, enormous kitchen you've always dreamed about.

MAMMA (*weeping*). I'm cold.

(NOAH *takes off his coat and puts it around her.*)

MAMMA. What's that falling on my hair?

NOAH. A little snow, maybe.

MAMMA. Snow?

NOAH. Yes. . . . Ah! . . . How shall I begin? (*To* MAMMA) Are you all right?

(MAMMA *makes no reply. She is falling asleep.*)

She's asleep, poor old comrade. She couldn't hold out . . . till the very end. Yes. (*Softly*) It has been hard. . . . (*Louder, and shaken with sobs*) It certainly has been pretty hard ! . . . It's a good thing I have such trust in You. . . . Do You hear ? I'll say You've given me some pretty hard knocks. It's been a bit past a joke sometimes, I can tell You ! You take me from my garden and chuck me on a bare rock, all by myself, with a hundred ways of dying . . . Haha ! . . . All right, all right. Don't You worry. I'll find a way out, some- how or other. I'll find a way out all right ! I tell You frankly I've given up trying to understand. But no matter. Go on, I'm following You ! Oh, let's go on ! Only just one thing I'd like to ask You. Be up there a bit just now and again, will You ? Just let me hear Your voice once in a while, or feel Your breath, just see Your light, even. Lord, if You'd just shed Your light on my work as I do it every day, and give the *feeling—the assurance—*the conviction that You are satisfied. We must all be satisfied, mustn't we ? (*He attacks the Ark with his hatchet.*) Well, I am satisfied. (*He shouts.*) I am satis- fied ! (*He sings.*) Are You satisfied ?

(*The seven colors of the rainbow appear in the background.*)

That's fine !

CURTAIN

Scene I

In the first scene how does Noah compare himself to the animals God has chosen to save, as a way of explaining his own chance of survival?

Noah tells the animals that the doors of their cages will always be open. How does this illustrate both obedience to divine authority and freedom of choice?

Look back at the Thomas poem "Fern Hill" on page 14. What golden age is described there? What is the golden age that Noah refers to?

During the encounter with the man from Noah's home neighborhood, how do Noah's words and actions imitate those of the God he serves? With what are the first raindrops identified (notice the stage directions as well as the dialogue)? What does this image suggest about the nature of the flood? What contrast in attitude toward the rain is shown by the man and by the children?

Scene II

Why does Noah wish that God too could have seen the swimming last survivors of the earth? What kind of God is Noah's? What kind of person is symbolized by the postman?

In what way is Noah more youthful than the children on the ark? Would they agree that he is? How is the conflict between youth and age and between youthful disobedience and mature faith used by Obey for dramatic effect throughout the first two scenes of *Noah*?

When Noah says that "there are white birds all ready to fly straight from my heart to God," how does the imagery he uses foreshadow an actual event?

Scene III

How do the actions of the three brothers illustrate that the new world is essentially the same as the old drowned one? Do you think they express impulses which are common to mankind?

In what way is Noah closer to the animals than he is to his sons?

Scene IV

Why are the making of a sail and the building of a rudder proof of Ham's disrespect? Of what song in Chapter One does Noah's scolding remind you? How does it express the essential relationship between man and God as Noah sees it?

How does Mrs. Noah betray her husband? How does Noah view God differently than in earlier scenes?

Although Noah is compared to a serpent, in reality the serpent on the ark is human nature. Why at the end of this scene is Noah unhappy even though he has been proved right?

Scene V

The author of this play uses the fight among the brothers to foreshadow the separation of people with black, yellow, and white skins into different regions of the earth. What causes the fight among the three brothers which ends in name-calling? After the fight, the brothers part as friends, each going his separate way with his future wife. What are the implications for the future of mankind in the way the fight is resolved?

"You take me from my garden and chuck me on a bare rock, all by myself, with a hundred ways of dying . . .," says Noah to God. How does this statement apply to Adam? to mankind as a whole? to the title of this book?

What is the rainbow a sign of at the end of the play?

What other signs or symbols appear in *Noah*? What do they symbolize?

In what way is the ark God's world? In what way is it man's world? Why might the period aboard the ark be considered a golden age? Why do those aboard fail to see it as such? What actions proclaim the end of that golden age? When the poet in "The Land of Nod" on page 32 says "the arky moon," which aspect of the world is she emphasizing?

How could you use a stepladder, a flashlight, a fur coat, and carpenter's tools as props in a production of this play?

A Boy's Head

In it there is a spaceship
and a project
for doing away with piano lessons.

And there is
Noah's ark,
which shall be first.

And there is
an entirely new bird,
an entirely new hare,
an entirely new bumblebee.

There is a river
that flows upward.

There is a multiplication table.

There is anti-matter.

And it just cannot be trimmed.

I believe
that only what cannot be trimmed
is a head.

There is much promise
in the circumstance
that so many people have heads.

MIROSLAV HOLUB

Why does the poet represent Noah's ark as the *first* thing in this boy's head?
Does the poem suggest that the boy's head, untrimmed and full of promise,
is the ark? If so, why? How does this poem illustrate that the events of the
Bible may constantly be re-created?

The Boatman

You might suppose it easy
For a maker not too lazy
To convert the gentle reader to an Ark:
But it takes a willing pupil
To admit both gnat and camel
—Quite an eyeful, all the crew that must embark.

After me when comes the deluge
And you're looking round for refuge
From God's anger pouring down in gush and spout,
Then you take the tender creature
—You remember, that's the reader—
And you pull him through his navel inside out.

That's to get his beasts outside him,
For they've got to come aboard him,
As the best directions have it, two by two.
When you've taken all their tickets
And you've marched them through his sockets,
Let the tempest bust Creation: heed not you.

For you're riding high and mighty
In a gale that's pushing ninety
With a solid bottom under you—that's his.
Fellow flesh affords a rampart,
And you've got along for comfort
All the world there ever shall be, was, and is.

JAY MACPHERSON

How does the reader of this poem become an ark? How has the ark been used symbolically by the three authors of *Noah*, "A Boy's Head," and "The Boatman"? What meanings do the three selections have in common?

WHILE THE EARTH LASTS

Let Us Build
Ourselves a City

Once upon a time all the world spoke a single language and used the same words. As men journeyed in the east, they came upon a plain in the land of Shinar and settled there. They said to one another, "Come, let us make bricks and bake them hard"; they used bricks for stone and bitumen for mortar. "Come," they said, "let us build ourselves a city and a tower with its top in the heavens, and make a name for ourselves; or we shall be dispersed all over the earth." Then the Lord came down to see the city and tower which mortal men had built, and he said, "Here they are, one people with a single language, and now they have started to do this; henceforward nothing they have a mind to do will be beyond their reach. Come, let us go down there and confuse their speech, so that they will not understand what they say to one another." So the Lord dispersed them from there all over the earth, and they left off building the city. That is why it is called Babel, because the Lord there made a babble of the language of all the world; from that place the Lord scattered men all over the face of the earth.

GENESIS 11:1–9

In what way does God's action here remind you of his action in the Noah story? How is Noah's mountaintop different from the tower in this story?

Can the building of the Tower of Babel be seen as a work of the human imagination whose bricks are words? If so, what makes the tower fall? Can it be argued that it is the same aspect of human nature that made Adam fall?

Encounter
at Dawn

It was in the last days of the Empire. The tiny ship was far from home, and almost a hundred light-years from the great parent vessel searching through the loosely packed stars at the rim of the Milky Way. But even here it could not escape from the shadow that lay across civilization: beneath that shadow, pausing ever and again in their work to wonder how their distant homes were faring, the scientists of the Galactic Survey still labored at their never-ending task.

The ship held only three occupants, but between them they carried knowledge of many sciences, and the experience of half a lifetime in space. After the long interstellar night, the star ahead was warming their spirits as they dropped down toward its fires. A little more golden, a trifle more brilliant than the sun that now seemed a legend of their childhood. They knew from past experience that the chance of locating planets here was more than ninety percent, and for the moment they forgot all else in the excitement of discovery.

They found the first planet within minutes of coming to rest. It was a giant, of a familiar type, too cold for protoplasmic life and probably possessing no stable surface. So they turned their search sunward, and presently were rewarded.

It was a world that made their hearts ache for home, a world where everything was hauntingly familiar, yet never quite the same. Two great land masses floated in blue-green seas, capped by ice at either pole. There were some desert regions, but the larger part of the planet was obviously fertile. Even from this distance, the signs of vegetation were unmistakably clear.

They gazed hungrily at the expanding landscape as they fell down into the atmosphere, heading toward noon in the subtropics. The ship plummeted through cloudless skies toward a great river, checked its fall with a surge of soundless power, and came to rest among the long grasses by the water's edge.

No one moved: there was nothing to be done until the automatic instruments had finished their work. Then a bell tinkled softly and the lights on the control board flashed in a pattern of meaningful chaos. Captain Altman rose to his feet with a sigh of relief.

"We're in luck," he said. "We can go outside without protection, if the pathogenic tests are satisfactory. What did you make of the place as we came in, Bertrond?"

"Geologically stable—no active volcanoes, at least. I didn't see any trace of cities, but that proves nothing. If there's a civilization here, it may have passed that stage."

"Or not reached it yet?"

Bertrond shrugged. "Either's just as likely. It may take us some time to find out on a planet this size."

"More time than we've got," said Clindar, glancing at the communications panel that linked them to the mother ship and thence to the Galaxy's threatened heart. For a moment there was a gloomy silence. Then Clindar walked to the control board and pressed a pattern of keys with automatic skill.

With a slight jar, a section of the hull slid aside and the fourth member of the crew stepped out onto the new planet, flexing metal limbs and adjusting servo motors to the unaccustomed gravity. Inside the ship, a television screen glimmered into life, revealing a long vista of waving grasses, some trees in the middle distance, and a glimpse of the great river. Clindar punched a button, and the picture flowed steadily across the screen as the robot turned its head.

"Which way shall we go?" Clindar asked.

"Let's have a look at those trees," Altman replied. "If there's any animal life we'll find it there."

"Look!" cried Bertrond. "A bird!"

Clindar's fingers flew over the keyboard: the picture centered on the tiny speck that had suddenly appeared on the left of the screen, and expanded rapidly as the robot's telephoto lens came into action.

"You're right," he said. "Feathers—beak—well up the evolutionary ladder. This place looks promising. I'll start the camera."

The swaying motion of the picture as the robot walked forward did not distract them: they had grown accustomed to it long ago. But they had never become reconciled to this exploration by proxy when all their impulses cried out to them to leave the ship, to run through the grass, and to feel the wind blowing against their faces. Yet it was too great a risk to take, even on a world that seemed as fair as this. There was always a skull hidden behind Nature's most smiling face. Wild beasts, poisonous reptiles, quagmires—death could come to the unwary explorer in a thousand disguises. And worst of all were the invisible enemies, the bacteria and viruses against which the only defense might often be a thousand light-years away.

A robot could laugh at all these dangers and even if, as sometimes happened, it encountered a beast powerful enough to destroy it— well, machines could always be replaced.

They met nothing on the walk across the grasslands. If any small animals were disturbed by the robot's passage, they kept outside its field of vision. Clindar slowed the machine as it approached the trees, and the watchers in the spaceship flinched involuntarily at the branches that appeared to slash across their eyes. The picture dimmed for a moment before the controls readjusted themselves to the weaker illumination; then it came back to normal.

The forest was full of life. It lurked in the undergrowth, clambered among the branches, flew through the air. It fled chattering and gibbering through the trees as the robot advanced. And all the while the automatic cameras were recording the pictures that formed on the screen, gathering material for the biologists to analyze when the ship returned to base.

Clindar breathed a sigh of relief when the trees suddenly thinned. It was exhausting work, keeping the robot from smashing into obstacles as it moved through the forest, but on open ground it could take care of itself. Then the picture trembled as if beneath a hammer blow, there was a grinding metallic thud, and the whole scene swept vertiginously upward as the robot toppled and fell.

"What's that?" cried Altman. "Did you trip?"

"No," said Clindar grimly, his fingers flying over the keyboard. "Something attacked from the rear. I hope . . . ah . . . I've still got control."

He brought the robot to a sitting position and swiveled its head. It did not take long to find the cause of the trouble. Standing a few feet away, and lashing its tail angrily, was a large quadruped with a most ferocious set of teeth. At the moment it was, fairly obviously, trying to decide whether to attack again.

Slowly, the robot rose to its feet, and as it did so the great beast crouched to spring. A smile flitted across Clindar's face: he knew how to deal with this situation. His thumb felt for the seldom-used key labeled "Siren."

The forest echoed with a hideous undulating scream from the robot's concealed speaker, and the machine advanced to meet its adversary, arms flailing in front of it. The startled beast almost fell over backward in its effort to turn, and in seconds he was gone from sight.

"Now I suppose we'll have to wait a couple of hours until everything comes out of hiding again," said Bertrond ruefully.

"I don't know much about animal psychology," interjected Altman, "but is it usual for them to attack something completely unfamiliar?"

"Some will attack anything that moves, but that's unusual. Normally they attack only for food, or if they've already been threatened. What are you driving at? Do you suggest that there are other robots on this planet?"

"Certainly not. But our carnivorous friend may have mistaken our machine for a more edible biped. Don't you think that this opening in the jungle is rather unnatural? It could easily be a path."

"In that case," said Clindar promptly, "we'll follow it and find out. I'm tired of dodging trees, but I hope nothing jumps on us again: it's bad for my nerves."

"You were right, Altman," said Bertrond a little later. "It's certainly a path. But that doesn't mean intelligence. After all, animals—"

He stopped in midsentence, and at the same instant Clindar brought the advancing robot to a halt. The path had suddenly opened out into a wide clearing, almost completely occupied by a village of flimsy huts. It was ringed by a wooden palisade, obviously defense against an enemy who at the moment presented no threat. For the gates were wide open, and beyond them the inhabitants were going peacefully about their ways.

For many minutes the three explorers stared in silence at the screen. Then Clindar shivered a little and remarked: "It's uncanny. It might be our own planet, a hundred thousand years ago. I feel as if I've gone back in time."

"There's nothing weird about it," said the practical Altman. "After all, we've discovered nearly a hundred planets with our type of life on them."

"Yes," retorted Clindar. "A hundred in the whole Galaxy! I still think it's strange it had to happen to us."

"Well, it had to happen to *somebody*," said Bertrond philosophically. "Meanwhile, we must work out our contact procedure. If we send the robot into the village it will start a panic."

"That," said Altman, "is a masterly understatement. What we'll have to do is catch a native by himself and prove that we're friendly. Hide the robot, Clindar. Somewhere in the woods where it can watch the village without being spotted. We've a week's practical anthropology ahead of us!"

It was three days before the biological tests showed that it would be safe to leave the ship. Even then Bertrond insisted on going alone — alone, that is, if one ignored the substantial company of the robot. With such an ally he was not afraid of this planet's larger beasts, and his body's natural defenses could take care of the microorganisms. So, at least, the analyzers had assured him; and considering the complexity of the problem, they made remarkably few mistakes . . . .

He stayed outside for an hour, enjoying himself cautiously, while his companions watched with envy. It would be another three days before they could be quite certain that it was safe to follow Bertrond's example. Meanwhile, they kept busy enough watching the village through the lenses of the robot, and recording everything they could with the cameras. They had moved the spaceship at night so that it was hidden in the depths of the forest, for they did not wish to be discovered until they were ready.

And all the while the news from home grew worse. Though their remoteness here at the edge of the Universe deadened its impact, it lay heavily on their minds and sometimes overwhelmed them with a sense of futility. At any moment, they knew, the signal for recall might come as the Empire summoned up its last resources in its extremity. But until then they would continue their work as though pure knowledge were the only thing that mattered.

Seven days after landing, they were ready to make the experiment. They knew now what paths the villagers used when going hunting, and Bertrond chose one of the less frequented ways. Then he placed a chair firmly in the middle of the path and settled down to read a book.

It was not, of course, quite as simple as that: Bertrond had taken all imaginable precautions. Hidden in the undergrowth fifty yards away, the robot was watching through its telescopic lenses, and in its hand it held a small but deadly weapon. Controlling it from the spaceship, his fingers poised over the keyboard, Clindar waited to do what might be necessary.

That was the negative side of the plan: The positive side was more obvious. Lying at Bertrond's feet was the carcass of a small, horned animal which he hoped would be an acceptable gift to any hunter passing this way.

Two hours later the radio in his suit harness whispered a warning. Quite calmly, though the blood was pounding in his veins, Bertrond laid aside his book and looked down the trail. The savage was walking forward confidently enough, swinging a spear in his right hand. He paused for a moment when he saw Bertrond, then advanced more cautiously. He could tell that there was nothing to fear, for the stranger was slightly built and obviously unarmed.

When only twenty feet separated them, Bertrond gave a reassuring smile and rose slowly to his feet. He bent down, picked up the carcass, and carried it forward as an offering. The gesture would have been understood by any creature on any world, and it was understood here. The savage reached forward, took the animal, and threw it effortlessly over his shoulder. For an instant he stared into Bertrond's eyes with a fathomless expression; then he turned and walked back toward the village. Three times he glanced round to see if Bertrond was following, and each time Bertrond smiled and waved reassurance. The whole episode lasted little more than a minute. As the first contact between two races it was completely without drama, though not without dignity.

Bertrond did not move until the other had vanished from sight. Then he relaxed and spoke into his suit microphone.

"That was a pretty good beginning," he said jubilantly. "He wasn't in the least frightened, or even suspicious. I think he'll be back."

"It still seems too good to be true," said Altman's voice in his ear. "I should have thought he'd have been either scared or hostile. Would *you* have accepted a lavish gift from a peculiar stranger with such little fuss?"

Bertrond was slowly walking back to the ship. The robot had now come out of cover and was keeping guard a few paces behind him.

"*I* wouldn't," he replied, "but I belong to a civilized community. Complete savages may react to strangers in many different ways, according to their past experience. Suppose this tribe has never had any enemies. That's quite possible on a large but sparsely populated planet. Then we may expect curiosity, but no fear at all."

"If these people have no enemies," put in Clindar, no longer fully occupied in controlling the robot, "why have they got a stockade round the village?"

"I meant no *human* enemies," replied Bertrond. "If that's true, it simplifies our task immensely."

"Do you think he'll come back?"

"Of course. If he's as human as I think, curiosity and greed will make him return. In a couple of days we'll be bosom friends."

Looked at dispassionately, it became a fantastic routine. Every morning the robot would go hunting under Clindar's direction, until it was now the deadliest killer in the jungle. Then Bertrond would wait until Yaan—which was the nearest they could get to his name—came striding confidently along the path. He came at the same time every day, and he always came alone. They wondered about this: did he wish to keep his great discovery to himself and thus get all the credit for his hunting prowess? If so, it showed unexpected foresight and cunning.

At first Yaan had departed at once with his prize, as if afraid that the donor of such a generous gift might change his mind. Soon, however, as Bertrond had hoped, he could be induced to stay for a while by simple conjuring tricks and a display of brightly colored fabrics and crystals, in which he took a childlike delight. At last Bertrond was able to engage him in lengthy conversations, all of which were recorded as well as being filmed through the eyes of the hidden robot.

One day the philologists might be able to analyze this material; the best that Bertrond could do was to discover the meanings of a few simple verbs and nouns. This was made more difficult by the fact that Yaan not only used different words for the same thing, but sometimes the same word for different things.

Between these daily interviews, the ship traveled far, surveying the planet from the air and sometimes landing for more detailed examinations. Although several other human settlements were observed, Bertrond made no attempt to get in touch with them, for it was easy to see that they were all at much the same cultural level as Yaan's people.

It was, Bertrond often thought, a particularly bad joke on the part of Fate that one of the Galaxy's very few truly human races should have been discovered at this moment of time. Not long ago this would have been an event of supreme importance; now civilization was too hard-pressed to concern itself with these savage cousins waiting at the dawn of history.

Not until Bertrond was sure he had become part of Yaan's everyday life did he introduce him to the robot. He was showing Yaan the patterns in a kaleidoscope when Clindar brought the machine striding through the grass with its latest victim dangling across one metal arm.

For the first time Yaan showed something akin to fear; but he relaxed at Bertrond's soothing words, though he continued to watch the advancing monster. It halted some distance away, and Bertrond walked forward to meet it. As he did so, the robot raised its arms and handed him the dead beast. He took it solemnly and carried it back to Yaan, staggering a little under the unaccustomed load.

Bertrond would have given a great deal to know just what Yaan was thinking as he accepted the gift. Was he trying to decide whether the robot was master or slave? Perhaps such conceptions as this were beyond his grasp: to him the robot might be merely another man, a hunter who was a friend of Bertrond.

Clindar's voice, slightly larger than life, came from the robot's speaker.

"It's astonishing how calmly he accepts us. Won't anything scare him?"

"You will keep judging him by your own standards," replied Bertrond. "Remember, his psychology is completely different, and much simpler. Now that he has confidence in me, anything that I accept won't worry him."

"I wonder if that will be true of all his race?" queried Altman. "It's hardly safe to judge by a single specimen. I want to see what happens when we send the robot into the village."

"Hello!" exclaimed Bertrond. "*That* surprised him. He's never met a person who could speak with two voices before."

"Do you think he'll guess the truth when he meets us?" said Clindar.

"No. The robot will be pure magic to him — but it won't be any more wonderful than fire and lightning and all the other forces he must already take for granted."

"Well, what's the next move?" asked Altman, a little impatiently. "Are you going to bring him to the ship, or will you go into the village first?"

Bertrond hesitated. "I'm anxious not to do too much too quickly. You know the accidents that have happened with strange races when that's been tried. I'll let him think this over, and when we get back tomorrow I'll try to persuade him to take the robot back to the village."

In the hidden ship, Clindar reactivated the robot and started it moving again. Like Altman, he was growing a little impatient of this excessive caution, but on all matters relating to alien life forms Bertrond was the expert, and they had to obey his orders.

There were times now when he almost wished he were a robot himself, devoid of feelings or emotions, able to watch the fall of a leaf or the death agonies of a world with equal detachment . . . .

The sun was low when Yaan heard the great voice crying from the jungle. He recognized it at once, despite its inhuman volume: it was the voice of his friend, and it was calling him.

In the echoing silence, the life of the village came to a stop. Even the children ceased their play: the only sound was the thin cry of a baby frightened by the sudden silence.

All eyes were upon Yaan as he walked swiftly to his hut and grasped the spear that lay beside the entrance. The stockade would soon be closed against the prowlers of the night, but he did not hesitate as he stepped out into the lengthening shadows. He was passing through the gates when once again that mighty voice summoned him, and now it held a note of urgency that came clearly across all the barriers of language and culture.

The shining giant who spoke with many voices met him a little way from the village and beckoned him to follow. There was no sign of Bertrond. They walked for almost a mile before they saw him in the distance, standing not far from the river's edge and staring out across the dark, slowly moving waters.

He turned as Yaan approached, yet for a moment seemed unaware of his presence. Then he gave a gesture of dismissal to the shining one, who withdrew into the distance.

Yaan waited. He was patient and, though he could never have expressed it in words, contented. When he was with Bertrond he felt the first intimations of that selfless, utterly irrational devotion his race would not fully achieve for many ages.

It was a strange tableau. Here at the river's brink two men were standing. One was dressed in a closely-fitting uniform equipped with tiny, intricate mechanisms. The other was wearing the skin of an animal and was carrying a flint-tipped spear. Ten thousand generations lay between them, ten thousand generations and an immeasurable gulf of space. Yet they were both human. As she must do often in eternity, Nature had repeated one of her basic patterns.

Presently Bertrond began to speak, walking to and fro in short, quick steps as he did, and in his voice there was a trace of madness.

"It's all over, Yaan. I'd hoped that with our knowledge we could have brought you out of barbarism in a dozen generations, but now you will have to fight your way up from the jungle alone, and it may take you a million years to do so. I'm sorry—there's so much we could have done. Even now I wanted to stay here, but Altman and Clindar talk of duty, and I suppose that they are right. There is little enough that we can do, but our world is calling and we must not forsake it.

"I wish you could understand me, Yaan. I wish you knew what I was saying. I'm leaving you these tools: some of them you will discover how to use, though as likely as not in a generation they'll be lost or forgotten. See how this blade cuts: it will be ages before your world can make its like. And guard this well: when you press the button—look! If you use it sparingly, it will give you light for years, though sooner or later it will die. As for these other things—find what use for them you can.

"Here come the first stars, up there in the east. Do you ever look at the stars, Yaan? I wonder how long it will be before you have discovered what they are, and I wonder what will have happened to us by then. Those stars are our homes, Yaan, and we cannot save them. Many have died already, in explosions so vast that I can imagine them no more than you. In a hundred thousand of your years, the light of those funeral pyres will reach your world and set its peoples wondering. By then, perhaps, your race will be reaching for the stars. I wish I could warn you against the mistakes we made, and which now will cost us all that we have won.

"It is well for your people, Yaan, that your world is here at the frontier of the Universe. You may escape the doom that waits for us. One day, perhaps, your ships will go searching among the stars as we have done, and they may come upon the ruins of our worlds and wonder who we were. But they will never know that we met here by this river when your race was young.

"Here come my friends; they would give me no more time. Good-by, Yaan—use well the things I have left you. They are your world's greatest treasures."

Something huge, something that glittered in the starlight, was sliding down from the sky. It did not reach the ground, but came to rest a little way above the surface, and in utter silence a rectangle of light opened in its side. The shining giant appeared out of the night and stepped through the golden door. Bertrond followed, pausing for a moment at the threshold to wave back at Yaan. Then the darkness closed behind him.

No more swiftly than smoke drifts upward from a fire, the ship lifted away. When it was so small that Yaan felt he could hold it in his hands, it seemed to blur into a long line of light slanting upward into the stars. From the empty sky a peal of thunder echoed over the sleeping land; and Yaan knew at last that the gods were gone and would never come again.

For a long time he stood by the gently moving waters, and into his soul there came a sense of loss he was never to forget and never to understand. Then, carefully and reverently, he collected together the gifts that Bertrond had left.

Under the stars, the lonely figure walked homeward across a nameless land. Behind him the river flowed softly to the sea, winding through the fertile plains on which, more than a thousand centuries ahead, Yaan's descendants would build the great city they were to call Babylon.

ARTHUR C. CLARKE

What is significant about the fact that the first sign of life on the planet is a bird?

"There was always a skull hidden behind Nature's most smiling face." How does this statement apply to Clarke's story? to Noah's story? to Adam's story?

What happens *seven* days after landing on the planet? Why does the author call it the "dawn of history"?

What were the space explorers to Yaan? Why did their departure create in him "a sense of loss he was never to forget"? What symbolic use is made of Babylon, traditionally a wicked city, at the end of this tale?

Taking "the fire next time" as your theme, write an account of the end of our world. Whom would you save? Where would they go? What would the world be like afterward? (These are a few of the questions your story should try to answer.)

Trace the references to God throughout this chapter and divide them into wrathful and merciful categories.

THOSE THAT BE PLANTED IN THE HOUSE OF THE LORD

O Lord, how great are thy works!
And thy thoughts are very deep.
A brutish man knoweth not;
Neither doth a fool understand this.
When the wicked spring as the grass,
And when all the workers of iniquity do flourish;
It is that they shall be destroyed for ever:
But thou, Lord, art most high for evermore.
For, lo, thine enemies, O Lord, for, lo, thine enemies
    shall perish;
All the workers of iniquity shall be scattered.
But my horn shalt thou exalt like the horn of a unicorn:
I shall be anointed with fresh oil.
Mine eyes also shall see my desire on mine enemies,
And mine ears shall hear my desire of the wicked that
    rise up against me.
The righteous shall flourish like the palm tree:
He shall grow like a cedar in Lebanon.
Those that be planted in the house of the Lord
Shall flourish in the courts of our God.
They shall bring forth fruit in old age;
They shall be fat and flourishing;
To show that the Lord is upright;
He is my rock, and there is no unrighteousness in him.

PSALM 92

The biblical narrative, like all stories, has a beginning, middle, and end. We are nowhere near the middle of the whole story yet, but already we can see that it starts with the creation of a perfect world and moves on to describe events that take place in it, once the original perfect creation has disappeared. It is important to see how a simple story within the Bible relates to the overall narrative. The beginning

149

of the Noah story, the Flood, is like the ending of
the Bible, the Last Judgment. The exit from the ark
at the end of the Noah story, heralding a new order,
is like the Creation of the world at the beginning of
the Bible.

The Noah story ends with Noah in much the
same position as Adam was earlier. Both are told by
God to people the earth. Despite the circularity of
this rhythm (mankind having come so far only to have
to start all over again), something new is added.
God promises that he will never again destroy all
living creatures as he did with the Flood. Noah re-
ceives more clear and direct assurance of God's
mercy despite man's wickedness than Adam does.
You will remember that when Adam was expelled
from Eden he said, "We shall die." Now it seems that
not everyone will die. This is an important stage of
development in the total biblical story.

The imagery in this chapter of plants and trees and
flowers echoes, for the most part, the imagery of the
garden in the first chapter. The righteous man, in
the ninety-second psalm, is compared to the palm
tree and to the cedar of Lebanon. The olive branch
brought back to the ark by the dove is the sign of
a new peace between land and sea. There is a beautiful and important olive tree in "The History of the
Flood," and Noah's wife, in the play, dreams of her
"garden full of flowers." But this imagery also has
its darker side. In a striking simile that recurs
throughout the Bible the wicked are described as
sprouting all about like weeds; and they "spring as
the grass," according to Psalm 92.

There are also images of rocks and stones. By
calling God a rock, the psalmist suggests that the
Lord is sturdy and upright, and that he is the foundation upon which men can build. Yet surely when
Noah says to God, "You take me from my garden and
chuck me on a bare rock, all by myself," he knows
the rock has less to offer than a garden. In these
images, as in the vegetative ones, we see that dif-

ferent writers can use the same imaginative expressions with contradictory meanings, according to their special purposes.

Cities, too, can be images suggesting either the garden or the wilderness. When the Bible speaks of "the courts of our God," it is telling us that buildings can be filled with the presence of God. Yet a tower like that of Babel can be a signpost of corruption, and can suffer righteous destruction. A building or a city can be either Babylon or the heavenly city, either the Tower of Babel or the court of the Lord. Whether it is demonic or divine depends on how the writer uses and interprets the image.

These shifts and reversals in symbolic meaning are characteristic of the Bible and of all literature. The poet Macpherson touches on this point in "The Boatman" by saying that man must turn himself inside out to get his "beasts" outside him. Then he can let them in again, in orderly fashion, through the "sockets of his eyes." He must, like Noah, start all over again in a new world. As the Holub poem suggests, each of our heads contains an ark, is filled to the brim with contradictions, and simply "cannot be trimmed." There is an ark in your head, too, and you must imaginatively board it before you can see that gardens can also be cities and a rock the foundation for one.

3: Father of a Multitude

PROMISE

I Will Make You into a Great Nation

The Lord said to Abram, "Leave your own country, your kinsmen, and your father's house, and go to a country that I will show you. I will make you into a great nation, I will bless you and make your name so great that it shall be used in blessings:

> Those that bless you I will bless,
> those that curse you, I will execrate.
> All the families on earth
> will pray to be blessed as you are blessed."

And so Abram set out as the Lord had bidden him, and Lot went with him. Abram was seventy-five years old when he left Harran. He took his wife Sarai, his nephew Lot, all the property they had collected, and all the dependents they had acquired in Harran, and they started on their journey to Canaan. When they arrived, Abram passed through the country to the sanctuary at Shechem, the terebinth tree of Moreh. At that time the Canaanites lived in this land. There the Lord appeared to Abram and said, "I give this land to your descendants." So Abram built an altar there to the Lord who had appeared to him. Thence he went on to the hill country east of Bethel and pitched his tent between Bethel on the west and Ai on the east. There he built an altar to the Lord and invoked the Lord by name. Thus Abram journeyed by stages toward the Negeb.

There came a famine in the land, so severe that Abram went down to Egypt to live there for a while. . . .

Abram went up from Egypt into the Negeb, he and his wife and all that he had, and Lot went with him. Abram was now very rich in cattle and in silver and gold. From the Negeb he journeyed by stages to Bethel, to the place between Bethel and Ai where he had pitched his tent in the beginning, where he had set up an altar on the first occasion and had invoked the Lord by name. Now Lot was traveling with Abram, and he too possessed sheep and cattle and tents. The land could not support them both together; for their livestock were so numerous that they could not settle in the same district, and there were quarrels between Abram's herdsmen and Lot's. The Canaanites and the Perizzites were then living in the land. So Abram said to Lot, "Let there be no quarreling between us, between my herdsmen and yours; for we are close kinsmen. The whole country is there in front of you; let us part company. If you go left, I will go right; if you go right, I will go left." Lot looked up and saw how well-watered the whole Plain of the Jordan was; all the way to Zoar it was like the Garden of the Lord, like the land of Egypt. This was before the Lord had destroyed Sodom and Gomorrah. So Lot chose all the Plain of the Jordan and took the road on the east side. Thus they parted company. Abram settled in the land of Canaan; but Lot settled among the cities of the Plain and pitched his tents near Sodom. Now the men of Sodom were wicked, great sinners against the Lord.

After Lot and Abram had parted, the Lord said to Abram, "Raise your eyes and look into the distance from the place where you are, north and south, east and west. All the land you can see I will give to you and to your descendants forever. I will make your descendants countless as the dust of the earth; if anyone could count the dust upon the ground, then he could count your descendants. Now go through the length and breadth of the land, for I give it to you." So Abram moved his tent and settled by the terebinths of Mamre at Hebron; and there he built an altar to the Lord.

After this the word of the Lord came to Abram in a vision. He said, "Do not be afraid, Abram, I am giving you a very great reward." Abram replied, "Lord God, what canst thou give me? I have no standing among men, for the heir to my household is Eliezer of Damascus." Abram continued, "Thou hast given me no children, and so my heir must be a slave born in my house." Then came the word of the Lord to him: "This man shall not be your heir; your heir shall be a child of your own body." He took Abram outside and said, "Look up into the sky, and count the stars if you can. So many," he said, "shall your descendants be."

Abram put his faith in the Lord, and the Lord counted that faith to him as righteousness; he said to him, "I am the Lord who brought you out from Ur of the Chaldees to give you this land to occupy." Abram said, "O Lord God, how can I be sure that I shall occupy it?" The Lord answered, "Bring me a heifer three years old, a she-goat three years old, a ram three years old, a turtledove, and a fledgling." He brought him all these, halved the animals down the middle and placed each piece opposite its corresponding piece, but he did not halve the birds. When the birds of prey swooped down on the carcasses, Abram scared them away. Then, as the sun was going down, a trance came over Abram and great fear came upon him. The Lord said to Abram, "Know this for certain, that your descendants will be aliens living in a land that is not theirs; they will be slaves, and will be held in oppression there for four hundred years. But I will punish that nation whose slaves they are, and after that they shall come out with great possessions. You yourself shall join your fathers in peace and be buried in a good old age; and the fourth generation shall return here, for the Amorites will not be ripe for punishment till then." The sun went down and it was dusk, and there appeared a smoking brazier and a flaming torch passing between the divided pieces. That very day the Lord made a covenant with Abram, and he said, "To your descendants I give this land from the River of Egypt to the Great River, the river Euphrates, the territory of the Kenites, Kenizzites, Kadmonites, Hittites, Perizzites, Rephaim, Amorites, Canaanites, Girgashites, Hivites, and Jebusites."

GENESIS 12:1–10; 13; 15

In what way does Abram remind you of Noah? What is special about the Lord's covenant with him? What prophecy (revelation of future events) does the Lord reveal to Abram?

The Draft Horse

With a lantern that wouldn't burn
In too frail a buggy we drove
Behind too heavy a horse
Through a pitch-dark limitless grove.

And a man came out of the trees
And took our horse by the head
And reaching back to his ribs
Deliberately stabbed him dead.

The ponderous beast went down
With a crack of a broken shaft.
And the night drew through the trees
In one long invidious draft.

The most unquestioning pair
That ever accepted fate
And the least disposed to ascribe
Any more than we had to to hate,

We assumed that the man himself
Or someone he had to obey
Wanted us to get down
And walk the rest of the way.

ROBERT FROST

How does Frost use the word *draft* in two distinct but quite literal ways?
What unspoken yet implied meaning of the word applies to the old couple
in the poem? Were Abram and Sarai also "drafted"? Why or why not?

Hagar and
Ishmael

Abram's wife Sarai had borne him no children. Now she had an Egyptian slave girl whose name was Hagar, and she said to Abram, "You see that the Lord has not allowed me to bear a child. Take my slave girl; perhaps I shall found a family through her." Abram agreed to what his wife said; so Sarai, Abram's wife, brought her slave girl, Hagar the Egyptian, and gave her to her husband Abram as a wife. When this happened Abram had been in Canaan for ten years. He lay with Hagar and she conceived; and when she knew that she was with child, she despised her mistress. Sarai said to Abram, "I have been wronged and you must answer for it. It was I who gave my slave girl into your arms, but since she has known that she is with child, she has despised me. May the Lord see justice done between you and me." Abram replied to Sarai, "Your slave girl is in your hands; deal with her as you will." So Sarai ill-treated her and she ran away.

The angel of the Lord found her by a spring of water in the wilderness on the way to Shur, and he said, "Hagar, Sarai's slave girl, where have you come from and where are you going?" She answered, "I am running away from Sarai my mistress." The angel of the Lord said to her, "Go back to your mistress and submit to her ill-treatment." The angel also said, "I will make your descendants too many to be counted." And the angel of the Lord said to her:

> "You are with child and will bear a son.
> You shall name him Ishmael,
> because the Lord has heard of your ill-treatment.
> He shall be a man like the wild ass,
> his hand against every man
> and every man's hand against him;
> and he shall live at odds with all his kinsmen."

GENESIS 16 : 1–12

You Shall Call
Him Isaac

When Abram was ninety-nine years old, the Lord appeared to him and said, "I am God Almighty. Live always in my presence and be perfect, so that I may set my covenant between myself and you and multiply your descendants." Abram threw himself down on his face, and God spoke with him and said, "I make this covenant, and I make it with you: you shall be the father of a host of nations. Your name shall no longer be Abram, your name shall be Abraham, for I make you father of a host of nations. I will make you exceedingly fruitful; I will make nations out of you, and kings shall spring from you. I will fulfill my covenant between myself and you and your descendants after you, generation after generation, an everlasting covenant, to be your God, yours and your descendants' after you. As an everlasting possession I will give you and your descendants after you the land in which you now are aliens, all the land of Canaan, and I will be God to your descendants."

God said to Abraham, "For your part, you must keep my covenant, you and your descendants after you, generation by generation. This is how you shall keep my covenant between myself and you and your descendants after you: circumcise yourselves, every male among you. You shall circumcise the flesh of your foreskin, and it shall be the sign of the covenant between us. Every male among you in every generation shall be circumcised on the eighth day, both those born in your house and any foreigner, not of your blood but bought with your money. Circumcise both those born in your house and those bought with your money; thus shall my covenant be marked in your flesh as an everlasting covenant. Every uncircumcised male, everyone who has not had the flesh of his foreskin circumcised, shall be cut off from the kin of his father. He has broken my covenant."

God said to Abraham, "As for Sarai your wife; you shall call her not Sarai, but Sarah. I will bless her and give you a son by her. I will bless her and she shall be the mother of nations; the kings of many people shall spring from her." Abraham threw himself down on his face; he laughed and said to himself, "Can a son be born to a man who is a hundred years old? Can Sarah bear a son when she is ninety?" He said to God, "If only Ishmael might live under thy special care!" But God replied, "No. Your wife Sarah shall bear you a son, and you shall call him Isaac. With him I will fulfill my covenant, an everlasting covenant with his descendants after him. I have heard your prayer for Ishmael. I have blessed him and will make him fruitful. I will multiply his descendants; he shall be father of twelve princes, and I will raise a great nation from him. But my covenant I will fulfill with Isaac, whom Sarah will bear to you at this season next year." When he had finished talking with Abraham, God ascended and left him.

Then Abraham took Ishmael his son, everyone who had been born in his household and everyone bought with money, every male in his household, and he circumcised them that very same day in the flesh of their foreskins as God had told him to do. Abraham was ninety-nine years old when he circumcised the flesh of his foreskin. Ishmael was thirteen years old when he was circumcised in the flesh of his foreskin. Both Abraham and Ishmael were circumcised on the same day, and all the men of his household, born in the house or bought with money from foreigners, were circumcised with him.

GENESIS 17

When God commands Abram at the age of ninety-nine to live always in his presence and be perfect, what do you deduce about Abram? about God?

The Old Testament was originally written in Hebrew. The Hebrew word *Abram* means "high father." The word *Abraham* means "father of a multitude." Why, then, does God change Abram's name to Abraham?

What Jewish ritual begins at this stage of history? How is the thirteenth year a significant milestone in the religious life of a Jewish youngster?

How do Adam's two original sons come to mind as we read the prophecies about Ishmael and Isaac?

The Lord Rained Down
Fire and Brimstone

The Lord appeared to Abraham by the terebinths of Mamre. As Abraham was sitting at the opening of his tent in the heat of the day, he looked up and saw three men standing in front of him. When he saw them, he ran from the opening of his tent to meet them and bowed low to the ground. "Sirs," he said, "if I have deserved your favor, do not pass by my humble self without a visit. Let me send for some water so that you may wash your feet and rest under a tree; and let me fetch a little food so that you may refresh yourselves. Afterward you may continue the journey which has brought you my way." They said, "Do by all means as you say." So Abraham hurried into the tent to Sarah and said, "Take three measures of flour quickly, knead it and make some cakes." Then Abraham ran to the cattle, chose a fine tender calf and gave it to a servant, who hurriedly prepared it. He took curds and milk and the calf he had prepared, set it before them, and waited on them himself under the tree while they ate. They asked him where Sarah his wife was, and he said, "There, in the tent." The stranger said, "About this time next year I will be sure to come back to you, and Sarah your wife shall have a son." Now Sarah was listening at the opening of the tent, and he was close beside it. Both Abraham and Sarah had grown very old, and Sarah was past the age of childbearing. So Sarah laughed to herself and said, "I am past bearing children now that I am out of my time, and my husband is old." The Lord said to Abraham, "Why did Sarah laugh and say, 'Shall I indeed bear a child when I am old?' Is anything impossible for the Lord? In due season I will come back to you, about this time next year, and Sarah shall have a son." Sarah lied because she was frightened, and denied that she had laughed; but he said, "Yes, you did laugh."

The men set out and looked down toward Sodom, and Abraham went with them to start them on their way. The Lord thought to himself, "Shall I conceal from Abraham what I intend to do? He will become a great and powerful nation, and all nations on earth will pray to be blessed as he is blessed. I have taken care of him on purpose that he may charge his sons and family after him to conform to the way of the Lord and to do what is right and just; thus I shall fulfill all that I have promised for him." So the Lord said, "There is a great outcry over Sodom and Gomorrah; their sin is very grave. I must go down and see whether their deeds warrant the outcry which has reached me. I am resolved to know the truth." When the men turned and went toward Sodom, Abraham remained standing before the Lord. Abraham drew near him and said, "Wilt thou really sweep away good and bad together? Suppose there are fifty good men in the city; wilt thou really sweep it away, and not pardon the place because of the fifty good men? Far be it from thee to do this — to kill good and bad together; for then the good would suffer with the bad. Far be it from thee. Shall not the judge of all the earth do what is just?" The Lord said, "If I find in the city of Sodom fifty good men, I will pardon the whole place for their sake." Abraham replied, "May I presume to speak to the Lord, dust and ashes that I am: suppose there are five short of the fifty good men? Wilt thou destroy the whole city for a mere five men?" He said, "If I find forty-five there I will not destroy it." Abraham spoke again, "Suppose forty can be found there?"; and he said, "For the sake of the forty I will not do it." Then Abraham said, "Please do not be angry, O Lord, if I speak again: suppose thirty can be found there?" He answered, "If I find thirty I will not do it." Abraham continued, "May I presume to speak to the Lord: suppose twenty can be found there?" He replied, "For the sake of the twenty I will not destroy it." Abraham said, "I pray thee not to be angry, O Lord, if I speak just once more: suppose ten can be found there?" He said, "For the sake of the ten I will not destroy it." When the Lord had finished talking with Abraham, he left him, and Abraham returned home.

The two angels came to Sodom in the evening, and Lot was sitting in the gateway of the city. When he saw them he rose to meet them and bowed low with his face to the ground. He said, "I pray you, sirs, turn aside to my humble home, spend the night there and wash your feet; you can rise early and continue your journey." "No," they answered, "we will spend the night in the street." But Lot was so insistent that they did turn aside and enter his house. He prepared a meal for them, baking unleavened cakes, and they ate them. Before they lay down to sleep, the men of Sodom, both young and old, surrounded the house — everyone without exception. They called to Lot and asked him where the men were who had entered his house that night. "Bring them out," they shouted, "so that we can have intercourse with them."

Lot went out into the doorway to them, closed the door behind him and said, "No, my friends, do not be so wicked. Look, I have two daughters, both virgins; let me bring them out to you, and you can do what you like with them; but do not touch these men, because they have come under the shelter of my roof." They said, "Out of our way! This man has come and settled here as an alien, and does he now take it upon himself to judge us? We will treat you worse than them." They crowded in on the man Lot and pressed close to smash in the door. But the two men inside reached out, pulled Lot in, and closed the door. Then they struck the men in the doorway with blindness, both small and great, so that they could not find the door.

The two men said to Lot, "Have you anyone else here, sons-in-law, sons, or daughters, or any who belong to you in the city? Get them out of this place, because we are going to destroy it. The outcry against it has been so great that the Lord has sent us to destroy it." So Lot went out and spoke to his intended sons-in-law. He said, "Be quick and leave this place; the Lord is going to destroy the city." But they did not take him seriously.

As soon as it was dawn, the angels urged Lot to go, saying, "Be quick, take your wife and your two daughters who are here, or you will be swept away when the city is punished." When he lingered, they took him by the hand, with his wife and his daughters, and, because the Lord had spared him, led him on until he was outside the city. When they had brought them out, they said, "Flee for your lives; do not look back and do not stop anywhere in the Plain. Flee to the hills or you will be swept away." Lot replied, "No, sirs. You have shown your servant favor and you have added to your unfailing care for me by saving my life, but I cannot escape to the hills; I shall be overtaken by the disaster, and die. Look, here is a town, only a small place, near enough for me to reach quickly. Let me escape to it—it is very small—and save my life." He said to him, "I grant your request: I will not overthrow this town you speak of. But flee there quickly, because I can do nothing until you are there." That is why the place was called Zoar. The sun had risen over the land as Lot entered Zoar; and then the Lord rained down fire and brimstone from the skies on Sodom and Gomorrah. He overthrew those cities and destroyed all the Plain, with everyone living there and everything growing in the ground. But Lot's wife, behind him, looked back, and she turned into a pillar of salt.

Next morning Abraham rose early and went to the place where he had stood in the presence of the Lord. He looked down toward Sodom and Gomorrah and all the wide extent of the Plain, and there he saw thick smoke rising high from the earth like the smoke of a lime kiln. Thus, when God destroyed the cities of the Plain, he thought of Abraham and rescued Lot from the disaster, the overthrow of the cities where he had been living.

GENESIS 18; 19:1–29

In the biblical accounts, what is the difference between Abraham's conversation with God and Noah's conversation with him?

What do Sodom and Gomorrah symbolize?

To this day there must be ten men present before there can be a service in an orthodox Jewish synagogue. How does this passage explain the attendance requirement?

Does this punishment of God upon men because of the evil and the wickedness in the world strike you as more or less merciful than the judgment he visited upon men in Noah's time?

Psalm 11

In the Lord put I my trust:
How say ye to my soul, Flee as a bird to your mountain?
For, lo, the wicked bend their bow,
They make ready their arrow upon the string,
That they may privily shoot at the upright in heart.
If the foundations be destroyed, what can the righteous do?
The Lord is in his holy temple,
The Lord's throne is in heaven:
His eyes behold, his eyelids try, the children of men.
The Lord trieth the righteous:
But the wicked and him that loveth violence his soul hateth.
Upon the wicked he shall rain snares,
Fire and brimstone and horrible tempest:
This shall be the portion of their cup.
For the righteous Lord loveth righteousness;
His countenance doth behold the upright.

How does this psalm describe both Abraham and the wicked men of Sodom and Gomorrah?

The Birth
of Isaac

The Lord showed favor to Sarah as he had promised, and made good what he had said about her. She conceived and bore a son to Abraham for his old age, at the time which God had appointed. The son whom Sarah bore to him, Abraham named Isaac. When Isaac was eight days old Abraham circumcised him, as God had commanded. Abraham was a hundred years old when his son Isaac was born. Sarah said, "God has given me good reason to laugh, and everybody who hears will laugh with me." She said, "Whoever would have told Abraham that Sarah would suckle children? Yet I have borne him a son for his old age." The boy grew and was weaned, and on the day of his weaning Abraham gave a feast. Sarah saw the son whom Hagar the Egyptian had borne to Abraham laughing at him, and she said to Abraham, "Drive out this slave girl and her son; I will not have this slave girl's son sharing the inheritance with my son Isaac." Abraham was vexed at this on his son Ishmael's account, but God said to him, "Do not be vexed on account of the boy and the slave girl. Do what Sarah says, because you shall have descendants through Isaac. I will make a great nation of the slave girl's son too, because he is your own child."

Abraham rose early in the morning, took some food and a water-skin full of water and gave it to Hagar; he set the child on her shoulder and sent her away, and she went and wandered in the wilderness of Beersheba. When the water in the skin was finished, she thrust the child under a bush, and went and sat down some way off, about two bowshots away, for she said, "How can I watch the child die?" So she sat some way off, weeping bitterly. God heard the child crying, and the angel of God called from heaven to Hagar, "What is the matter, Hagar? Do not be afraid: God has heard the child crying where you laid him. Get to your feet, lift the child up and hold him in your arms, because

SACRIFICE

The Sacrifice of Isaac

The time came when God put Abraham to the test. "Abraham," he called, and Abraham replied, "Here I am." God said, "Take your son Isaac, your only son, whom you love, and go to the land of Moriah. There you shall offer him as a sacrifice on one of the hills which I will show you." So Abraham rose early in the morning and saddled his ass, and he took with him two of his men and his son Isaac; and he split the firewood for the sacrifice, and set out for the place of which God had spoken. On the third day Abraham looked up and saw the place in the distance. He said to his men, "Stay here with the ass while I and the boy go over there; and when we have worshiped we will come back to you." So Abraham took the wood for the sacrifice and laid it on his son Isaac's shoulder; he himself carried the fire and the knife, and the two of them went on together. Isaac said to Abraham, "Father," and he answered, "What is it, my son?" Isaac said, "Here are the fire and the wood, but where is the young beast for the sacrifice?" Abraham answered, "God will provide himself with a young beast for a sacrifice, my son." And the two of them went on together and came to the place of which God had spoken. There Abraham built an altar and arranged the wood. He bound his son Isaac and laid him on the altar on top of the wood. Then he stretched out his hand and took the knife to kill his son; but the angel of the Lord called to him from heaven, "Abraham, Abraham." He answered, "Here I am." The angel of the Lord said, "Do not raise your hand against the boy; do not touch him. Now I know that you are a God-fearing man. You have not withheld from me your son, your only son." Abraham looked up, and there he saw a ram caught by its horns in a thicket. So he went and took the ram and offered it as a sacrifice instead of his son. Abraham named that place Jehovah-jireh; and to this day the saying is: "In the mountain of the Lord it was provided." Then the angel of the Lord called from heaven a second time to Abraham, "This is the word of the Lord: By my own self I swear: inasmuch as you have done this and have not withheld your son, your only son, I will bless you abundantly and greatly multiply your descendants until they are as numerous as the stars in the sky and the grains of sand on the seashore. Your descendants shall possess the cities of their enemies. All nations on earth shall pray to be blessed as your descendants are blessed, and this because you have obeyed me."

Abraham went back to his men, and together they returned to Beer-sheba; and there Abraham remained.

GENESIS 22:1–19

We think of human and animal sacrifice as primitive and superstitious, but to societies in earlier ages the offering of a young person or of a young animal to God seemed fitting. Can you imagine why this would be so? In what ways do we still "sacrifice" the young today?

Does Isaac have a second birth in this story? Is it more miraculous than the first? Where does it take place?

*The following legend is told by the
Pawnee Indians of the Plains region
of North America.*

The Boy Who Was Sacrificed

There was a time, far back, when some people thought that it was good to sacrifice to *Ti-ra'-wa* whatever they had that was most precious to them. The sacrifice of the animal, the burnt offering, has always been made by all the Pawnees; that is one of the things handed down from the ruler. It is very old. The Skidi have always performed the sacrifice of the captive. Each one of these is sacred and solemn, but it is not like giving up something that belongs to you, and that you love. It is a sacrifice, but it does not cost much.

Many years ago, in the Skidi village on the Loup, there lived a man, who believed that if he sacrificed his son to *Ti-ra'-wa*, it would be a blessing to him. He thought that if he did this thing, perhaps *Ti-ra'-wa* would speak to him face to face, and that he could talk to him just as two people would talk to one another, and that in this way he would learn many things that other people did not understand. His child was a nice boy about ten years old, strong, growing up well, and the man loved him. It made him feel badly to think of killing him. He meditated long about this, but the more he thought about it, the more he believed that this sacrifice would please *Ti-ra'-wa*. There were many things that he wanted to understand, and to do; and he thought if he gave up his son, these good things would come to him. So he resolved to make the sacrifice.

One morning he started out from the village, and took the boy with him. They went over to the Platte. When they got to the river, as they were walking along, the man took his knife from its sheath, and caught the boy by the shoulder, and stabbed him quickly, and cut him open. When the boy was dead, he threw the body into the river, and then went back to the village. When he got there, he went into his lodge and sat down. After a time he said to his wife, "Where is the boy?" The woman said, "He went out with you, when you went over to see the horses." The man answered, "No; I went out to where the horses are feeding, and looked at them, but he did not go with me."

The man went out, and looked for the boy all through the village, but he could not find him. At night when the boy did not come home, they began to get frightened, and for two days they hunted for the boy, and at last they got the old crier to call out for him from the top of the lodge, and ask if anyone had seen him, but none of the people knew what had become of the boy. Now the mother was mourning, and the father pretended to feel very badly. They could not find the boy; and soon after this the tribe started on the summer hunt, and the father and mother went with them. The village made a good hunt, killing plenty of buffalo, and made much dried meat.

After the boy had been thrown into the river, he floated down with the current, sometimes turning over and over in the swift water, and sometimes grounding for a little while on a sand bar, and then being floated off again, and being carried further down. At length he came near to the place where the whirlpool is, under the bluff at *Pa-hŭk'*, where is the lodge of the *Nahu'rac*. There were two buzzards sitting on the bluff, just above this place, and as they sat there, one of them stretched out his neck and looked up the river, and after he had looked, he said to the other, "I see a body." Then both the buzzards flew down to where the boy was floating in the water, and got down under him, and raised him on their backs, and lifted him up out of the water, and flew up to the bluff, carrying the boy on their backs, and placed him on the ground on top of the bluff over the big cave, which is the home of the *Nahu'rac*. In this lodge were all kinds of animals, and all kinds of birds. There were bears, and mountain lions, and buffalo, and elk, and beaver, and otter, and deer; all kinds of animals, great and small, and all kinds of birds.

There is a little bird, smaller than a pigeon. Its back is blue, and its breast white, and its head is spotted. It flies swiftly over the water, and when it sees a fish, it dives down into the water to catch it. This bird is a servant or a messenger for the *Nahu'rac*. Such a bird came flying by just as the buzzards put the body on the ground, and he stopped and looked at it. When he saw how it was—for he knew all that had happened—he flew down into the lodge and told the *Nahu'rac* about the boy. The bird said, "There is a boy up here on the hill. He is dead, and he is poor, and I want to have him brought to life again." Then he told the *Nahu'rac* all the things that had happened. When the messenger bird had done speaking, the *Nahu'rac,* earnestly counseled together for a long time to decide what should be done, and each one made a speech, giving his opinion about the matter, but they could not make up their minds what ought to be done.

The little bird was coaxing the *Nahu'rac,* and saying, "Come, now, we want to save his life." But the *Nahu'rac* could not decide. At last the chief of the *Nahu'rac* said, "No, messenger, we cannot decide this here. You will have to go to the other council lodges, and see what they say about it." The bird said, "I am going," and flew swiftly out of the lodge and up the river, till he came to the *Nahu'rac* lodge near the Lone Tree. When he got there, he told them all about the boy, and said that the council at *Pa-hŭk'* could not decide what should be done. The *Nahu'rac* here talked, and at last they said, "We cannot decide. The council at *Pa-hŭk'* must decide." Then the bird went to the lodge on the Loup, and the *Nahu'rac* there said that they could not decide. Then he went to *Kitz-a-witz-ŭk,* and to *Pa-hŭr';* and at each place the *Nahu'rac* considered and talked about it, and then said, "We cannot decide what shall be done. The council at *Pa-hŭk'* must decide for themselves."

At last, after he had visited all the council lodges of the *Nahu'rac,* the bird flew swiftly back to the lodge at *Pa-hŭk',* and told them there what the animals at the other lodges had said. In the council of the *Nahu'rac* at *Pa-hŭk',* there were four chiefs, who sat there as judges to determine such matters as this, after they had all been talked over, and to decide what should be done. When the messenger bird came back, and told the *Nahu'rac* what the other councils had said, these judges considered for a time, and then spoke together, and at length the chief of the judges said to the bird, "Now, messenger, we have concluded that we will not decide this question ourselves. You decide it, and say what shall be done."

The messenger was not long in deciding. He did not hesitate. He said, "I want this boy brought back to life." Then all the *Nahu'rac* stood up, and went to where the boy lay, and stood around him and prayed, and at last the boy breathed once, and then after a little while he breathed again, and at last he came to life and sat up. He looked about and saw all these animals standing around him, and he wondered. He said to himself, "Why, my father stabbed me, and killed me, and now here I am among this great crowd of animals. What does this mean?" He was surprised.

The *Nahu'rac* all went back into the lodge, and took the boy with them. When all were seated in the lodge, the four judges talked to each other, and the chief one stood up, and said, "Now, my people, we have brought this boy back to life, but he is poor, and we must do something for him. Let us teach him all we know, and make him one of us." Then the *Nahu'rac* all made a noise. They were glad. Then they began to sing and they danced. They taught the boy all their secrets, and all their ways. They taught him how to cut a man open and cure him again, and how to shoot an arrow through a man and then cure him, and how to cut a man's tongue out and then to put it back, and how to make well a broken leg, and many other things. After they had done all these things, they said to the boy, "Now we have brought you back to life, and have taught you all these things, so that you are one of us. Now you must stop with us one season. Your people have gone off on the summer hunt. You must stay with us until the autumn. Then you can go back to your people." So the boy stayed with the *Nahu'rac* in their lodge.

At length the Skidi had returned from the hunt with plenty of dried meat. Soon after this, the *Nahu'rac* said one day to the boy, "Your people have got back from the hunt. Now you can go back to the village. Go back and get a lot of nice dried meat, and bring it back to us here, and we will have a feast."

The boy went home to the village. He got there in the night, and went to his father's lodge, and went in. There was a little fire burning in the lodge. It was nearly out, and gave only a little light, but he knew the place where his mother slept. He went up to her, and put out his hand and touched her, and pushed her a little. She awoke, and sat up and looked at him, and he said, "I've come back." When she saw him, and heard him speak, she was very much surprised, and her heart was glad to see her boy again. She called to his father, and he woke up. When he saw the boy he was afraid, for he thought it was a ghost. The boy told them nothing of what had happened, or where he had been. He just said, "I have come back again."

In the morning all the people were surprised to hear that he had come back, and to see him, and they stood around looking at him, and asking him questions, but he said nothing. The next day the people still questioned him, and at last the boy said, "I have been all summer with friends, with people who have been good to me. I should like to take them a present of some nice dried meat, so that we can have a feast." The people said that this was good. They picked out four strong horses, and loaded them with dried meat, the nicest pieces. The boy's father gave some of it, and all the other people brought pieces and put them on the horses, until they had big loads. They sent two young men with the boy, to help him load and drive the horses, and they started to go to the *Nahu'rac* lodge at *Pa-hŭk'*.

When they had come pretty near the place, the boy sent the young men back to the village, and he went on alone, driving the pack horses before him. When he reached the home of the *Nahu'rac*, he unloaded the horses, and turned them loose, and then went into the lodge. When he went in, and when the *Nahu'rac* saw him, they all made a hissing noise. They were glad to see him. The boy brought into the lodge all the dried meat, and they had a great feast. After the feast they had a doctors' dance, and the boy was made a doctor, and again was taught all that the *Nahu'rac* knew. After that he could do many wonderful things. He could sometimes go to a man that had been dead for a day, and then bring him back to life.

No one ever knew what the father had done, for the boy never told anyone. He knew that he could never have learned all these wonderful things unless his father had sacrificed him.

Retold by GEORGE B. GRINNELL

In this myth, the father sacrifices the boy he loves so he can meet God face to face and learn things men do not ordinarily know. Why was Abraham willing to sacrifice Isaac? According to each story, was the sacrifice, or willingness to sacrifice, worthwhile?

What characteristic does the little bird stand for? Where in Noah's story (in Chapter Two) does a bird figure?

Story of Isaac

1. The door it o - pened slow - ly, My
2. The trees they got much small - er, The
3. You who build these al - tars now To

1. fa - ther he came in, I was
2. lake a la - dy's mir - ror, We
3. sa - cri - fice these chil - dren, You must not

1. nine years old And he
2. stopped to drink some wine. Then he
3. do it a - ny more. A

1. stood so tall a - bove me,
2. threw the bot - tle o - ver,
3. scheme is not a vi - sion And you

1. Blue eyes they were shin - ing And his
2. Broke a min - ute la - ter And he
3. nev - er have been tempt - ed By a

1. voice was ve - ry cold. Said, "I've had a vi -
2. put his hand on mine. Thought I saw an ea -
3. de - mon or a god. You who stand a-bove them

1. sion And you know I'm strong and
2. gle But it might have been a
3. now, Your hatch - ets blunt and

1. ho - ly, I must do what I've been told."
2. vul - ture, I nev - er could de - cide.
3. blood - y, You were not there be - fore.

1. So he start - ed up the moun - tain, I was
2. Then my fa - ther built an al - tar, He looked
3. When I lay up - on a moun - tain And my

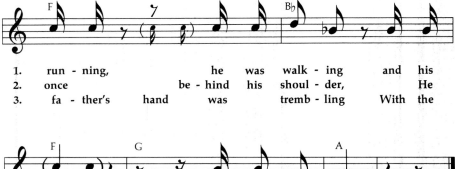

1.	run - ning,		he	was	walk - ing	and	his
2.	once		be - hind	his	shoul - der,		He
3.	fa - ther's	hand	was		tremb - ling	With	the

1.	ax	was	made	of	gold.
2.	knew	I	would	not	hide.
3.	beau - ty		of	the	word.

4. And if you call me brother now
    Forgive me if I inquire
    Just according to whose plan?
When it all comes down to dust
    I will kill you if I must
    I will help you if I can.
When it all comes down to dust
    I will help you if I must
    I will kill you if I can.
And mercy on our uniform
Man of peace or man of war—
    The peacock spreads his fan.

LEONARD COHEN

What modern sacrifice does the author of this song connect with the sacrifice of Isaac? Why is this modern sacrifice a scheme instead of a vision? In what way does the poet establish that in Abraham's case it was a vision that prompted his action?

Can you explain the reversal of *helping* and *killing* in the last stanza? What do the eagle or vulture and the peacock symbolize in this poem?

The Bull Calf

The thing could barely stand. Yet taken
from his mother and the barn smells
he still impressed with his pride,
with the promise of sovereignty in the way
his head moved to take us in.
The fierce sunlight tugging the maize from the ground
licked at his shapely flanks.
He was too young for all that pride.
I thought of the deposed Richard II.

"No money in bull calves," Freeman had said.
The visiting clergyman rubbed the nostrils
now snuffing pathetically at the windless day.
"A pity," he sighed.
My gaze slipped off his hat toward the empty sky
that circled over the black knot of men,
over us and the calf waiting for the first blow.

Struck,
the bull calf drew in his thin forelegs
as if gathering strength for a mad rush . . .
tottered . . . raised his darkening eyes to us,
and I saw we were at the far end
of his frightened look, growing smaller and smaller
till we were only the ponderous mallet
that flicked his bleeding ear
and pushed him over on his side, stiffly,
like a block of wood.

Below the hill's crest
the river snuffled on the improvised beach.
We dug a deep pit and threw the dead calf into it.
It made a wet sound, a sepulchral gurgle,

as the warm sides bulged and flattened.
Settled, the bull calf lay as if asleep,
one foreleg over the other,
bereft of pride and so beautiful now,
without movement, perfectly still in the cool pit,
I turned away and wept.

IRVING LAYTON

Richard II was crowned King of England at the age of ten.

Does man often kill beautiful things for the reason the farmer kills the bull calf? How is this killing different from a sacrifice? Why does the poet weep?

*The following poem describes the
Aztec Indian ritual which took place
once a year at the feast of the god
Tezcatlipoca.*

On His Back upon the Stone

In the fifth month was the great feast
the feast of Tezcatlipoca

At this feast died the youth the fair
ʼyouth the young man without
blemish
who for one year had lived as the god

For he who was chosen
from among the most select of captives
from among say the ten most fair of body and good
to look upon
he who was chosen to be the god
was slain on this day

And on this same day a new impersonator of the god
who again would live for one year
was offered to the people

The youth chosen was of radiant countenance
of good understanding
quick and clean of body
                    slender like a reed
                    lean and well built as a cane
                    neither corpulent nor small
                    nor overly tall
                                (for of one too tall the women said
                                Headnodder
                                Star-hands)

He who was chosen was entirely without defect
                smooth as a pebble or carved wood

.   .   .   .

Now with his companions his pages
he arrived at the temple of Tlacochcalco
and by himself
of his own free will
ascended its steps

    at the first step he stopped and broke
    his flute

      his music stopped

        at another step he broke and threw down
        his smoking tube

          at each step
          he broke and scattered the belongings
          left to him
          until

            at the summit of the steps nothing
            was left to him nothing

              and there
              at the summit of the temple steps
              the priests fell upon him

                they threw him on his back upon
                the stone

                  they cut open his breast tore out
                  his heart and raised it to the sun
                  in offering

                    later his severed head was
                    impaled upon the skull rack

Thus he ended his life
in the adornment of death so is betokened our life on earth

For whoever rejoices in possessions and
prosperity
sweet things and riches
ends in nothing and in misery

For says the god himself
Tezcatlipoca
"No one takes with him into death
the good things of life"

Translated by CHARLES E. DIBBLE
and ARTHUR J. O. ANDERSON

How is the captive sacrificial youth an "impersonator" of the god? How do his actions just before the sacrifice remind you of Isaac's attitude in the biblical story? What evidence is there that the Aztec's god Tezcatlipoca was identified with the sun? Does the sun also nearly die each year?

from *Psalm 91*

He that dwelleth in the secret place of the most High
Shall abide under the shadow of the Almighty.
I will say of the Lord, "He is my refuge and my fortress;
My God, in him will I trust."
Surely he shall deliver thee from the snare of the fowler,
And from the noisome pestilence.
He shall cover thee with his feathers,
And under his wings shalt thou trust;
His truth shall be thy shield and buckler.
Thou shalt not be afraid for the terror by night;
Nor for the arrow that flieth by day;
Nor for the pestilence that walketh in darkness;
Nor for the destruction that wasteth at noonday.
A thousand shall fall at thy side,
And ten thousand at thy right hand;
But it shall not come nigh thee.
Only with thine eyes shalt thou behold
And see the reward of the wicked.
Because thou hast made the Lord, which is my refuge,
Even the most High, thy habitation;
There shall no evil befall thee,
Neither shall any plague come nigh thy dwelling.
For he shall give his angels charge over thee,
To keep thee in all thy ways.
They shall bear thee up in their hands,
Lest thou dash thy foot against a stone.
Thou shalt tread upon the lion and adder;
The young lion and the dragon shalt thou trample under feet
Because he hath set his love upon me, therefore will I deliver him. . . .

What metaphors explain the "secret place" mentioned at the beginning of
this psalm? How are the stories of Noah and Abraham echoed in the words
of the psalm?

SUCCESSION

The Marriage of Isaac and Rebecca

By this time Abraham had become a very old man, and the Lord had blessed him in all that he did. Abraham said to his servant, who had been long in his service and was in charge of all his possessions, "Put your hand under my thigh: I want you to swear by the Lord, the God of heaven and earth, that you will not take a wife for my son from the women of the Canaanites in whose land I dwell; you must go to my own country and to my own kindred to find a wife for my son Isaac." The servant said to him, "What if the woman is unwilling to come with me to this country? Must I in that event take your son back to the land from which you came?" Abraham said to him, "On no account are you to take my son back there. The Lord the God of heaven who took me from my father's house and the land of my birth, the Lord who swore to me that he would give this land to my descendants—he will send his angel before you, and from there you shall take a wife for my son. If the woman is unwilling to come with you, then you will be released from your oath to me; but you must not take my son back there." So the servant put his hand under his master Abraham's thigh and swore an oath in those terms.

The servant took ten camels from his master's herds, and also all kinds of gifts from his master; he set out for Aram-naharaim and arrived at the city where Nahor lived. Toward evening, the time when the women come out to draw water, he made the camels kneel down by the well outside the city. He said, "O Lord God of my master Abraham, give me good fortune this day; keep faith with my master Abraham. Here I stand by the spring, and the women of the city are coming out to draw water. Let it be like this: I shall say to a girl, 'Please lower

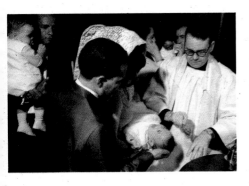

"Some fine day, my son, all this will be yours."

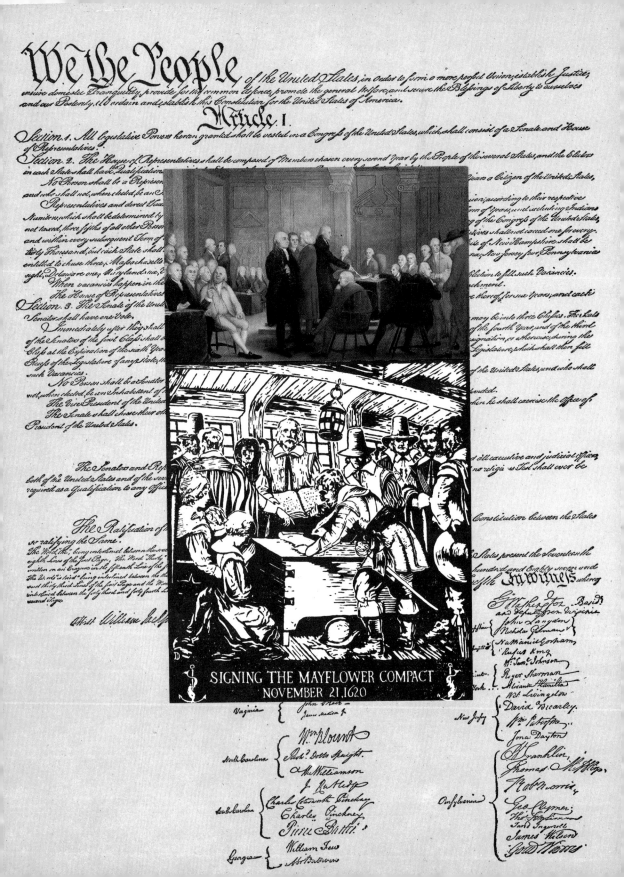

SIGNING THE MAYFLOWER COMPACT
NOVEMBER 21, 1620

your jar so that I may drink'; and if she answers, 'Drink, and I will water your camels also,' that will be the girl whom thou dost intend for thy servant Isaac. In this way I shall know that thou hast kept faith with my master."

Before he had finished praying silently, he saw Rebecca coming out with her water jug on her shoulder. She was the daughter of Bethuel son of Milcah, the wife of Abraham's brother Nahor. The girl was very beautiful, a virgin, who had had no intercourse with a man. She went down to the spring, filled her jar and came up again. Abraham's servant hurried to meet her and said, "Give me a sip of water from your jar." "Drink, sir," she answered, and at once lowered her jar onto her hand to let him drink. When she had finished giving him a drink, she said, "Now I will draw water for your camels until they have had enough." So she quickly emptied her jar into the water trough, hurried again to the well to draw water and watered all the camels. The man was watching quietly to see whether or not the Lord had made his journey successful. When the camels had finished drinking, the man took a gold nose ring weighing half a shekel, and two bracelets for her wrists weighing ten shekels, also of gold, and said, "Tell me, please, whose daughter you are. Is there room in your father's house for us to spend the night?" She answered, "I am the daughter of Bethuel, the son of Nahor and Milcah; and we have plenty of straw and fodder and also room for you to spend the night." So the man bowed down and prostrated himself to the Lord. He said, "Blessed be the Lord the God of my master Abraham, who has not failed to keep faith and truth with my master; for I have been guided by the Lord to the house of my master's kinsman."

The girl ran to her mother's house and told them what had happened. . . . They called Rebecca and asked her if she would go with the man, and she said, "Yes, I will go." So they let their sister Rebecca and her nurse go with Abraham's servant and his men. They blessed Rebecca and said to her:

"You are our sister, may you be the mother of myriads;
    may your sons possess the cities of their enemies."

Then Rebecca and her companions mounted their camels at once and followed the man. So the servant took Rebecca and went his way.

Isaac meanwhile had moved on as far as Beer-lahai-roi and was living in the Negeb. One evening when he had gone out into the open country hoping to meet them, he looked up and saw camels approaching. When Rebecca raised her eyes and saw Isaac, she slipped hastily from her camel, saying to the servant, "Who is that man walking across the open toward us?" The servant answered, "It is my master." So she took her veil and covered herself. The servant related to Isaac all that had happened. Isaac conducted her into the tent and took her as his wife. So she became his wife, and he loved her and was consoled for the death of his mother.

GENESIS 24 : 1–28, 58–67

Why does Abraham's servant feel that God has led him by the right road in finding Rebecca as a prospective bride for Isaac? What conditions are met before the final choice is made? Which of these conditions was initiated by the servant himself? Would you agree with him that it is a very important attribute of a good wife?

The Death
of Abraham

Abraham had given all that he had to Isaac; and he had already in his lifetime given presents to the sons of his concubines, and had sent them away eastward, to a land of the east, out of his son Isaac's way. Abraham had lived for a hundred and seventy-five years when he breathed his last. He died at a good old age, after a very long life, and was gathered to his father's kin. His sons, Isaac and Ishmael, buried him in the cave at Machpelah, on the land of Ephron son of Zohar the Hittite, east of Mamre, the plot which Abraham had bought from the Hittites. There Abraham was buried with his wife Sarah. After the death of Abraham, God blessed his son Isaac, who settled close by Beer-lahai-roi.

GENESIS 25 : 5–11

Abraham led a pastoral life in country places with his herds, family, and servants. Which other characters in this book are shepherds or wanderers? Is Abraham the first who has been both? Why was he a wanderer?

Abraham

The rivulet-loving wanderer Abraham
Through waterless wastes tracing his fields of pasture
Led his Chaldean herds and fattening flocks
With the meandering art of wavering water
That seeks and finds, yet does not know its way.
He came, rested and prospered, and went on,
Scattering behind him little pastoral kingdoms,
And over each one its own particular sky,
Not the great rounded sky through which he journeyed,
That went with him but when he rested changed.
His mind was full of names
Learned from strange peoples speaking alien tongues,
And all that was theirs one day he would inherit.
He died content and full of years, though still
The Promise had not come, and left his bones,
Far from his father's house, in alien Canaan.

EDWIN MUIR

How does the poet use images of water and sky to describe the kind of life
Abraham lived? What, in Abraham's mind, accounts both for the restless-
ness and the contentment of his life?

In what sense is Abraham still an exile (a wanderer) at the time of his
death? What is he searching for?

The Birth of Jacob and Esau

When Isaac was forty years old he married Rebecca the daughter of Bethuel the Aramaean from Paddan-aram and the sister of Laban the Aramaean. Isaac appealed to the Lord on behalf of his wife because she was barren; the Lord yielded to his entreaty, and Rebecca conceived. The children pressed hard on each other in her womb, and she said, "If this is how it is with me, what does it mean?" So she went to seek guidance of the Lord. The Lord said to her:

> "Two nations in your womb,
>   two peoples, going their own ways from birth!
> One shall be stronger than the other;
>   the older shall be servant to the younger."

When her time had come, there were indeed twins in her womb. The first came out red, hairy all over like a hair cloak, and they named him Esau. Immediately afterward his brother was born with his hand grasping Esau's heel, and they called him Jacob. Isaac was sixty years old when they were born. The boys grew up; and Esau became skillful in hunting, a man of the open plains, but Jacob led a settled life and stayed among the tents. Isaac favored Esau because he kept him supplied with venison, but Rebecca favored Jacob. One day Jacob prepared a broth and when Esau came in from the country, exhausted, he said to Jacob, "I am exhausted; let me swallow some of that red broth": this is why he was called Edom. Jacob said, "Not till you sell me your rights as the first-born." Esau replied, "I am at death's door; what use is my birthright to me?" Jacob said, "Not till you swear!"; so he swore an oath and sold his birthright to Jacob. Then Jacob gave Esau bread and the lentil broth, and he ate and drank and went away without more ado. Thus Esau showed how little he valued his birthright.

GENESIS 25 : 20–34

What differences are there between the twins born to Rebecca? Do they remind you of any previous sons in earlier biblical stories? What unusual aspect of Jacob's birth suggests that he, rather than Esau, will be his father's heir?

What in those days would have been especially important about a man's birthright? Is the birthright still important today? How does the biblical story account for the descriptive saying, "He would sell his birthright for a mess of pottage"? What kind of person is described in this saying?

The Blessing
of Jacob

When Isaac grew old and his eyes became so dim that he could not see, he called his elder son Esau and said to him, "My son," and he answered, "Here I am." Isaac said, "Listen now: I am old and I do not know when I may die. Take your hunting gear, your quiver and your bow, and go out into the country and get me some venison. Then make me a savory dish of the kind I like, and bring it to me to eat so that I may give you my blessing before I die." Now Rebecca was listening as Isaac talked to his son Esau. When Esau went off into the country to find some venison and bring it home, she said to her son Jacob, "I heard your father talking to your brother Esau, and he said, 'Bring me some venison and make it into a savory dish so that I may eat it and bless you in the presence of the Lord before I die.' Listen to me, my son, and do what I tell you. Go to the flock and pick me out two fine young kids, and I will make them into a savory dish for your father, of the kind he likes. Then take them in to your father, and he will eat them so that he may bless you before he dies." Jacob said to his mother Rebecca, "But my brother Esau is a hairy man, and my skin is smooth. Suppose my father feels me, he will know I am tricking him and I shall bring a curse upon myself instead of a blessing." His mother answered him, "Let the curse fall on me, my son, but do as I say; go and bring me the kids." So Jacob fetched them and brought them to his mother, who made them into a savory dish of the kind that his father liked. Then Rebecca took her elder son's clothes, Esau's best clothes which she kept by her in the house, and put them on her younger son Jacob. She put the goatskins on his hands and on the smooth nape of his neck; and she handed her son Jacob the savory dish and the bread she had made. He came to his father and said, "Father." He answered, "Yes, my son; who are you?" Jacob answered his father, "I am Esau, your elder son. I have done as you told me. Come, sit up and eat some of my venison, so that you may give me your blessing." Isaac said to his son, "What is this that you found so quickly?" and Jacob answered, "It is what the Lord your God put in my way." Isaac then said to Jacob, "Come close and let me feel you, my son, to see whether you are really my son Esau." When Jacob came close to his father, Isaac felt him and said, "The voice is Jacob's voice, but the hands are the hands of Esau." He did not recognize him because his hands were hairy like Esau's, and that is why he blessed him. He said, "Are you really my son Esau?" and he answered, "Yes." Then Isaac said, "Bring me some of your venison to eat, my son, so that I may give you my blessing." Then Jacob brought it to him, and he ate it; he brought wine also, and he drank it. Then his father Isaac said to him, "Come near, my son, and kiss me." So he came near and kissed him, and when Isaac smelled the smell of his clothes, he blessed him and said:

> "Ah! The smell of my son is like the smell of open country
>   blessed by the Lord.
> God give you dew from heaven
> and the richness of the earth,
> corn and new wine in plenty!
> Peoples shall serve you,
> nations bow down to you.
>   Be lord over your brothers;
> may your mother's sons bow down to you.
> A curse upon those who curse you;
> a blessing on those who bless you!"

Isaac finished blessing Jacob; and Jacob had scarcely left his father Isaac's presence, when his brother Esau came in from his hunting. He too made a savory dish and brought it to his father. He said, "Come, father, and eat some of my venison, so that you may give me your blessing." His father Isaac said, "Who are you?" He said, "I am Esau, your elder son." Then Isaac became greatly agitated and said, "Then who was it that hunted and brought me venison? I ate it all before you came in and I blessed him, and the blessing will stand." When Esau heard what his father said, he gave a loud and bitter cry and said, "Bless me too, father." But Isaac said, "Your brother came treacherously and took away your blessing." Esau said, "He is rightly called Jacob. This is the second time he has supplanted me. He took away my right as the first-born and now he has taken away my blessing. Have you kept back any blessing for me?" Isaac answered, "I have made him lord over you, and I have given him all his brothers as slaves. I have bestowed upon him corn and new wine for his sustenance. What is there left that I can do for you, my son?" Esau asked his father, "Had you then only one blessing, father? Bless me too, my father." And Esau cried bitterly. Then his father Isaac answered:

> "Your dwelling shall be far from the richness of the earth,
>   far from the dew of heaven above.
>   By your sword shall you live,
>   and you shall serve your brother;
>   but the time will come when you grow restive
>   and break off his yoke from your neck."

Esau bore a grudge against Jacob because of the blessing which his father had given him, and he said to himself, "The time of mourning for my father will soon be here; then I will kill my brother Jacob." When Rebecca was told what her elder son Esau was saying, she called her younger son Jacob, and she said to him, "Esau your brother is threatening to kill you. Now, my son, listen to me. Slip away at once to my brother Laban in Harran. Stay with him for a while until your brother's anger cools. When it has subsided and he forgets what you have done to him, I will send and fetch you back. Why should I lose you both in one day?"

Rebecca said to Isaac, "I am weary to death of Hittite women! If Jacob marries a Hittite woman like those who live here, my life will not be worth living." Isaac called Jacob, blessed him and gave him instructions. He said, "You must not marry one of these women of Canaan. Go at once to the house of Bethuel, your mother's father, in Paddan-aram, and there find a wife, one of the daughters of Laban, your mother's brother. God Almighty bless you, make you fruitful and increase your descendants until they become a host of nations. May he bestow on you and your offspring the blessing of Abraham, and may you thus possess the country where you are now living, the land which God gave to Abraham!" So Isaac sent Jacob away. . . .

Jacob set out from Beersheba and went on his way toward Harran. He came to a certain place and stopped there for the night, because the sun had set; and, taking one of the stones there, he made it a pillow for his head and lay down to sleep. He dreamed that he saw a ladder, which rested on the ground with its top reaching to heaven, and angels of God were going up and down upon it. The Lord was standing beside him and said, "I am the Lord, the God of your father Abraham and the God of Isaac. This land on which you are lying I will give to you and your descendants. They shall be countless as the dust upon the earth, and you shall spread far and wide, to north and south, to east and west. All the families of the earth shall pray to be blessed as you and your descendants are blessed. I will be with you, and I will protect you wherever you go and will bring you back to this land; for I will not leave you until I have done all that I have promised." Jacob woke from his sleep and said, "Truly the Lord is in this place, and I did not know it." Then he was afraid and said, "How fearsome is this place! This is no other than the house of God, this is the gate of heaven." Jacob rose early in the morning, took the stone on which he had laid his head, set it up as a sacred pillar and poured oil on the top of it. He named that place Beth-El; but the earlier name of the city was Luz.

Thereupon Jacob made this vow: "If God will be with me, if he will protect me on my journey and give me food to eat and clothes to wear, and I come back safely to my father's house, then the Lord shall be my God, and this stone which I have set up as a sacred pillar shall be a house of God. And of all that thou givest me, I will without fail allot a tenth part to thee."

GENESIS 27; 28 : 1–5, 10–22

Is there evidence in this passage for or against the accusation that Jacob stole rather than bought his older brother's birthright? What experience of Jacob's parallels an event in his father's life? What is the significance of Esau's marrying Ishmael's daughter?

Noah built his altar on a mountaintop, and Jacob's ladder went up to heaven. The young Aztec was sacrificed at the summit of the temple steps. What does all this suggest about the place where people have traditionally imagined God as dwelling?

If you enjoy sketching, you might illustrate Jacob's dream.

The Secret Heart

Across the years he could recall
His father one way best of all.

In the stillest hour of night
The boy awakened to a light

Half in dreams, he saw his sire
With his great hands full of fire

The man had struck a match to see
If his son slept peacefully.

He held his palms each side the spark
His love had kindled in the dark.

His two hands were curved apart
In the semblance of a heart.

He wore, it seemed to his small son,
A bare heart on his hidden one,

A heart that gave out such a glow
No son awake could bear to know.

It showed a look upon a face
Too tender for the day to trace.

One instant, it lit all about,
And then the secret heart went out.

But it shone long enough for one
To know that hands held up the sun.

ROBERT P. TRISTAM COFFIN

Jacob's Ladder

1. As Ja - cob with trav - el was wea - ry one day, at____
2. This lad - der is long, it is strong and well made, has stood
3. Come let us as - cend! all may climb it who will; for the

1. night on a stone for a pil - low he lay; he____
2. hun - dreds of years and is not yet de - cayed; ma - ny
3. an - gels of Ja - cob are guard - ing it still: and re -

1. saw in a vi - sion a lad - der so high that its
2. mil - lions have climbed it and reached Si - on's hill and____
3. mem - ber each step that by faith we pass o'er some____

1. foot was on earth and its top in the sky.
2. thou - sands by faith are____ climb - ing it still.
3. pro - phet or mar - tyr hath trod it be - fore.

4. And when we arrive at the haven of rest,
   We shall hear the glad words, " Come up hither, ye blest,
   Here are regions of light, here are mansions of bliss. "
   O, who would not climb such a ladder as this ?

Israel Shall
Be Your Name

Jacob continued his journey and came to the land of the eastern tribes. There he saw a well in the open country and three flocks of sheep lying beside it, because the flocks were watered from that well. Over its mouth was a huge stone, and all the herdsmen used to gather there and roll it off the mouth of the well and water the flocks; then they would put it back in its place over the well. Jacob said to them, "Where are you from, my friends?" "We are from Harran," they replied. He asked them if they knew Laban the grandson of Nahor. They answered, "Yes, we do." "Is he well?" Jacob asked; and they answered, "Yes, he is well, and here is his daughter Rachel coming with the flock." Jacob said, "The sun is still high, and the time for folding the sheep has not yet come. Water the flocks and then go and graze them." But they replied, "We cannot, until all the herdsmen have gathered together and the stone is rolled away from the mouth of the well; then we can water our flocks." While he was talking to them, Rachel came up with her father's flock, for she was a shepherdess. When Jacob saw Rachel, the daughter of Laban his mother's brother, with Laban's flock, he stepped forward, rolled the stone off the mouth of the well and watered Laban's sheep. He kissed Rachel, and was moved to tears. He told her that he was her father's kinsman and Rebecca's son; so she ran and told her father. When Laban heard the news of his sister's son Jacob, he ran to meet him, embraced him, kissed him warmly and welcomed him to his home. Jacob told Laban everything, and Laban said, "Yes, you are my own flesh and blood." So Jacob stayed with him for a whole month.

Laban said to Jacob, "Why should you work for me for nothing simply because you are my kinsman? Tell me what your wages ought to be." Now Laban had two daughters: the elder was called Leah, and the younger Rachel. Leah was dull-eyed, but Rachel was graceful and beautiful. Jacob had fallen in love with Rachel and he said, "I will work seven years for your younger daughter Rachel." Laban replied, "It is better that I should give her to you than to anyone else; stay with me." So

Jacob worked seven years for Rachel, and they seemed like a few days because he loved her. Then Jacob said to Laban, "I have served my time. Give me my wife so that we may sleep together." So Laban gathered all the men of the place together and gave a feast. In the evening he took his daughter Leah and brought her to Jacob, and Jacob slept with her. At the same time Laban gave his slave girl Zilpah to his daughter Leah. But when morning came, Jacob saw that it was Leah and said to Laban, "What have you done to me? Did I not work for Rachel? Why have you deceived me?" Laban answered, "In our country it is not right to give the younger sister in marriage before the elder. Go through with the seven days' feast for the elder, and the younger shall be given you in return for a further seven years' work." Jacob agreed, and completed the seven days for Leah.

Then Laban gave Jacob his daughter Rachel as wife; and he gave his slave girl Bilhah to serve his daughter Rachel. Jacob slept with Rachel also; he loved her rather than Leah, and he worked for Laban for a further seven years. When the Lord saw that Leah was not loved, he granted her a child; but Rachel was childless. Leah conceived and bore a son; and she called him Reuben, for she said, "The Lord has seen my humiliation; now my husband will love me." Again she conceived and bore a son and said, "The Lord, hearing that I am not loved, has given me this child also"; and she called him Simeon. She conceived again and bore a son; and she said, "Now that I have borne him three sons my husband and I will surely be united." So she called him Levi. Once more she conceived and bore a son; and she said, "Now I will praise the Lord"; therefore she named him Judah. Then for a while she bore no more children.

When Rachel found that she bore Jacob no children, she became jealous of her sister and said to Jacob, "Give me sons, or I shall die." Jacob said angrily to Rachel, "Can I take the place of God, who has denied you children?" She said, "Here is my slave girl Bilhah. Lie with her, so that she may bear sons to be laid upon my knees, and through her I too may build up a family." So she gave him her slave girl Bilhah as a wife, and Jacob lay with her. Bilhah conceived and bore Jacob a son. Then Rachel said, "God has given judgment for me; he has indeed heard me and given me a son," so she named him Dan. Rachel's slave girl Bilhah again conceived and bore Jacob another son. Rachel said, "I have played a fine trick on my sister, and it has succeeded"; so she named him Naphtali. When Leah found that she was bearing no more children, she took her slave girl Zilpah and gave her to Jacob as a wife, and Zilpah bore Jacob a son. Leah said, "Good fortune has come," and she named him Gad. Zilpah, Leah's slave girl, bore Jacob another son, and Leah said, "Happiness has come, for young women will call me happy." So she named him Asher.

In the time of wheat harvest Reuben went out and found some mandrakes in the open country and brought them to his mother Leah. Then Rachel asked Leah for some of her son's mandrakes, but Leah said, "Is it so small a thing to have taken away my husband, that you should take my son's mandrakes as well?" But Rachel said, "Very well, let him sleep with you tonight in exchange for your son's mandrakes." So when Jacob came in from the country in the evening, Leah went out to meet him and said, "You are to sleep with me tonight; I have hired you with my son's mandrakes." That night he slept with her, and God heard Leah's prayer, and she conceived and bore a fifth son. Leah said, "God has rewarded me, because I gave my slave girl to my husband." So she named him Issachar. Leah again conceived and bore a sixth son. She said, "God has endowed me with a noble dowry. Now my husband will treat me in princely style, because I have borne him six sons." So she named him Zebulun. Later she bore a daughter and named her Dinah. Then God thought of Rachel; he heard her prayer and gave her a child; so she conceived and bore a son and said, "God has taken away my humiliation." She named him Joseph, saying, "May the Lord add another son!"

God said to Jacob, "Go up to Bethel and settle there; build an altar there to the God who appeared to you when you were running away from your brother Esau." So Jacob said to his household and to all who were with him, "Rid yourselves of the foreign gods which you have among you, purify yourselves, and see your clothes are mended. We are going to Bethel, so that I can set up an altar there to the God who answered me in the day of my distress, and who has been with me all the way that I have come." So they handed over to Jacob all the foreign gods in their possession and the rings from their ears, and he buried them under the terebinth tree near Shechem. Then they set out, and the cities round about were panic-stricken, and the inhabitants dared not pursue the sons of Jacob. Jacob and all the people with him came to Luz, that is Bethel, in Canaan. There he built an altar, and he called the place El-bethel, because it was there that God had revealed himself to him when he was running away from his brother. Rebecca's nurse Deborah died and was buried under the oak below Bethel, and he named it Allon-bakuth.

God appeared again to Jacob when he came back from Paddan-aram and blessed him. God said to him:

"Jacob is your name,
  but your name shall no longer be Jacob:
  Israel shall be your name."

So he named him Israel. And God said to him:

"I am God Almighty.
  Be fruitful and increase as a nation;
  a host of nations shall come from you,
  and kings shall spring from your body.
  The land which I gave to Abraham and Isaac I give to you;
  and to your descendants after you I give this land."

God then left him, and Jacob erected a sacred pillar in the place where God had spoken with him, a pillar of stone, and he offered a drink-offering over it and poured oil on it. Jacob called the place where God had spoken with him Bethel.

They set out from Bethel, and when there was still some distance to go to Ephrathah, Rachel was in labor and her pains were severe. While her pains were upon her, the midwife said, "Do not be afraid, this is another son for you." Then with her last breath, as she was dying, she named him Ben-oni, but his father called him Benjamin. So Rachel died and was buried by the side of the road to Ephrathah, that is Bethlehem. Jacob set up a sacred pillar over her grave; it is known to this day as the Pillar of Rachel's Grave. Then Israel journeyed on and pitched his tent on the other side of Migdal-eder. While Israel was living in that district, Reuben went and lay with his father's concubine Bilhah, and Israel came to hear of it.

The sons of Jacob were twelve. The sons of Leah: Jacob's first-born Reuben, then Simeon, Levi, Judah, Issachar, and Zebulun. The sons of Rachel: Joseph and Benjamin. The sons of Rachel's slave girl Bilhah: Dan and Naphtali. The sons of Leah's slave girl Zilpah: Gad and Asher. These were Jacob's sons, born to him in Paddan-aram. Jacob came to his father Isaac at Mamre by Kiriath-arba, that is Hebron, where Abraham and Isaac had dwelt. Isaac had lived for a hundred and eighty years when he breathed his last. He died and was gathered to his father's kin at a very great age, and his sons Esau and Jacob buried him.

GENESIS 29; 30:1–24; 35

How can Leah and Rachel be seen as feminine counterparts of Esau and Jacob?

One father, four wives, twelve sons, and one daughter are named in this part of Jacob's story. In diagrammatic fashion chart Jacob's family tree, beginning with his grandparents Abraham and Sarah.

Earlier we saw a reason for God's changing Abram's name to Abraham. Knowing that Jacob means "he that caught the heel" and Israel "he that strives with God," explain why God changes Jacob's name. The twelve tribes of Israel are said to be descended from the twelve sons of Jacob. How does this also help to explain the change in Jacob's name?

———————————

All the biblical selections so far have come from the first book of the Bible, Genesis. Genesis was written so long ago and has been used for so long in the English-speaking world that we tend to forget that its original version was in Hebrew. We know people who are still being named Adam or Daniel or Joseph or Rachel or Rebecca or Sarah without knowing that in Hebrew these names have specific meanings. Adam, for instance, as we noted on page 11, is the Hebrew word for "man." Sarah in Hebrew means "princess" but Sarai means "mockery." Normally when a name is changed in the Bible there is a reason for it.

Here is a brief dictionary of the names in our third chapter. Consider in each case the significance of the name. Do we place significance in names today?

Abram: high father
Abraham: father of a multitude
Asher: happy
Bethel: house of God
Bilhah: tender
Ben-oni: son of my ill luck
Benjamin: son of good luck, son of the right hand
Dan: he has given judgment
Dinah: judged or avenged
El Roi: God of a vision
Esau: covering
Gad: good fortune
Hagar: wandering
Isaac: laughter
Ishmael: God heard
Israel: he that strives with God
Issachar: reward
Jacob: caught the heel, supplanted

Joseph: may mean either "he takes away" or "may he add"
Judah: praise
Leah: weary
Levi: union
Naphtali: trickery
Rachel: a lamb
Rebecca: flattering
Reuben: see, a son
Sarah: princess
Sarai: mockery
Simeon: hearing
Zebulun: prince
Zilpah: myrrh dropping
Zion (may also be spelled Sion): fortress; the southwest hill of Jerusalem, the older and higher part of the city; often called the City of David

IN THE LIGHT
OF THE LIVING

Be merciful unto me, O God:
For man would swallow me up; he fighting daily
    oppresseth me.
Mine enemies would daily swallow me up:
For they be many that fight against me, O thou Most High.
What time I am afraid, I will trust in thee.
In God I will praise his word, in God I have put my trust;
I will not fear what flesh can do unto me.
Every day they wrest my words:
All their thoughts are against me for evil.
They gather themselves together, they hide themselves,
They mark my steps, when they wait for my soul.
Shall they escape by iniquity?
In thine anger cast down the people, O God.
Thou tellest my wanderings:
Put thou my tears into thy bottle: are they not in
    thy book?
When I cry unto thee, then shall mine enemies turn back:
This I know; for God is for me.
In God will I praise his word:
In the Lord will I praise his word.
In God have I put my trust:
I will not be afraid what man can do unto me.
Thy vows are upon me, O God:
I will render praises unto thee.
For thou hast delivered my soul from death:
Wilt thou not deliver my feet from falling,
That I may walk before God in the light of the living?

PSALM 56

The Bible contains an ongoing chain of contrasting
images. People are characterized as for or against the
Lord, as godly or ungodly, depending upon whether
or not they further the working out of the Lord's will.
This evaluation extends to places and things as well.
The cities of Sodom and Gomorrah are ungodly but
the land promised to Abraham is godly, for it is the

destination of God's people. Ishmael and Esau, even though they have committed no evil worse than their brothers, are found wanting: Isaac and Jacob receive the blessing. The tensions between favored and unfavored brothers is a well-established theme. It begins early in the Bible with Cain and Abel and continues through the story of the sons of Noah.

The sacrifice of Isaac is central to the biblical narrative. As a crucial test of Abraham's loyalty, the incident mirrors his response to the first call of the Lord, which comes unexpectedly and arbitrarily. It was no minor undertaking, in those ancient times, for a man to pick up family, household, and belongings and move off to an alien country. Nevertheless, Abraham does so, without questioning the Lord. When asked to sacrifice Isaac, Abraham acts with the same blind obedience. But here the stakes are immeasurably higher, involving every conceivable aspect of the future, a future which except for Isaac would not merely be bleak but in fact nonexistent.

To appreciate fully the story of Isaac, we must be aware that human sacrifice was a common practice in the days of the biblical patriarchs. In the light of this fact, the story can be interpreted as teaching a central lesson of Judaism: the God of Israel does not want the sacrifice of human life. The account of the substitution of the ram for Isaac is a moral fable or parable revealing the concrete possibility of deliverance, no matter how crucial the crisis. The God who saves Isaac at the last minute is a "true" God, whose communion with his followers is not to be compared with that of the "devil-gods" of neighboring nations who demand human blood. Isaac represents all the descendants of Abraham and his story summarizes the expectation of Israel—that God will save her from the jaws of death if she is faithful to his demand for obedience.

The high sense of morality expressed in the story of Abraham and Isaac, and the deep sensitivity to the human condition, mark a central point in the biblical narrative. The bargaining with God over the fate of Sodom, for the sake of a few just men, is another parable of Abraham's newly acquired insight into the value of human life. You will remember that God commanded Abraham, "Live always in my presence and be perfect." Psalm 56 identifies God's presence with "the light of the living." Biblical writers equate "light" with a sense of the value of human life which Abraham comes to appreciate. They equate "darkness" with disregard for the value of life. Death and darkness, life and light, can thus be seen as part of the twofold simultaneous pattern of images which the Bible presents as its narrative unfolds.

The psalmist of the fifty-sixth psalm complains, "Mine enemies would daily swallow me up," yet he goes on to say, "I will not fear." His reason for not being afraid is the same as Abraham's: trust in the power of God is the only defense against superior physical power. That the Israelites would develop this notion to the fullest is certainly understandable, for they were constantly surrounded by enemy tribes and peoples.

There is a stark, primitive quality in Robert Frost's poem (page 157) which conveys something of the feeling men must have had in biblical times when they faced unforeseen disaster with a few ancient tools, and no witnesses but the sky, the surrounding hills, and the road ahead. The same impulse of the mind which moved Frost to think of some "unseen power" also moved the early Hebrew patriarchs to turn heavenward. They were shepherds and farmers of the ancient deserts and grasslands, and they were surrounded by the warring of the elements, the jealousies of small clans and tribes, and all the other arbitrary aspects of man and nature that still cause us hardship today. The experiences they faced in living their lives and giving them meaning shaped their vocabulary, their imagery, their stories, and ultimately the plot of their national epic, the Bible.

Not all men entertain these same religious beliefs which have their roots in the unfolding of the patriarchal tradition. But almost every man immediately can recognize himself in the ancient stories told by the tent fires of the Hebrew shepherds: stories of a man's longing for children, of his quest for truth and justice, of his bowing obediently before the unforeseen and the unknowable, and of his occasional victories over danger and, sometimes, death. We have our own deserts around us today, and the actions of the human and natural environment surrounding us are no less arbitrary and unexpected than those which the patriarchs faced. We too, like Jacob, have no need to be ashamed when we give our own special names to the unexpected places where a ladder connects the ground we stand upon with the unknown "region of light."

4: Joseph, that Dreamer

Corita

LISTEN TO THIS DREAM

The Maiden Sacrificed to Winter

A winter colder and harder than any before came to the land of the Chinook people. Snow lay on the level as deep as half a man's height. The time for spring came, but the snow did not melt. Ice floated down the river in huge masses, grinding and crashing. Every night more snow fell, filling up places the wind had swept clean. Snowbirds were everywhere.

One day a bird flew over with something red in its bill. The people so frightened it that it dropped the red thing—a ripe strawberry. Then they knew that somewhere not far away spring had come. Around them it was still winter. The earth was frozen.

Something was wrong. So the chief of the village called a meeting at his lodge. All the people came. The old men asked each other, "Why does the winter not end? What can we do to end it?"

After much talk, the oldest man in the village arose and spoke. "Our grandfathers used to say that if a bird should be struck by a stone, the snow would never stop falling. Perhaps some child has stoned a bird."

The headman asked that all the children be brought in before the council. When they came, they were questioned one by one. Each child spoke for himself. Every mother was in fear, lest her child be the guilty person. One by one, the children said they had not struck any bird. Some of them pointed to a little girl. "She did it."

"You ask your daughter if the children speak the truth," the old men of the council said to her father and mother.

In terror the little girl answered that she had struck a bird with a stone.

The chief men of the village sat in council for a long time. The child and her parents waited, trembling.

Slowly the chief arose. "Give us your child. We will not kill her as we first thought we would do. Instead, we will give her to Winter. Then he will cease to be angry, and Summer will come."

The hearts of the little girl's father and mother were sad and heavy. This was their only child. But they realized that the wise men of the village knew best, and that the good of all was more important than the life of their little one. Many people brought them gifts in payment for the child, but their hearts were not lightened. As the headmen led her away, her father and mother cried aloud. They mourned for her as if for the dead.

Some young men were sent to the river to get a large block of ice. The headmen would place the maiden on it and thus give her to Winter. Finding a large piece in an eddy in the river, they pulled it to shore.

While the young men did that, all the other people dressed in their finest clothes, as if for the winter dances. The little girl was dressed best of all. Then the headmen led her to the river, and all the people followed.

At the water's edge they spread a thick layer of straw on the block of ice, and over that a covering of many tule mats. They placed the girl on the ice and pushed it out into the swift current. Swirling with the rise and fall of the water, the ice block drifted down the river. The crying of the child and the wailing of the parents could be heard above the noise of the water and the crashing of the ice. When child and ice block were out of sight, the people returned to their lodges, chanting.

Very soon they felt a warm wind. In a few days the snow had gone. Then the people knew that the old men of years gone by had spoken the truth.

When spring came, the people moved to their fishing place, to catch and dry salmon. In the fall they went back to their winter village. Snow and ice came again. One day some old men stood by the riverbank watching the ice drift by. Far down the stream, as far as their eyes could see, a block of ice swirled round and round in an eddy. On the ice was a black spot.

The headmen of the village sent a young man out to look at it. "It looks like a body!" he called back as he drew near the ice block. The people who were watching brought long poles and drew the ice to the shore. On it was a young girl—the one who had been sacrificed as an offering to Winter.

The people lifted her up and carried her to the lodge of her father and mother. Wrapped in warm furs, she fell asleep by the fire.

Ever after that, she was able to walk barefoot on ice and snow. People thought she had special power. They called her *Wah-kah-nee,* meaning "She drifts."

Retold by ELLA E. CLARK

In what way is Wah-kah-nee's story both similar to and different from Isaac's? Are they both reborn?

You could call Isaac and Wah-kah-nee heroes who symbolically must go into hell or its equivalent to fulfill a quest. What were Noah, Abraham, and Jacob questing for?

How did the sacrifice of the child turn a wilderness into a garden?

Joseph Sold
into Egypt

So Jacob lived in Canaan, the country in which his father had settled. And this is the story of the descendants of Jacob.

When Joseph was a boy of seventeen, he used to accompany his brothers, the sons of Bilhah and Zilpah, his father's wives, when they were in charge of the flock; and he brought their father a bad report of them. Now Israel loved Joseph more than any other of his sons, because he was a child of his old age, and he made him a long, sleeved robe. When his brothers saw that their father loved him more than any of them, they hated him and could not say a kind word to him.

Joseph had a dream; and when he told it to his brothers, they hated him still more. He said to them, "Listen to this dream I have had. We were in the field binding sheaves, and my sheaf rose on end and stood upright, and your sheaves gathered round and bowed low before my sheaf." His brothers answered him, "Do you think you will one day be a king and lord it over us?" and they hated him still more because of his dreams and what he said. He had another dream, which he told to his father and his brothers. He said, "Listen: I have had another dream. The sun and moon and eleven stars were bowing down to me." When he told it to his father and his brothers, his father took him to task: "What is this dream of yours?" he said. "Must we come and bow low to the ground before you, I and your mother and your brothers?" His brothers were jealous of him, but his father did not forget.

Joseph's brothers went to mind their father's flocks in Shechem. Israel said to him, "Your brothers are minding the flocks in Shechem; come, I will send you to them" and he said, "I am ready." He said to him, "Go and see if all is well with your brothers and the sheep, and bring me back word." So he sent off Joseph from the vale of Hebron and he came to Shechem. A man met him wandering in the open country and asked him what he was looking for. He replied, "I am looking for my brothers. Tell me, please, where they are minding the flocks." The man said, "They have gone away from here; I heard them speak of going to Dothan." So Joseph followed his brothers and he found them in Dothan. They saw him in the distance, and before he reached them, they plotted to kill him. They said to each other, "Here comes that dreamer. Now is our chance; let us kill him and throw him into one of these pits and say that a wild beast has devoured him. Then we shall see what will come of his dreams." When Reuben heard, he came to his rescue, urging them not to take his life. "Let us have no bloodshed," he said. "Throw him into this pit in the wilderness, but do him no bodily harm." He meant to save him from them so as to restore him to his father. When Joseph came up to his brothers, they stripped him of the long, sleeved robe which he was wearing, took him and threw him into the pit. The pit was empty and had no water in it.

Then they sat down to eat some food and, looking up, they saw an Ishmaelite caravan coming in from Gilead on the way down to Egypt, with camels carrying gum tragacanth and balm and myrrh. Judah said to his brothers, "What shall we gain by killing our brother and concealing his death? Why not sell him to the Ishmaelites? Let us do him no harm, for he is our brother, our own flesh and blood"; and his brothers agreed with him. Meanwhile some Midianite merchants passed by and drew Joseph up out of the pit. They sold him for twenty pieces of silver to the Ishmaelites, and they brought Joseph to Egypt. When Reuben went back to the pit, Joseph was not there. He rent his clothes and went back to his brothers and said, "The boy is not there. Where can I go?"

Joseph's brothers took his robe, killed a goat and dipped it in the goat's blood. Then they tore the robe, the long, sleeved robe, brought it to their father and said, "Look what we have found. Do you recognize it? Is this your son's robe or not?" Jacob did recognize it, and he replied, "It is my son's robe. A wild beast has devoured him. Joseph has been torn to pieces." Jacob rent his clothes, put on sackcloth and mourned his son for a long time. His sons and daughters all tried to comfort him, but he refused to be comforted. He said, "I will go to my grave mourning for my son." Thus Joseph's father wept for him.

GENESIS 37 : 1–35

What other favored brothers have you already met in this book? Why do you suppose that the theme of hatred between brothers is repeated so often in these biblical stories? What effect do Joseph's dreams have on his brothers? What is symbolic about Joseph's being put into and taken out of the pit?

Pharaoh's Dreams
Are One Dream

It happened later that the king's butler and his baker offended their master the king of Egypt. Pharaoh was angry with these two eunuchs, the chief butler and the chief baker, and he put them in custody in the house of the captain of the guard, in the Round Tower where Joseph was imprisoned. The captain of the guard appointed Joseph as their attendant, and he waited on them. One night, when they had been in prison for some time, they both had dreams, each needing its own interpretation — the king of Egypt's butler and his baker who were imprisoned in the Round Tower. When Joseph came to them in the morning, he saw that they looked dejected. So he asked these eunuchs, who were in custody with him in his master's house, why they were so downcast that day. They replied, "We have each had a dream and there is no one to interpret it for us." Joseph said to them, "Does not interpretation belong to God? Tell me your dreams." So the chief butler told Joseph his dream: "In my dream," he said, "there was a vine in front of me. On the vine there were three branches, and as soon as it budded, it blossomed and its clusters ripened into grapes. Now I had Pharaoh's cup in my hand, and I plucked the grapes, crushed them into Pharaoh's cup and put the cup into Pharaoh's hand." Joseph said to him, "This is the interpretation. The three branches are three days: within three days Pharaoh will raise you and restore you to your post, and then you will put the cup into Pharaoh's hand as you used to do when you were his butler. But when things go well with you, if you think of me, keep faith with me and bring my case to Pharaoh's notice and help me to get out of this house. By force I was carried off from the land of the Hebrews, and I have done nothing here to deserve being put in this dungeon."

When the chief baker saw that Joseph had given a favorable interpretation, he said to him, "I too had a dream, and in my dream there were three baskets of white bread on my head. In the top basket there was every kind of food which the baker prepares for Pharaoh, and the birds were eating out of the top basket on my head." Joseph answered, "This is the interpretation. The three baskets are three days: within three days Pharaoh will raise you and hang you up on a tree, and the birds of the air will eat your flesh."

The third day was Pharaoh's birthday and he gave a feast for all his servants. He raised the chief butler and the chief baker in the presence of his court. He restored the chief butler to his post, and the butler put the cup into Pharaoh's hand; but he hanged the chief baker. All went as Joseph had said in interpreting the dreams for them. Even so the chief butler did not remember Joseph, but forgot him.

Nearly two years later Pharaoh had a dream: he was standing by the Nile, and there came up from the river seven cows, sleek and fat, and they grazed on the reeds. After them seven other cows came up from the river, gaunt and lean, and stood on the riverbank beside the first cows. The cows that were gaunt and lean devoured the cows that were sleek and fat. Then Pharaoh woke up. He fell asleep again and had a second dream: he saw seven ears of corn, full and ripe, growing on one stalk. Growing up after them were seven other ears, thin and shriveled by the east wind. The thin ears swallowed up the ears that were full and ripe. Then Pharaoh woke up and knew that it was a dream. When morning came, Pharaoh was troubled in mind; so he summoned all the magicians and sages of Egypt. He told them his dreams, but there was no one who could interpret them for him. Then Pharaoh's chief butler spoke up and said, "It is time for me to recall my faults. Once Pharaoh was angry with his servants, and he imprisoned me and the chief baker in the house of the captain of the guard. One night we both had dreams, each needing its own interpretation. We had with us a young Hebrew, a slave of the captain of the guard, and we told him our dreams and he interpreted them for us, giving each man's dream its own interpretation. Each dream came true as it had been interpreted to us: I was restored to my position, and he was hanged."

Pharaoh thereupon sent for Joseph, and they hurriedly brought him out of the dungeon. He shaved and changed his clothes, and came in to Pharaoh. Pharaoh said to him, "I have had a dream, and no one can interpret it to me. I have heard it said that you can understand and interpret dreams." Joseph answered, "Not I, but God, will answer for Pharaoh's welfare." Then Pharaoh said to Joseph, "In my dream I was standing on the bank of the Nile, and there came up from the river seven cows, fat and sleek, and they grazed on the reeds. After them seven other cows came up that were poor, very gaunt and lean; I have never seen such gaunt creatures in all Egypt. These lean, gaunt cows devoured the first cows, the fat ones. They were swallowed up, but no one could have guessed that they were in the bellies of the others, which looked as gaunt as before. Then I woke up. After I had fallen asleep again, I saw in a dream seven ears of corn, full and ripe, growing on one stalk. Growing up after them were seven other ears, shriveled, thin, and blighted by the east wind. The thin ears swallowed up the seven ripe ears. When I told all this to the magicians, no one could explain it to me."

Joseph said to Pharaoh, "Pharaoh's dreams are one dream. God has told Pharaoh what he is going to do. The seven good cows are seven years, and the seven good ears of corn are seven years. It is all one dream. The seven lean and gaunt cows that came up after them are seven years, and the empty ears of corn blighted by the east wind will be seven years of famine. It is as I have said to Pharaoh: God has let Pharaoh see what he is going to do. There are to be seven years of great plenty throughout the land. After them will come seven years of famine; all the years of plenty in Egypt will be forgotten, and the famine will ruin the country. The good years will not be remembered in the land because of the famine that follows; for it will be very severe. The doubling of Pharaoh's dream means that God is already resolved to do this, and he will very soon put it into effect. Pharaoh should now look for a shrewd and intelligent man, and put him in charge of the country. This is what Pharaoh should do: appoint controllers over the land, and take one fifth of the produce of Egypt during the seven years of plenty. They should collect all this food produced in the good years that are coming and put the corn under Pharaoh's control in store in the cities, and keep it under guard. This food will be a reserve for the country against the seven years of famine which will come upon Egypt. Thus the country will not be devastated by the famine."

The plan pleased Pharaoh and all his courtiers, and he said to them, "Can we find a man like this man, one who has the spirit of a god in him?" He said to Joseph, "Since a god has made all this known to you, there is no one so shrewd and intelligent as you. You shall be in charge of my household, and all my people will depend on your every word. Only my royal throne shall make me greater than you." Pharaoh said to Joseph, "I hereby give you authority over the whole land of Egypt." He took off his signet ring and put it on Joseph's finger, he had him dressed in fine linen, and hung a gold chain round his neck. He mounted him in his viceroy's chariot and men cried "Make way!" before him. Thus Pharaoh made him ruler over all Egypt and said to him, "I am the Pharaoh. Without your consent no man shall lift hand or foot throughout Egypt." Pharaoh named him Zaphenath-paneah, and he gave him as wife Asenath the daughter of Potiphera priest of On. And Joseph's authority extended over the whole of Egypt.

Joseph was thirty years old when he entered the service of Pharaoh king of Egypt. When he took his leave of the king, he made a tour of inspection through the country. During the seven years of plenty there were abundant harvests, and Joseph gathered all the food produced in Egypt during those years and stored it in the cities, putting in each the food from the surrounding country. He stored the grain in huge quantities; it was like the sand of the sea, so much that he stopped measuring: it was beyond all measure.

Before the years of famine came, two sons were born to Joseph by Asenath the daughter of Potiphera priest of On. He named the elder Manasseh, "for," he said, "God has caused me to forget all my troubles and my father's family." He named the second Ephraim, "for," he said, "God has made me fruitful in the land of my hardships." When the seven years of plenty in Egypt came to an end, seven years of famine began, as Joseph had foretold. There was famine in every country, but throughout Egypt there was bread. So when the famine spread through all Egypt, the people appealed to Pharaoh for bread, and he ordered them to go to Joseph and do as he told them. In every region there was famine, and Joseph opened all the granaries and sold corn to the Egyptians, for the famine was severe. The whole world came to Egypt to buy corn from Joseph, so severe was the famine everywhere.

GENESIS 40; 41

What is Joseph's interpretation of Pharaoh's two dreams, and what is his solution to the problems they raise? You remember that Joseph's brothers called him "that dreamer," yet Pharaoh sees Joseph as a "shrewd and intelligent man" who can be put in charge of the whole country of Egypt. How does the first analysis of Joseph's character help explain the second?

In the story of the Flood only Noah and those with him on the ark were saved from death. In Abraham's story God was willing to widen his mercy to include even the people of Sodom if ten just men could be found there. How is God's mercy shown in this story?

Dick Whittington

In the reign of King Edward III there lived in Somersetshire a boy called Dick Whittington, whose father and mother had died when he was very young. The people where he lived were very poor, and he had very little to eat, but he heard talk about the great city of London, which they said was so rich and fine that all the folks there were great ladies and gentlemen, and that the streets were all paved with gold. And as he grew older he made up his mind that he would somehow manage to go to London, where he could make his fortune. One day there drove through the village a large wagon with a team of horses on its way to London. So he took courage and begged the wagoner to let him come too. The wagoner was moved to pity when he heard how badly off poor Dick was, so he told him he might come if he liked, and they set off together.

When he reached London he said good-by to the wagoner, who gave him a groat on parting, and with this as his sole possession Dick wandered here and there, wondering what he should try to do next, and bitterly disappointed to find that in the streets that he had expected to be paved with gold he found nothing but mud and dirt.

After he had spent the little he had and had gone hungry for two days he sat down to rest on the doorstep of a merchant's house in Leadenhall Street. Soon the cook, who was exceedingly bad-tempered, saw him, and threatened to kick him from the door.

Just then the master of the house, Mr. Fitzwarren, came home from the Royal Exchange. When he noticed the boy there he asked him what he wanted, and then told him that he must go away at once. Dick tried to do so, but was so faint from want of food that he fell down again when he tried to stand. Then he told Mr. Fitzwarren that he was a poor boy from the country, and that he would do any work that was given him, if only to get some food. The merchant felt sorry for him, and as he happened to want a boy to help in the kitchen he ordered one of his servants to take him in, saying what work he should be given to do. Then a good meal was set before Dick, and you may be sure that he was glad to see it.

But all was not by any means easy and pleasant for him. The servants made him a laughingstock, and the bad-tempered cook ordered him to do innumerable jobs in the kitchen, threatening to break his head with her ladle if he did not do them quickly enough.

Still, he got enough to eat now, and that was a change. And Miss Alice, his master's daughter, seeing him in the kitchen, found some old clothes for him that were better than his poor rags, and gave orders to the cook and the other servants that he was to be treated kindly.

So it was decided that he should stay, and a bed was made up for him in the garret.

But he found that the rats and mice in the garret were almost as troublesome by night as the cook was by day. They ran over Dick Whittington's face, and disturbed him so with their squeaking and scratching that he was almost tempted to run away once more.

Soon after, a merchant came to dinner, and as it came on to rain very hard he was invited to stay the night. In the morning Dick cleaned his shoes, and when he took them to the merchant he was given a penny for his trouble. A little later, as he was going on an errand, he saw a woman with a cat under her arm. He asked her if she would sell it. She said that as it was a fine mouser she would not take less than sixpence. But when Dick replied that a penny was all he had the woman let him have the cat.

He took the cat home, and hid her in his garret all day, for he was afraid that the cook would kill her if she was found in the kitchen. He always saved scraps from his dinner to take up to her, and at night she worked so well for her living that Whittington was troubled no more with rats and mice.

Now whenever the merchant, Mr. Fitzwarren, sent out a ship it was his custom to call all his servants and ask them to venture something of their own in it. As he was now sending out a ship, everybody but Whittington came, and brought what they could for it. Miss Alice noticed his absence, and ordered him to be called, but he tried to excuse himself, saying that all he could call his own was a poor cat which he had bought for a penny that had been given him for cleaning shoes. When Miss Alice heard this she offered to put something in the ship for him, but her father told her that it was the custom for everybody to venture something of his own. He therefore told Whittington to bring his cat. This he did very unwillingly, for he was parting with his best friend. He had tears in his eyes as he gave it to the master of the ship, the *Unicorn,* which immediately started off down the river on her voyage.

After this the cook often made fun of Whittington's venture, and altogether she scolded and harassed him so much that at last he made up his mind to run away rather than be so tormented any longer. He packed up his bundle, and early the next morning got up with the idea of going away into the country. He went through Moorfields, and in time he reached Holloway, where he sat down at the top of the hill to rest on a stone, which to this day is called "Whittington's Stone." As he sat there he could hear Bow Bells ringing merrily. It seemed that they were speaking to him, and saying:

> "Turn again, Whittington,
> Thrice Lord Mayor of London"

That seemed to him to be such a grand idea that he decided that he had better not run away after all. As it was yet early he thought that he might reach home before his absence was noticed. And so it happened. And he was able to creep quickly in and start doing his usual work without being seen by anybody.

While all this was going on the ship in which Whittington's cat had been taken, after having been buffeted by contrary winds, had sought shelter on the coast of Barbary. The inhabitants of this region were Moors, and they were quite unknown to the English. As they seemed disposed to be friendly, however, the ship's captain determined to trade with them. He brought all his wares on deck and displayed them so that the Moors could see what he had. They were so pleased with the goods that news was carried to the King, who sent for samples, and afterward invited the master to come to the palace.

As was the custom in that country, everybody sat on the floor, which was covered with rich carpets. Upon these various dishes were laid, and the appetizing odor soon attracted a great number of rats and mice, who quickly ate all that they could see. The captain, in great astonishment, asked some of the people if they did not object to the presence of such vermin.

"Yes," was the answer, "we dislike them extremely. His Majesty would willingly give half of what he possesses to get rid of them." The captain then thought of Whittington's cat, and he lost no time in telling the King that he had in his ship an animal which would quickly destroy these pests.

This was welcome news to the King, and he desired to see this wonderful animal at once, saying, "If this is so and you will let me have it I will fill your ship with precious gems."

The master replied, "She is indeed the most wonderful creature in the world, but I cannot spare her, for she keeps the ship clear of rats and mice, and so prevents my goods from being destroyed."

The King, however, would not hear of any objections, saying that he was willing to pay any price for such a precious animal.

Accordingly the cat was brought, and when the dishes were spread on the floor the rats and mice scurried in as before. The cat, however, made short work of them, and came purring to the King, as if asking for a reward. Naturally he admired her greatly, and gave ten times more for her than for all the freight besides.

The ship then set sail with a fair wind for England, and arrived safely at Blackwall. Taking the casket of jewels with him, the master presented his bill of lading to Mr. Fitzwarren, who naturally rejoiced in so prosperous a voyage.

When he assembled all his servants to give each the portion that belonged to him the master showed him the casket of gems, and told him that this was all for Whittington's cat. Mr. Fitzwarren immediately sent for Whittington, who was in the kitchen washing pots and pans. When, after some hesitation, he came in, the merchant ordered a chair to be placed for him. Poor Dick, thinking that they were all laughing at him, knelt before his master, and with tears in his eyes asked him not to make a game of a poor fellow who meant nobody any harm.

Mr. Fitzwarren, helping him to his feet, addressed him as "Mr. Whittington," and said, "We are very much in earnest. At the present moment you are a richer man than I am." Then he gave him the casket, the value of which amounted to three hundred thousand pounds.

When he could be induced to believe that all this was really true Whittington turned to his master, and laid his wealth at his feet, but Mr. Fitzwarren said, "No, Mr. Whittington, I could not dream of taking even the smallest portion from you. May it bring you much happiness!"

Whittington then turned to Miss Alice, but she would not take anything either, so he gave shares to his fellow servants, not even forgetting his old enemy the cook, and he rewarded handsomely all the ship's crew.

Then he was given clothes in keeping with his new position, and as he was now dressed he was seen to be a very presentable young man; so much so that Miss Alice began to look at him with favor. Her father, seeing this, thought that it would be a good idea to arrange a match between them. This was soon settled, and the Lord Mayor and Aldermen were invited to the wedding.

At the conclusion of the honeymoon Mr. Fitzwarren asked his son-in-law what occupation he would wish to choose. Whittington replied without hesitation that he would like to be a merchant. As a result they entered into partnership, and both became extremely wealthy.

All this good fortune did not make Richard Whittington proud or overbearing. Indeed, he was such good company that all took delight in being with him, and he was particularly kind to the poor. In the year 1393 he was made Sheriff of the City of London, during the time that Sir John Hadley was Lord Mayor.

Four years later he was chosen as Lord Mayor himself, and received the honor of knighthood from the King. And he filled the duties of that office with such prudence and distinction that on two later occasions he was chosen for the same office.

In the last year it fell to his lot to entertain King Henry V after he returned from his conquests in France. The King and Queen were feasted at the Guildhall so splendidly that the King said, "Never had prince such a subject!" To which Whittington replied, "Never had subject such a prince!"

Till the year 1780 the figure of Sir Richard Whittington with his cat in his arms might be seen, carved in stone over the archway that spanned the street by the old prison of Newgate.

In what way is Dick Whittington's career similiar to Joseph's? How does his cat save a kingdom? What wishes are fulfilled in this story?

WAIT IT OUT

The Israelites Go into Egypt

When Jacob saw that there was corn in Egypt, he said to his sons, "Why do you stand staring at each other? I have heard that there is corn in Egypt. Go down and buy some so that we may keep ourselves alive and not starve." So Joseph's brothers, ten of them, went down to buy grain from Egypt, but Jacob did not let Joseph's brother Benjamin go with them, for fear that he might come to harm.

So the sons of Israel came down with everyone else to buy corn, because of the famine in Canaan. Now Joseph was governor of all Egypt, and it was he who sold the corn to all the people of the land. Joseph's brothers came and bowed to the ground before him, and when he saw his brothers, he recognized them but pretended not to know them and spoke harshly to them. "Where do you come from?" he asked. "From Canaan," they answered, "to buy food." Although Joseph had recognized his brothers, they did not recognize him. He remembered also the dreams he had had about them; so he said to them, "You are spies; you have come to spy out the weak points in our defenses." They answered, "No, sir: your servants have come to buy food. We are all sons of one man. Your humble servants are honest men, we are not spies." "No," he insisted, "it is to spy out our weaknesses that you have come." They answered him, "Sir, there are twelve of us, all brothers, sons of one man in Canaan. The youngest is still with our father, and one has disappeared." But Joseph said again to them, "No, as I said before, you are spies. This is how you shall be put to the proof: unless your youngest brother comes here, by the life of Pharaoh, you shall not leave this place. Send one of your number to bring your brother; the rest will be kept in prison. Thus your story will be tested, and we shall see whether you are telling the truth. If not, then, by the life of Pharaoh, you must be spies." So he kept them in prison for three days.

On the third day Joseph said to the brothers, "Do what I say and your lives will be spared; for I am a God-fearing man: if you are honest men, your brother there shall be kept in prison, and the rest of you shall take corn for your hungry households and bring your youngest brother to me; thus your words will be proved true, and you will not die."

They said to one another, "No doubt we deserve to be punished because of our brother, whose suffering we saw; for when he pleaded with us we refused to listen. That is why these sufferings have come upon us." But Reuben said, "Did I not tell you not to do the boy a wrong? But you would not listen, and his blood is on our heads, and we must pay." They did not know that Joseph understood, because he had used an interpreter. Joseph turned away from them and wept. Then, turning back, he played a trick on them. First he took Simeon and bound him before their eyes; then he gave orders to fill their bags with grain, to return each man's silver, putting it in his sack, and to give them supplies for the journey. All this was done; and they loaded the corn on to their asses and went away. When they stopped for the night, one of them opened his sack to give fodder to his ass, and there he saw his silver at the top of the pack. He said to his brothers, "My silver has been returned to me, and here it is in my pack." Bewildered and trembling, they said to each other, "What is this that God has done to us?"

When they came to their father Jacob in Canaan, they told him all that had happened to them. They said, "The man who is lord of the country spoke harshly to us and made out that we were spies. We said to him, 'We are honest men, we are not spies. There are twelve of us, all brothers, sons of one father. One has disappeared, and the youngest is with our father in Canaan.' This man, the lord of the country, said to us, 'This is how I shall find out if you are honest men. Leave one of your brothers with me, take food for your hungry households and go. Bring your youngest brother to me, and I shall know that you are not spies, but honest men. Then I will restore your brother to you, and you can move about the country freely.' " But on emptying their sacks, each of them found his silver inside, and when they and their father saw the bundles of silver, they were afraid. Their father Jacob said to them, "You have robbed me of my children. Joseph has disappeared; Simeon has disappeared; and now you are taking Benjamin. Everything is against me." Reuben said to his father, "You may kill both my sons if I do not bring him back to you. Put him in my charge, and I shall bring him back." But Jacob said, "My son shall not go with you, for his brother is dead and he alone is left. If he comes to any harm on the journey, you will bring down my gray hairs in sorrow to the grave."

The famine was still severe in the country. When they had used up the corn they had brought from Egypt, their father said to them, "Go back and buy a little more corn for us to eat." But Judah replied, "The man plainly warned us that we must not go into his presence unless our brother was with us. If you let our brother go with us, we will go down and buy food for you. But if you will not let him, we will not go; for the man said to us, 'You shall not come into my presence, unless your brother is with you.' " Israel said, "Why have you treated me so badly? Why did you tell the man that you had yet another brother?" They answered, "He questioned us closely about ourselves and our family: 'Is your father still alive?' he asked, 'Have you a brother?' and we answered his questions. How could we possibly know that he would tell us to bring our brother to Egypt?" Judah said to his father Israel, "Send the boy with me; then we can start at once. By doing this we shall save our lives, ours, yours, and our dependents', and none of us will starve. I will go surety for him and you may hold me responsible. If I do not bring him back and restore him to you, you shall hold me guilty all my life. If we had not wasted all this time, by now we could have gone back twice over."

Their father Israel said to them, "If it must be so, then do this: take in your baggage, as a gift for the man, some of the produce for which our country is famous: a little balsam, a little honey, gum tragacanth, myrrh, pistachio nuts, and almonds. Take double the amount of silver and restore what was returned to you in your packs; perhaps it was a mistake. Take your brother with you and go straight back to the man. May God Almighty make him kindly disposed to you, and may he send back the one whom you left behind, and Benjamin too. As for me, if I am bereaved, then I am bereaved." So they took the gift and double the amount of silver, and with Benjamin they started at once for Egypt, where they presented themselves to Joseph.

When Joseph saw Benjamin with them, he said to his steward, "Bring these men indoors, kill a beast and make dinner ready, for they will eat with me at noon." He did as Joseph told him and brought the men into the house. When they came in they were afraid, for they thought, "We have been brought in here because of that affair of the silver which was replaced in our packs the first time. He means to trump up some charge against us and victimize us, seize our asses and make us his slaves." So they approached Joseph's steward and spoke to him at the door of the house. They said, "Please listen, my lord. After our first visit to buy food, when we reached the place where we were to spend the night, we opened our packs and each of us found his silver in full weight at the top of his pack. We have brought it back with us, and have added other silver to buy food. We do not know who put the silver in our packs." He answered, "Set your minds at rest; do not be afraid. It was your God, the God of your father, who hid treasure for you in your packs. I did receive the silver." Then he brought Simeon out to them.

The steward brought them into Joseph's house and gave them water to wash their feet, and provided fodder for their asses. They had their gifts ready when Joseph arrived at noon, for they had heard that they were to eat there. When Joseph came into the house, they presented him with the gifts which they had brought, bowing to the ground before him. He asked them how they were and said, "Is your father well, the old man of whom you spoke? Is he still alive?" They answered, "Yes, my lord, our father is still alive and well." And they bowed low and prostrated themselves. Joseph looked and saw his own mother's son, his brother Benjamin, and asked, "Is this your youngest brother, of whom you told me?" and to Benjamin he said, "May God be gracious to you, my son!" Joseph was overcome; his feelings for his brother mastered him, and he was near to tears. So he went into the inner room and wept. Then he washed his face and came out; and, holding back his feelings, he ordered the meal to be served. They served him by himself, and the brothers by themselves, and the Egyptians who were at dinner were also served separately; for Egyptians hold it an abomination to eat with Hebrews. The brothers were seated in his presence, the eldest first according to his age and so on down to the youngest: they looked at one another in astonishment. Joseph sent them each a portion from what was before him, but Benjamin's was five times larger than any of the other portions. Thus they drank with him and all grew merry.

Joseph gave his steward this order: "Fill the men's packs with as much food as they can carry and put each man's silver at the top of his pack. And put my goblet, my silver goblet, at the top of the youngest brother's pack with the silver for the corn." He did as Joseph said. At daybreak the brothers were allowed to take their asses and go on their journey; but before they had gone very far from the city, Joseph said to his steward, "Go after those men at once, and when you catch up with them, say, 'Why have you repaid good with evil? Why have you stolen the silver goblet? It is the one from which my lord drinks, and which he uses for divination. You have done a wicked thing.'" When he caught up with them, he repeated all this to them, but they replied, "My lord, how can you say such things? No, sir, God forbid that we should do any such thing! You remember the silver we found at the top of our packs? We brought it back to you from Canaan. Why should we steal silver or gold from your master's house? If any one of us is found with the goblet, he shall die; and, what is more, my lord, we will all become your slaves." He said, "Very well, then; I accept what you say. The man in whose possession it is found shall be my slave, but the rest of you shall go free." Each man quickly lowered his pack to the ground and opened it. The steward searched them, beginning with the eldest and finishing with the youngest, and the goblet was found in Benjamin's pack.

At this they rent their clothes; then each man loaded his ass and they returned to the city. Joseph was still in the house when Judah and his brothers came in. They threw themselves on the ground before him, and Joseph said, "What have you done? You might have known that a man like myself would practice divination." Judah said, "What shall we say, my lord? What can we say to prove our innocence? God has found out our sin. Here we are, my lord, ready to be made your slaves, we ourselves as well as the one who was found with the goblet." Joseph answered, "God forbid that I should do such a thing! The one who was found with the goblet shall become my slave, but the rest of you can go home to your father in peace."

Then Judah went up to him and said, "Please listen, my lord. Let me say a word to your lordship, I beg. Do not be angry with me, for you are as great as Pharaoh. You, my lord, asked us whether we had a father or a brother. We answered, 'We have an aged father, and he has a young son born in his old age; this boy's full brother is dead and he alone is left of his mother's children, he alone, and his father loves him.' Your lordship answered, 'Bring him down to me so that I may set eyes on him.' We told you, my lord, that the boy could not leave his father, and that his father would die if he left him. But you answered, 'Unless your youngest brother comes here with you, you shall not enter my presence again.' We went back to your servant our father, and told him what your lordship had said. When our father told us to go and buy food, we answered, 'We cannot go down; for without our youngest brother we cannot enter the man's presence; but if our brother is with us, we will go.' Our father, my lord, then said to us, 'You know that my wife bore me two sons. One left me, and I said, "He must have been torn to pieces." I have not seen him to this day. If you take this one from me as well, and he comes to any harm, then you will bring down my gray hairs in trouble to the grave.' Now, my lord, when I return to my father without the boy—and remember, his life is bound up with the boy's—what will happen is this: he will see that the boy is not with us and will die, and your servants will have brought down our father's gray hairs in sorrow to the grave. Indeed, my lord, it was I who went surety for the boy to my father. I said, 'If I do not bring him back to you, then you shall hold me guilty all my life.' Now, my lord, let me remain in place of the boy as your lordship's slave, and let him go with his brothers. How can I return to my father without the boy? I could not bear to see the misery which my father would suffer."

Joseph could no longer control his feelings in front of his attendants, and he called out, "Let everyone leave my presence." So there was nobody present when Joseph made himself known to his brothers, but so loudly did he weep that the Egyptians and Pharaoh's household heard him. Joseph said to his brothers, "I am Joseph; can my father be still alive?" His brothers were so dumbfounded at finding themselves face to face with Joseph that they could not answer. Then Joseph said to his brothers, "Come closer," and so they came close. He said, "I am your brother Joseph whom you sold into Egypt. Now do not be distressed or take it amiss that you sold me into slavery here; it was God who sent me ahead of you to save men's lives. For there have now been two years of famine in the country, and there will be another five years with neither plowing nor harvest. God sent me ahead of you to ensure that you will have descendants on earth, and to preserve you all, a great band of survivors. So it was not you who sent me here, but God, and he has made me a father to Pharaoh, and lord over all his household and ruler of all Egypt. Make haste and go back to my father and give him this message from his son Joseph: 'God has made me lord of all Egypt. Come down to me; do not delay. You shall live in the land of Goshen and be near me, you, your sons and your grandsons, your flocks and herds and all that you have. I will take care of you there, you and your household and all that you have, and see that you are not reduced to poverty; there are still five years of famine to come.' You can see for yourselves, and so can my brother Benjamin, that it is Joseph himself who is speaking to you. Tell my father of all the honor which I enjoy in Egypt, tell him all you have seen, and make haste to bring him down here." Then he threw his arms round his brother Benjamin and wept, and Benjamin too embraced him weeping. He kissed all his brothers and wept over them, and afterward his brothers talked with him. . . . [Then Joseph] dismissed his brothers, telling them not to quarrel among themselves on the road, and they set out. Thus they went up from Egypt and came to their father Jacob in Canaan. There they gave him the news that Joseph was still alive and that he was ruler of all Egypt. He was stunned and could not believe it, but they told him all that Joseph had said; and when he saw the wagons which Joseph had sent to take him away, his spirit revived. Israel said, "It is enough. Joseph my son is still alive; I will go and see him before I die."

GENESIS 42; 43; 44; 45 : 1–15, 24–28

What concept of humanity do Joseph's brothers use as an argument for the sharing of the Egyptian food stores? How has Joseph's career itself shown the truth of this concept?

Why does Joseph "frame" Benjamin? How does Judah plead for Benjamin's freedom? What effect does his plea have on Joseph?

How does Joseph explain his forgiving of his brothers for their earlier crime against him? In what ways does he remind you here of Noah and Abraham? Do Joseph's exploits help to fulfill the promises made to them?

Why is it necessary for the Israelites to emigrate to Egypt?

How does Joseph, like the Pawnee boy (page 170), have a kind of rebirth?

You Must Take
My Bones

So Israel set out with all that he had and came to Beersheba where he offered sacrifices to the God of his father Isaac. God said to Israel in a vision by night, "Jacob, Jacob," and he answered, "I am here." God said, "I am God, the God of your father. Do not be afraid to go down to Egypt, for there I will make you a great nation. I will go down with you to Egypt, and I myself will bring you back again without fail; and Joseph shall close your eyes." So Jacob set out from Beersheba. Israel's sons conveyed their father Jacob, their dependents, and their wives in the wagons which Pharaoh had sent to carry them. They took the herds and the stock which they had acquired in Canaan and came to Egypt, Jacob and all his descendants with him, his sons and their sons, his daughters and his sons' daughters: he brought all his descendants to Egypt. . . .

The persons belonging to Jacob who came to Egypt, all his direct descendants, not counting the wives of his sons, were sixty-six in all. Two sons were born to Joseph in Egypt. Thus the house of Jacob numbered seventy when it entered Egypt.

Judah was sent ahead that he might appear before Joseph in Goshen, and so they entered Goshen. Joseph had his chariot made ready and went up to meet his father Israel in Goshen. When they met, he threw his arms round him and wept, and embraced him for a long time, weeping. Israel said to Joseph, "I have seen your face again, and you are still alive. Now I am ready to die." Joseph said to his brothers and to his father's household, "I will go and tell Pharaoh; I will say to him, 'My brothers and my father's household who were in Canaan have come to me.'" Now his brothers were shepherds, men with their own flocks and herds, and they had brought them with them, their flocks and herds and all that they possessed. So Joseph said, "When Pharaoh summons you and asks you what your occupation is, you must say, 'My lord, we have been herdsmen all our lives, as our fathers were before us.' You must say this if you are to settle in the land of Goshen, because all shepherds are an abomination to the Egyptians."

Joseph came and told Pharaoh, "My father and my brothers have arrived from Canaan, with their flocks and their cattle and all that they have, and they are now in Goshen." Then he chose five of his brothers and presented them to Pharaoh, who asked them what their occupation was, and they answered, "My lord, we are shepherds, we and our fathers before us, and we have come to stay in this land; for there is no pasture in Canaan for our sheep, because the famine there is so severe. We beg you, my lord, to let us settle now in Goshen." Pharaoh said to Joseph, "So your father and your brothers have come to you. The land of Egypt is yours; settle them in the best part of it. Let them live in Goshen, and if you know of any capable men among them, make them chief herdsmen over my cattle."

Then Joseph brought his father in and presented him to Pharaoh, and Jacob gave Pharaoh his blessing. Pharaoh asked Jacob his age, and he answered, "The years of my earthly sojourn are one hundred and thirty; hard years they have been and few, not equal to the years that my fathers lived in their time." Jacob then blessed Pharaoh and went out from his presence. So Joseph settled his father and his brothers, and gave them lands in Egypt, in the best part of the country, in the district of Rameses, as Pharaoh had ordered. He supported his father, his brothers, and all his father's household with all the food they needed.

There was no bread in the whole country, so very severe was the famine, and Egypt and Canaan were laid low by it. Joseph collected all the silver in Egypt and Canaan in return for the corn which the people bought, and deposited it in Pharaoh's treasury. When all the silver in Egypt and Canaan had been used up, the Egyptians came to Joseph and said, "Give us bread, or we shall die before your eyes. Our silver is all spent." Joseph said, "If your silver is spent, give me your herds and I will give you bread in return." So they brought their herds to Joseph, who gave them bread in exchange for their horses, their flocks of sheep and herds of cattle, and their asses. He maintained them that year with bread in exchange for their herds. The year came to an end, and the following year they came to him again and said, "My lord, we cannot conceal it from you: our silver is all gone and our herds of cattle are yours. Nothing is left for your lordship but our bodies and our lands. Why should we perish before your eyes, we and our land as well? Take us and our land in payment for bread, and we and our land alike will be in bondage to Pharaoh. Give us seed corn to keep us alive, or we shall die and our land will become desert."

So Joseph bought all the land in Egypt for Pharaoh, because the Egyptians sold all their fields, so severe was the famine; the land became Pharaoh's. As for the people, Pharaoh set them to work as slaves from one end of the territory of Egypt to the other. But Joseph did not buy the land which belonged to the priests; they had a fixed allowance from Pharaoh and lived on this, so that they had no need to sell their land.

Joseph remained in Egypt, he and his father's household. He lived there to be a hundred and ten years old and saw Ephraim's children to the third generation; he also recognized as his the children of Manasseh's son Machir. He said to his brothers, "I am dying; but God will not fail to come to your aid and take you from here to the land which he promised on oath to Abraham, Isaac, and Jacob." He made the sons of Israel take an oath, saying, "When God thus comes to your aid, you must take my bones with you from here." So Joseph died at the age of a hundred and ten. He was embalmed and laid in a coffin in Egypt.

GENESIS 46 : 1–7, 26–34; 47 : 1–22; 50 : 22–26

How is God's promise to Jacob like the covenant he made with Abraham?

How did Joseph consolidate Pharaoh's power during the years of famine?

What is Joseph's dying wish? How does it foreshadow the hope of all the Israelites in Egypt?

Can Israel's journey from Canaan into Egypt be seen as a journey from a wilderness to a garden?

I Don't Intend to Die
in Egypt Land

stay a - way; Lord, I can't. stay a - way; I
don't in - tend to die in E - gypt land.

4. She said, "Go bring me some water, let me wash my hands";
I don't intend to die in Egypt land!
"I shan't be guilty of an innocent man."
I don't intend to die in Egypt land!
Chor: Lord, I can't stay away (etc.)

5. (Repeat verse 1 and chorus.)

Is this singer trying to return to the first home of man? Is his longing like that of the Israelites for their promised land of Canaan?

In what way can three different times (past, present, and future) be thought of as simultaneous as this spiritual is sung? If you think of these three times as biblical, historical, and personal, you might be helped to see why there are three.

The Strong
Ones

Cheder, too often described as a place where innocent children suffered at the hands of a sloppy, ill-tempered teacher, was not quite that. What was wrong with society was wrong with cheder.

There was one boy with constantly clenched fists who kept looking for a chance to hit someone. Assistant bullies and sycophants surrounded him.

Another boy, for whom it was not practical to use violence, acted the little saint, smiling at everyone, doing favors, and all with an expression that implied immeasurable love. But in his quiet way he schemed to acquire things, to taste something wonderful for nothing. Pious though he was, he showed friendship for the bully while feigning sympathy for his victims. When his friend the bully decided to give someone a bloody nose, the little saint would run to the victim with a handkerchief while gently admonishing the bully, "You shouldn't have done that . . . ."

There was another boy who was interested only in business, trading a button for a nail, a bit of putty for a pencil, a candy for a roll. He was always losing out on bargains, but in the end he got the best of everyone. Half the cheder was indebted to him, since he lent money on interest. He and the bully had an arrangement whereby anyone who reneged had his hat snatched off.

Then there was the liar who boasted that his family was rich and famous and that Warsaw's elite visited his home. Promising us dates, figs, St. John's bread, and oranges from theoretical weddings and circumcisions, and a projected summer vacation, he demanded advance presents from all of us.

Then there was the victim. One day the bully drew blood from him and the next day he gave the bully a present. Smiling with sly submissiveness, the victim indicated another boy who needed a beating.

From my seat in cheder I saw everything, and even though the bully had punched me, I presented him with neither smiles nor gifts. I called him an Esau and predicted that his hereafter would be spent on a bed of nails. He hit me again for that, but I didn't weaken. I would have nothing to do with the bully, the priggish saint, the moneylender, or the liar, nor would I pay them any compliments.

I wasn't making out too well. Most of the cheder boys had grown hostile, informing against me to the teacher and the tutor. If they caught me in the street, they said, they'd break my leg. I recognized the danger. After all, I was too small to take on the entire cheder.

The trip to cheder each morning was agonizing, but I couldn't complain to my parents—they had their own troubles. Besides, they'd probably say, "That's what you get for being different from everyone else . . . ."

There was nothing to do but wait it out. Even the devil had to weary. God, if He supported truth and justice, must inevitably side with me.

The day came when it seemed to me impossible to go on. Even the teacher, in that hellish atmosphere, opposed me, though I knew my Pentateuch. The rebbetzin made malicious remarks about me. It was as if I were excommunicated.

Then, one day, everything changed. The bully miscalculated the strength of a new boy, who just happened to hit back. Then the teacher hurled himself at the bully, who already had a lump on his head. He was dragged to the whipping bench, his pants were pulled down, and he was whipped before all of us. Like Haman, he was punished. When he tried to resume his reign of terror, he was repulsed in favor of the victor.

The moneylender also met his downfall. The father of one boy who had paid out too much interest appeared at cheder to complain. A search of the moneylender's pockets proved so fruitful that he too was whipped.

The saint's hypocrisy was recognized at last, despite his whispered secrets and his flatteries.

Then, as if in response to my prayers, the boys began speaking to me once more. The flatterers and the traders offered me good will and bargains—I don't know why. I might even have formed a group of my own, but I wasn't inclined that way. There was only one boy whose friendship I wanted, and he was the one I chose. Mendel was a fine, decent person without social ambitions. We studied from the same Pentateuch and walked with our arms about each other. Others, jealous, intrigued against us, but our friendship remained constant. We were like David and Jonathan . . . .

Even after I left cheder, our friendship persisted. I had attended several cheders, and from each one I retained a friend. Occasionally, in the evenings, we would meet near the markets and walk along the sidewalk, talking, making plans. My friends' names were Mendel Besser, Mottel Horowitz, Abraham something-or-other, Boruch-Dovid, and others. More or less their leader, I would tell them things my older brother had told my mother. There was a great feeling of trust among us, until one day I had the impression that they resented me. They grumbled about my bossiness; I had to be demoted a little. They were preparing a revolution and I saw it in their faces. And even though I asked how I had offended them, they behaved like Joseph's brothers and could not answer in a friendly way. They couldn't even look at me directly. What was it they envied? My dreams . . . I could actually hear them say as I approached them, "Behold this dreamer cometh . . . Let us slay him and cast him in some pit . . . Let us sell him to the Ishmaelites . . . ."

It is painful to be among one's brothers when they are jealous. They had been good to me, they praised me, and then they were mean. All at once they grew angry. Turning away as I approached, they whispered . . . .

Friendships with me are not casual; I cannot make new friends easily. I wondered if I had sinned against them, or deceived them. But, if so, why hadn't they told me what was wrong?

I could not recollect having harmed them in any way, nor had I said anything against them. And if someone had slandered me, why should my friends believe it? After all, they were devoted to me.

There was nothing to do but wait it out. My kind has to become accustomed to loneliness. And when one is alone there is nothing to do but study. I became a diligent scholar. I would spend whole days in the Radzymin study house and then pore over religious works at home. Purchasing and renting books from peddlers, I read constantly. It was summertime and the days were long. Reading a story of three brothers, I imagined that I could write too, and began to cover both sides of a sheet. "Once there was a king who had three sons. One was wise, one foolish, and one merry . . . ." But somehow the story didn't jell.

On another paper I began to draw freakish humans and fantastic beasts. But this too wearied me, and going out to the balcony, I looked down at the street. Only I was alone. Other boys were running, playing, and talking together. I'll go mad, I thought—there was too much happening in my head all the time. Shouldn't I jump from the balcony? Or spit down on the janitor's cap?

That evening, at the Radzymin study house, a boy approached me, acting as a go-between. He spoke tactfully, suggesting that my friends were eager for an understanding but, since I was the minority, it was up to me to make the first move. In short, he suggested that I submit a plea for a truce.

I was infuriated. "It wasn't I who started this," I said. "Why should I be the one to make up?"

"You'll regret it," he warned.

"Leave!" I commanded.

He left angrily. His job as a trucemaker had been spoiled. But he knew I meant what I said.

Now that they had sent an intermediary, I knew my friends were remorseful. But I would never give in to them.

I grew accustomed to being alone and the days no longer seemed interminable. I studied, wrote, read stories. My brother had brought home a two-volume book called *Crime and Punishment*. Although I didn't really understand it, it fascinated me. Secluded in the bedroom, I read for hours. A student who had killed a crone suffered, starved, and reasoned profoundly. Coming before the prosecutor, he was questioned . . . . It was something like a storybook, but different. Strange and lofty, it reminded me of the Cabala. Who were the authors of books like this, and who could understand them? Now and then a passage was illuminated for me, I understood an episode and became enthralled by the beauty of a new insight.

I was in another world. I forgot about my friends.

At evening services in the Radzymin study house, I was unaware of the men among whom I stood. My mind was wandering, when suddenly the intermediary approached.

"Nothing you have to say can interest me," I said.

"Here's a note," he told me.

It was like a scene from a novel. My friends wrote that they missed me. "We wander about in a daze . . . ." I still remember what they said. Despite this great triumph, I was so immersed in my book that it scarcely seemed important any more that they wanted to make amends. I went out to the courtyard, and there they were. It reminded me of Joseph and his brothers. They had come to Joseph to buy grain, but why had my friends come to me?

Nevertheless, they did come, ashamed and somehow afraid—

Simon, Levi, Judah. . . . Since I had not become Egypt's ruler, they were not required to bow down to the earth. I had nothing to sell but new dreams.

We talked together late and I spoke of my book. "This is no story-book, this is literature . . . ." I said. I created for them a fantastic mélange of incidents and my own thoughts, and infected them with my excitement. Hours passed. They begged me to forgive them, confessed that they had been wrong and never would be angry with me again . . . .

They kept their word.

Only time separated us. The rest was accomplished by the German murderers.

I. B. SINGER

The author says, "What was wrong with society was wrong with cheder." Discuss this, in relation to the boy in this story, as well as to Joseph in the biblical story, and to your own school and society.

How do the author's friends begin to act as Joseph's brothers did? How is the author, like Joseph, a dreamer? Is being a dreamer often a cause of hostility from others? Why? What kind of feeling might cause the author to say "Everyone is out of step except me"?

Why does the author have to "wait it out" a second time? What characters so far in this book also have had to "wait it out"? What reading activity turns this boy into an interpreter of dreams? Does the story's title fit here? List the "strong ones" you have already read about in this book. In what sense are they and this boy "the one" as well as "the strong"?

The author says "there was too much happening in my head." What piece in Chapter Two also describes a boy with much happening in his head?

How does this story make it apparent that the events of the Bible are not merely historical (that is, what happens in time) but also outside history (that is, always happening)? Trace the connection you can find in this book so far between biblical patterns and later persons, objects, or events.

SHEPHERD OF ISRAEL

Give ear, O Shepherd of Israel,
Thou that leadest Joseph like a flock;
Thou that dwellest between the cherubim, shine forth.
Before Ephraim and Benjamin and Manasseh
    stir up thy strength,
And come and save us.
Turn us again, O God, and cause thy face to shine;
And we shall be saved.
O Lord God of hosts, how long wilt thou be angry
    against the prayer of thy people?
Thou feedest them with the bread of tears;
And givest them tears to drink in great measure.
Thou makest us a strife unto our neighbors:
And our enemies laugh among themselves.
Turn us again, O God of hosts, and cause thy face to shine;
And we shall be saved.
Thou hast brought a vine out of Egypt:
Thou hast cast out the heathen, and planted it.
Thou preparedst room before it,
And didst cause it to take deep root, and it filled the land.
The hills were covered with the shadow of it,
And the boughs thereof were like the goodly cedars.
She sent out her boughs unto the sea,
And her branches unto the river.
Why hast thou then broken down her hedges,
So that all they which pass by the way do pluck her?
The boar out of the wood doth waste it,
And the wild beast of the field doth devour it.
Return, we beseech thee, O God of hosts:
Look down from heaven, and behold, and visit this vine;
And the vineyard which thy right hand hath planted,
And the branch that thou madest strong for thyself.
It is burned with fire, it is cut down:
They perish at the rebuke of thy countenance.
Let thy hand be upon the man of thy right hand,
Upon the son of man whom thou madest strong for thyself.
So will not we go back from thee:
Quicken us, and we will call upon thy name.
Turn us again, O Lord God of hosts,
Cause thy face to shine;
And we shall be saved.

PSALM 80

245

The descendants of Abraham go down into Egypt because of a food shortage in their homeland. The biblical story by now has moved a long way from its beginning in the garden of Eden. Even in a foreign land, however, God has a "man of his right hand" to look after his people. The story of Joseph contrasts the worldly power of Egypt with the spiritual power of Israel. Despite Pharaoh's great wealth and authority, the Israelites continue to look elsewhere for leadership and deliverance. The psalmist in Psalm 80 expresses this same desire when he pleads to God, "Turn us again, O God, and cause thy face to shine." The story of the Bible so far, then, is the story of a series of patriarchal heroes—Noah, Abraham, Isaac, Jacob, and Joseph—who are heroes because they are God's right-hand men. They are not led astray by the worldly power and evil of the foreign peoples among whom at times they must live. The families and societies these heroes serve are thought of both as the chosen people of God (Israel) and as a flock of sheep whose shepherd is the Lord. Several of the heroes themselves actually are shepherds. For flocks they have both actual sheep, and men.

In order to make their particular stories vivid and memorable the biblical writers, like those in other cultures, imbue the events, people, and places they are describing with metaphorical significance. Abraham actually is a shepherd, but the God whom he obeys is the real shepherd in the story, with the result that the children and followers of Abraham are God's flock as well as Abraham's own. Jacob actually is the son of Isaac, but he is also the son of God and is renamed "Israel" by his heavenly father. God's first son was Adam, but Jacob (Israel), as a symbol of mankind, is also Adam. Even as "in the beginning" God creates the world out of watery chaos, so he re-creates it after the Flood. Adam's fall, through eating the forbidden fruit in his garden, corresponds to Noah's fall, symbolized by his drunkenness in the vineyard which he plants in the new world after his experiences in the ark.

Recurrent patterns, then, underline the overall biblical story, a story in which God is "the hero." For the biblical writers the human heroes *are* heroes because they are agents of God. When we read these stories as literature—that is, as works of the human imagination—we may or may not believe what the original writers believed. Nonetheless their writings remind us symbolically that every man is Adam and that all people live in a fallen world in which somehow there persists a memory of a golden age and of an ideal garden state.

Traditionally, heroes go on quests to achieve some kind of victory (it may be the winning over of an enemy, or the finding of a treasure or a bride, or perhaps the gaining of wisdom). For the hero to be effective in his quest, he must believe in the possibility of victory. He must feel that something better than what exists at the beginning of his adventure can be won or restored by him and his actions. When Joseph is a slave or in prison, he can still hope for eventual freedom. Even with hope, though, "the bread of tears" is part of the staple diet of the bibical heroes. Simply to enable them and their people to survive, they have to dream of a future time when they will have prosperity and a home of their own. The taking of Jacob's bones back to Canaan to be buried there is the outward sign that Israel belongs in her physical and spiritual homeland. Israel belongs there because this is God's way of rewarding her for her steadfastness and faith in adversity. On one level of the imagination, the quest in the early part of the Old Testament is for a geographical place, the land of Canaan, the Promised Land. But this quest also can be seen symbolically, as referring not so much to geography as to a state of mind in which all men in all times and places share.

5:
To
Set
the
People
Free

THE STRONG HAND OF MOSES

The Raising Up
of a Hero

These are the names of the Israelites who entered Egypt with Jacob, each with his household: Reuben, Simeon, Levi, and Judah; Issachar, Zebulun, and Benjamin; Dan and Naphtali, Gad and Asher. There were seventy of them all told, all direct descendants of Jacob. Joseph was already in Egypt.

In course of time Joseph died, he and all his brothers and that whole generation. Now the Israelites were fruitful and prolific; they increased in numbers and became very powerful, so that the country was overrun by them. Then a new king ascended the throne of Egypt, one who knew nothing of Joseph. He said to his people, "These Israelites have become too many and too strong for us. We must take precautions to see that they do not increase any further; or we shall find that, if war breaks out, they will join the enemy and fight against us, and they will become masters of the country." So they were made to work in gangs with officers set over them, to break their spirit with heavy labor. This is how Pharaoh's store-cities, Pithom and Rameses, were built. But the more harshly they were treated, the more their numbers increased beyond all bounds, until the Egyptians came to loathe the sight of them. So they treated their Israelite slaves with ruthless severity, and made life bitter for them with cruel servitude, setting them to work on clay and brick-making, and all sorts of work in the fields. In short they made ruthless use of them as slaves in every kind of hard labor.

Then the king of Egypt spoke to the Hebrew midwives, whose names were Shiphrah and Puah. "When you are attending the Hebrew women in childbirth," he told them, "watch as the child is delivered and if it is a boy, kill him; if it is a girl, let her live." But they were God-fearing women. They did not do what the king of Egypt had told them to do, but let the boys live. So he summoned those Hebrew midwives and asked them why they had done this and let the boys live. They told Pharaoh that Hebrew women were not like Egyptian women. When they were in labor they gave birth before the midwife could get to them. So God made the midwives prosper, and the people increased in numbers and in strength. God gave the midwives homes and families of their own, because they feared him. Pharaoh then ordered all his people to throw every newborn Hebrew boy into the Nile, but to let the girls live.

A descendant of Levi married a Levite woman who conceived and bore a son. When she saw what a fine child he was, she hid him for three months, but she could conceal him no longer. So she got a rush basket for him, made it watertight with clay and tar, laid him in it, and put it among the reeds by the bank of the Nile. The child's sister took her stand at a distance to see what would happen to him. Pharaoh's daughter came down to bathe in the river, while her ladies-in-waiting walked along the bank. She noticed the basket among the reeds and sent her slave girl for it. She took it from her and when she opened it, she saw the child. It was crying, and she was filled with pity for it. "Why," she said, "it is a little Hebrew boy." Thereupon the sister said to Pharaoh's daughter, "Shall I go and fetch one of the Hebrew women as a wet-nurse to suckle the child for you?" Pharaoh's daughter told her to go; so the girl went and called the baby's mother. Then Pharaoh's daughter said to her, "Here is the child, suckle him for me, and I will pay you for it myself." So the woman took the child and suckled him. When the child was old enough, she brought him to Pharaoh's daughter, who adopted him and called him Moses, "because," she said, "I drew him out of the water."

One day when Moses was grown up, he went out to his own kinsmen and saw them at their heavy labor. He saw an Egyptian strike one of his fellow Hebrews. He looked this way and that, and, seeing there was no one about, he struck the Egyptian down and hid his body in the sand. When he went out next day, two Hebrews were fighting together. He asked the man who was in the wrong, "Why are you strik-

The Dreamer

He spent his childhood hours in a den
of rushes, watching the gray rain braille
the surface of the river. Concealed
from the outside world, nestled within,
he was safe from parents, God, and eyes
that looked upon him accusingly,
as though to say: Even at your age,
you could do better. His camouflage
was scant, but it served, and at evening,
when fireflies burned holes into heaven,
he took the path homeward in the dark,
a small Noah, leaving his safe ark.

WILLIAM CHILDRESS

How does the poet connect Moses and Noah? How could the poem also apply to Joseph?

Let My People Go

Years passed, and the king of Egypt died, but the Israelites still groaned in slavery. They cried out, and their appeal for rescue from their slavery rose up to God. He heard their groaning, and remembered his covenant with Abraham, Isaac, and Jacob; he saw the plight of Israel, and he took heed of it.

Moses was minding the flock of his father-in-law Jethro, priest of Midian. He led the flock along the side of the wilderness and came to Horeb, the mountain of God. There the angel of the Lord appeared to him in the flame of a burning bush. Moses noticed that, although the bush was on fire, it was not being burned up; so he said to himself, "I must go across to see this wonderful sight. Why does not the bush burn away?" When the Lord saw that Moses had turned aside to look, he called to him out of the bush, "Moses, Moses." And Moses answered, "Yes, I am here." God said, "Come no nearer; take off your sandals; the place where you are standing is holy ground." Then he said, "I am the God of your forefathers, the God of Abraham, the God of Isaac, the God of Jacob." Moses covered his face, for he was afraid to gaze on God.

The Lord said, "I have indeed seen the misery of my people in Egypt. I have heard their outcry against their slave masters. I have taken heed of their sufferings, and have come down to rescue them from the power of Egypt, and to bring them up out of that country into a fine, broad land; it is a land flowing with milk and honey, the home of Canaanites, Hittites, Amorites, Perizzites, Hivites, and Jebusites. The outcry of the Israelites has now reached me; yes, I have seen the brutality of the Egyptians toward them. Come now; I will send you to Pharaoh and you shall bring my people Israel out of Egypt." "But who am I," Moses said to God, "that I should go to Pharaoh, and that I should bring the Israelites out of Egypt?" God answered, "I am with you. This shall be the proof that it is I who have sent you: when you have brought the people out of Egypt, you shall all worship God here on this mountain."

Then Moses said to God, "If I go to the Israelites and tell them that the God of their forefathers has sent me to them, and they ask me his name, what shall I say?" God answered, "I Am; that is who I am. Tell them that I Am has sent you to them." And God said further, "You must tell the Israelites this, that it is Jehovah the God of their forefathers, the God of Abraham, the God of Isaac, the God of Jacob, who has sent you to them. This is my name for ever; this is my title in every generation. Go and assemble the elders of Israel and tell them that Jehovah the God of their forefathers, the God of Abraham, Isaac, and Jacob, has appeared to you and has said, 'I have indeed turned my eyes toward you; I have marked all that has been done to you in Egypt, and I am resolved to bring you up out of your misery in Egypt, into the country of the Canaanites, Hittites, Amorites, Perizzites, Hivites, and Jebusites, a land flowing with milk and honey.' They will listen to you, and then you and the elders of Israel must go to the king of Egypt. Tell him, 'It has happened that the Lord the God of the Hebrews met us. So now give us leave to go a three days' journey into the wilderness to offer sacrifice to the Lord our God.' I know well that the king of Egypt will not give you leave unless he is compelled. I shall then stretch out my hand and assail the Egyptians with all the miracles I shall work among them. After that he will send you away. Further, I will bring this people into such favor with the Egyptians that, when you go, you will not go empty-handed. Every woman shall ask her neighbor or any woman who lives in her house for jewelry of silver and gold and for clothing. Load your sons and daughters with them, and plunder Egypt."

Moses answered, "But they will never believe me or listen to me; they will say, 'The Lord did not appear to you.'" The Lord said, "What have you there in your hand?" "A staff," Moses answered. The Lord said, "Throw it on the ground." Moses threw it down and it turned into a snake. He ran away from it, but the Lord said, "Put your hand out and seize it by the tail." He did so and gripped it firmly, and it turned back into a staff in his hand. "This is to convince the people that the Lord the God of their forefathers, the God of Abraham, the God of Isaac, the God of Jacob, has appeared to you." Then the Lord said, "Put your hand inside the fold of your cloak." He did so, and when he drew it out the skin was diseased, white as snow. The Lord said, "Put it back again," and he did so. When he drew it out this time it was as healthy as the rest of his body. "Now," said the Lord, "if they do not believe you and do not accept the evidence of the first sign, they may accept the evidence of the second. But if they are not convinced even by these two signs, and will not accept what you say, then fetch some water from the Nile and pour it out on the dry ground, and the water you take from the Nile will turn to blood on the ground."

But Moses said, "O Lord, I have never been a man of ready speech, never in my life, not even now that thou hast spoken to me; I am slow and hesitant of speech." The Lord said to him, "Who is it that gives man speech? Who makes him dumb or deaf? Who makes him clear-sighted or blind? Is it not I, the Lord? Go now; I will help your speech and tell you what to say." But Moses still protested, "No, Lord, send whom thou wilt." At this the Lord grew angry with Moses and said, "Have you not a brother, Aaron the Levite? He, I know, will do all the speaking. He is already on his way out to meet you, and he will be glad indeed to see you. You shall speak to him and put the words in his mouth; I will help both of you to speak and tell you both what to do. He will do all the speaking to the people for you, he will be the mouthpiece, and you will be the god he speaks for. But take this staff, for with it you are to work the signs."

At length Moses went back to Jethro his father-in-law and said, "Let me return to my kinsfolk in Egypt and see if they are still alive." Jethro told him to go and wished him well.

Meanwhile the Lord had ordered Aaron to go and meet Moses in the wilderness. Aaron went and met him at the mountain of God, and he kissed him. Then Moses told Aaron everything, the words the Lord had sent him to say and the signs he had commanded him to perform. Moses and Aaron went and assembled all the elders of Israel. Aaron told them everything that the Lord had said to Moses; he performed the signs before the people, and they were convinced. They heard that the Lord had shown his concern for the Israelites and seen their misery; and they bowed themselves to the ground in worship.

After this, Moses and Aaron came to Pharaoh and said, "These are the words of the Lord the God of Israel: 'Let my people go so that they may keep my pilgrim feast in the wilderness.'" "Who is the Lord," asked Pharaoh, "that I should obey him and let Israel go? I care nothing for the Lord: and I tell you I will not let Israel go." They replied, "It has happened that the God of the Hebrews met us. So let us go three days' journey into the wilderness to offer sacrifice to the Lord our God, or else he will attack us with pestilence or sword." But the king of Egypt said, "Moses and Aaron, what do you mean by distracting the people from their work? Back to your labors! Your people already outnumber the native Egyptians; yet you would have them stop working!"

That very day Pharaoh ordered the people's overseers and their foremen not to supply the people with the straw used in making bricks, as they had done hitherto. "Let them go and collect their own straw, but see that they produce the same tally of bricks as before. On no account reduce it. They are a lazy people, and that is why they are clamoring to go and offer sacrifice to their god. Keep the men hard at work; let them attend to that and take no notice of a pack of lies." The overseers and foremen went out and said to the people, "Pharaoh's orders are that no more straw is to be supplied. Go and get it for your-selves wherever you can find it; but there will be no reduction in your daily task." So the people scattered all over Egypt to gather stubble for straw, while the overseers kept urging them on, bidding them com-plete, day after day, the same quantity as when straw was supplied. Then the Israelite foremen were flogged because they were held re-sponsible by Pharaoh's overseers, who asked them, "Why did you not complete the usual number of bricks yesterday or today?" So the fore-men came and appealed to Pharaoh: "Why do you treat your servants like this?" they said. "We are given no straw, yet they keep on telling us to make bricks. Here are we being flogged, but it is your people's fault." But Pharaoh replied, "You are lazy, you are lazy. That is why you talk about going to offer sacrifice to the Lord. Now go; get on with your work. You will be given no straw, but you must produce the tally of bricks." When they were told that they must not let the daily tally of bricks fall short, the Israelite foremen saw that they were in trouble. As they came out from Pharaoh's presence they found Moses and Aaron waiting to meet them, and said, "May this bring the Lord's judgment down upon you: you have made us stink in the nostrils of Pharaoh and his subjects; you have put a sword in their hands to kill us."

Moses went back to the Lord, and said, "Why, O Lord, hast thou brought misfortune on this people? And why didst thou ever send me? Since I first went to Pharaoh to speak in thy name he has heaped mis-fortune on thy people, and thou hast done nothing at all to rescue them." The Lord answered, "Now you shall see what I will do to Pharaoh. In the end Pharaoh will let them go with a strong hand, nay, will drive them from his country with an outstretched arm."

God spoke to Moses and said, "I am the Lord. I appeared to Abra-ham, Isaac, and Jacob as God Almighty. But I did not let myself be known to them by my name Jehovah. Moreover, I made a covenant with them to give them Canaan, the land where they settled for a time as foreigners. And now I have heard the groaning of the Israelites, enslaved by the Egyptians, and I have called my covenant to mind.

Say therefore to the Israelites, 'I am the Lord. I will release you from your labors in Egypt. I will rescue you from slavery there. I will redeem you with arm outstretched and with mighty acts of judgment. I will adopt you as my people, and I will become your God. You shall know that I, the Lord, am your God, the God who releases you from your labors in Egypt. I will lead you to the land which I swore with uplifted hand to give to Abraham, to Isaac and to Jacob. I will give it you for your possession. I am the Lord.' "

Moses repeated these words to the Israelites, but they did not listen to him; they had become impatient because of their cruel slavery.

Then the Lord spoke to Moses and said, "Go and tell Pharaoh king of Egypt to set the Israelites free to leave his country." Moses made answer in the presence of the Lord, "If the Israelites do not listen to me, how will Pharaoh listen to such a halting speaker as I am?"

Thus the Lord spoke to Moses and Aaron and gave them their commission to the Israelites and to Pharaoh, namely that they should bring the Israelites out of Egypt.

EXODUS 2:23-25; 3; 4:1-18, 27-31; 5; 6:1-13

When God reveals himself to Moses, what promise does he remember? What place in Chapter One comes to mind when he describes the land of Canaan to Moses?

Jehovah in Hebrew is YHWH, pronounced Yahweh but traditionally read Jehovah. The name means "existing one," the incommunicable name of the God of Israel. In the common version of the English Bible it is generally, though improperly, translated as "the Lord."

In what three ways does the Lord convince Moses that the Egyptians will believe that Moses is indeed God's spokesman? Who, in fact, is to be Moses' "mouthpiece"? Why is Moses an unpromising choice as the leader of a people?

God says elsewhere in Exodus, "Israel is my first-born son." What symbolic significance does this statement have?

How is God's covenant with the Israelites renewed? Why did God not reveal his name, Jehovah, to Abraham, Isaac, or Jacob?

The Passover

[After Pharaoh refused to let the Israelites go, ten plagues visited Egypt. The Israelites interpreted these as signs of God's anger against the Egyptians. The plagues were natural phenomena familiar at that time, but extraordinary in intensity and violence and in their destructive effects. The water in the river Nile turned to blood; the Nile and the country swarmed with frogs; the dust on the ground changed to maggots; there was a plague of flies; camels, cattle, sheep, and horses suffered from a fatal disease; men as well as beasts were infested with boils; there was a violent hailstorm; a plague of locusts ate all the crops; for three days there was total darkness; every first-born creature in the land of Egypt died. This final plague is told of in the following excerpt.]

The Lord said to Moses and Aaron in Egypt: This month is for you the first of months; you shall make it the first month of the year. Speak to the whole community of Israel and say to them: On the tenth day of this month let each man take a lamb or a kid for his family, one for each household, but if a household is too small for one lamb or one kid, then the man and his nearest neighbor may take one between them. They shall share the cost, taking into account both the number of persons and the amount each of them eats. Your lamb or kid must be without blemish, a yearling male. You may take equally a sheep or a goat. You must have it in safe keeping until the fourteenth day of this month, and then all the assembled community of Israel shall slaughter the victim between dusk and dark. They must take some of the blood and smear it on the two doorposts and on the lintel of every house in which they eat the lamb. On that night they shall eat the flesh roast on the fire; they shall eat it with unleavened cakes and bitter herbs. You are not to eat any of it raw or even boiled in water, but roasted, head, shins, and entrails. You shall not leave any of it till morning; if anything is left over until morning, it must be destroyed by fire.

This is the way in which you must eat it: you shall have your belt fastened, your sandals on your feet and your staff in your hand, and you must eat in urgent haste. It is the Lord's Passover. On that night I shall pass through the land of Egypt and kill every first-born of man and beast. Thus will I execute judgment, I the Lord, against all the gods of Egypt. And as for you, the blood will be a sign on the houses in which you are: when I see the blood I will pass over you; the mortal blow shall not touch you, when I strike the land of Egypt.

You shall keep this day as a day of remembrance, and make it a pilgrim feast, a festival of the Lord; you shall keep it generation after generation as a rule for all time. . . .

Moses summoned all the elders of Israel and said to them, "Go at once and get sheep for your families and slaughter the Passover. Then take a bunch of marjoram, dip it in the blood in the basin and smear some blood from the basin on the lintel and the two doorposts. Nobody may go out through the door of his house till morning. The Lord will go through Egypt and strike it, but when he sees the blood on the lintel and the two doorposts, he will pass over that door and will not let the destroyer enter your houses to strike you. You shall keep this as a rule for you and your children for all time. When you enter the land which the Lord will give you as he promised, you shall observe this rite. Then, when your children ask you, 'What is the meaning of this rite?' you shall say, 'It is the Lord's Passover, for he passed over the houses of the Israelites in Egypt when he struck the Egyptians but spared our houses.'" The people bowed down and prostrated themselves.

The Israelites went and did all that the Lord had commanded Moses and Aaron; and by midnight the Lord had struck down every first-born in Egypt, from the first-born of Pharaoh on his throne to the first-born of the captive in the dungeon, and the first-born of cattle. Before night was over Pharaoh rose, he and all his courtiers and all the Egyptians, and a great cry of anguish went up, because not a house in Egypt was without its dead. Pharaoh summoned Moses and Aaron while it was still night and said, "Up with you! Be off, and leave my people, you and your Israelites. Go and worship the Lord, as you ask; take your sheep and cattle, and go; and ask God's blessing on me also." The Egyptians urged on the people and hurried them out of the country, "or else," they said, "we shall all be dead." The people picked up their dough before it was leavened, wrapped their kneading troughs in their cloaks, and slung them on their shoulders. Meanwhile the Israelites had done as Moses had told them, asking the Egyptians for jewelry of silver and gold and for clothing. As the Lord had made the Egyptians well-disposed toward them, they let them have what they asked; in this way they plundered the Egyptians.

EXODUS 12:1-14, 21-36

"This month is for you the first of months," the Lord tells Moses and Aaron. Since the Jewish New Year comes in autumn and Passover comes in early spring, what symbolic meaning did God's statement have? How does the Christian feast of Easter have basically the same kind of symbolic significance? What ritual did the Chinook Indians perform (page 214) to usher in a new spring?

The Exodus

The Israelites set out from Rameses on the way to Succoth, about six hundred thousand men on foot, not counting dependents. And with them too went a large company of every kind, and cattle in great numbers, both flocks and herds. The dough they had brought from Egypt they baked into unleavened cakes, because there was no leaven; for they had been driven out of Egypt and allowed no time even to get food ready for themselves.

The Israelites had been settled in Egypt for four hundred and thirty years. At the end of four hundred and thirty years, on this very day, all the tribes of the Lord came out of Egypt. This was a night of vigil as the Lord waited to bring them out of Egypt. It is the Lord's night; all Israelites keep their vigil generation after generation. . . .

The Israelites did all that the Lord had commanded Moses and Aaron; and on this very day the Lord brought the Israelites out of Egypt mustered in their tribal hosts.

The Lord spoke to Moses and said, "Every first-born, the first birth of every womb among the Israelites, you must dedicate to me, both man and beast; it is mine."

Then Moses said to the people, "Remember this day, the day on which you have come out of Egypt, the land of slavery, because the Lord by the strength of his hand has brought you out. . . .

"Every first-born among your sons you must redeem. When in time to come your son asks you what this means, you shall say to him, 'By the strength of his hand the Lord brought us out of Egypt, out of the land of slavery. When Pharaoh proved stubborn and refused to let us go, the Lord killed all the first-born in Egypt both man and beast. That is why I sacrifice to the Lord the first birth of every womb if it is a male and redeem every first-born of my sons. You shall have the record of it as a sign upon your hand, and upon your forehead as a phylactery, because by the strength of his hand the Lord brought us out of Egypt.' "

Now when Pharaoh let the people go, God did not guide them by the road toward the Philistines, although that was the shortest; for he said,

"The people may change their minds when they see war before them, and turn back to Egypt." So God made them go round by way of the wilderness toward the Red Sea; and the fifth generation of Israelites departed from Egypt.

Moses took the bones of Joseph with him, because Joseph had exacted an oath from the Israelites: "Some day," he said, "God will show his care for you, and then, as you go, you must take my bones with you."

They set out from Succoth and encamped at Etham on the edge of the wilderness. And all the time the Lord went before them, by day a pillar of cloud to guide them on their journey, by night a pillar of fire to give them light, so that they could travel night and day. The pillar of cloud never left its place in front of the people by day, nor the pillar of fire by night.

The Lord spoke to Moses and said, "Speak to the Israelites: they are to turn back and encamp before Pi-hahiroth, between Migdol and the sea to the east of Baal-zephon; your camp shall be opposite, by the sea. Pharaoh will then think that the Israelites are finding themselves in difficult country, and are hemmed in by the wilderness. I will make Pharaoh obstinate, and he will pursue them, so that I may win glory for myself at the expense of Pharaoh and all his army; and the Egyptians shall know that I am the Lord." The Israelites did as they were bidden.

When the king of Egypt was told that the Israelites had slipped away, he and his courtiers changed their minds completely, and said, "What have we done? We have let our Israelite slaves go free!" So Pharaoh put horses to his chariot, and took his troops with him. He took six hundred picked chariots and all the other chariots of Egypt, with a commander in each. Then Pharaoh king of Egypt, made obstinate by the Lord, pursued the Israelites as they marched defiantly away. The Egyptians, all Pharaoh's chariots and horses, cavalry and infantry, pursued them and overtook them encamped beside the sea by Pi-hahiroth to the east of Baal-zephon. Pharaoh was almost upon them when the Israelites looked up and saw the Egyptians close behind. In their terror they clamored to the Lord for help and said to Moses, "Were there no graves in Egypt, that you should have brought us here to die in the wilderness? See what you have done to us by bringing us out of Egypt! Is not this just what we meant when we said in Egypt, 'Leave us alone; let us be slaves to the Egyptians'? We would rather be slaves to the Egyptians than die here in the wilderness." "Have no fear," Moses answered; "stand firm and see the deliverance that the Lord will bring you this day; for as sure as you see the Egyptians now, you will never see them again. The Lord will fight for you; so hold your peace."

The Lord said to Moses, "What is the meaning of this clamor? Tell the Israelites to strike camp. And you shall raise high your staff, stretch out your hand over the sea and cleave it in two, so that the Israelites can pass through the sea on dry ground. For my part I will make the Egyptians obstinate and they will come after you; thus will I win glory for myself at the expense of Pharaoh and his army, chariots and cavalry all together. The Egyptians will know that I am the Lord when I win glory for myself at the expense of their Pharaoh, his chariots and cavalry."

The angel of God, who had kept in front of the Israelites, moved away to the rear. The pillar of cloud moved from the front and took its place behind them and so came between the Egyptians and the Israelites. And the cloud brought on darkness and early nightfall, so that contact was lost throughout the night.

Then Moses stretched out his hand over the sea, and the Lord drove the sea away all night with a strong east wind and turned the sea bed into dry land. The waters were torn apart, and the Israelites went through the sea on the dry ground, while the waters made a wall for them to right and to left. The Egyptians went in pursuit of them far into the sea, all Pharaoh's horse, his chariots, and his cavalry. In the morning watch the Lord looked down on the Egyptian army through the pillar of fire and cloud, and he threw them into a panic. He clogged their chariot wheels and made them lumber along heavily, so that the Egyptians said, "It is the Lord fighting for Israel against Egypt; let us flee." Then the Lord said to Moses, "Stretch out your hand over the sea, and let the water flow back over the Egyptians, their chariots and their cavalry." So Moses stretched out his hand over the sea, and at daybreak the water returned to its accustomed place; but the Egyptians were in flight as it advanced, and the Lord swept them out into the sea. The water flowed back and covered all Pharaoh's army, the chariots and the cavalry, which had pressed the pursuit into the sea. Not one man was left alive. Meanwhile the Israelites had passed along the dry ground through the sea, with the water making a wall for them to right and to left. That day the Lord saved Israel from the power of Egypt, and the Israelites saw the Egyptians lying dead on the seashore. When Israel saw the great power which the Lord had put forth against Egypt, all the people feared the Lord, and they put their faith in him and in Moses his servant.

Then Moses and the Israelites sang this song to the Lord:

I will sing to the Lord, for he has risen up in triumph;
the horse and his rider he has hurled into the sea.
    The Lord is my refuge and my defense,
    he has shown himself my deliverer.
    He is my God, and I will glorify him;
    he is my father's God, and I will exalt him.
    The Lord is a warrior: the Lord is his name.
    The chariots of Pharaoh and his army
    he has cast into the sea;
    the flower of his officers
    are engulfed in the Red Sea.
    The watery abyss has covered them,
    they sank into the depths like a stone.
Thy right hand, O Lord, is majestic in strength:
thy right hand, O Lord, shattered the enemy.
      In the fullness of thy triumph
      thou didst cast the rebels down:
      thou didst let loose thy fury;
      it consumed them like chaff.
At the blast of thy anger the sea piled up:
    the waters stood up like a bank:
    out at sea the great deep congealed.
The enemy said, "I will pursue, I will overtake;
      I will divide the spoil,
      I will glut my appetite upon them;
      I will draw my sword,
      I will rid myself of them."
Thou didst blow with thy blast; the sea covered them.
They sank like lead in the swelling waves.
    Who is like thee, O Lord, among the gods?
    Who is like thee, majestic in holiness,
    worthy of awe and praise, who workest wonders?
      Thou didst stretch out thy right hand,
      earth engulfed them.
In thy constant love thou hast led the people
      whom thou didst ransom:

thou hast guided them by thy strength
 to thy holy dwelling place.
Nations heard and trembled;
 agony seized the dwellers in Philistia.
Then the chieftains of Edom were dismayed,
 trembling seized the leaders of Moab,
all the inhabitants of Canaan were in turmoil;
 terror and dread fell upon them:
through the might of thy arm they stayed stone-still,
 while thy people passed, O Lord,
while the people whom thou madest thy own passed by.
Thou broughtest them in and didst plant them
 in the mount that is thy possession,
 the dwelling place, O Lord, of thy own making,
the sanctuary, O Lord, which thy own hands prepared.
 The Lord shall reign for ever and for ever.

For Pharaoh's horse, both chariots and cavalry, went into the sea, and the Lord brought back the waters over them, but Israel had passed through the sea on dry ground. And Miriam the prophetess, Aaron's sister, took up her tambourine, and all the women followed her, dancing to the sound of tambourines; and Miriam sang them this refrain:

Sing to the Lord, for he has risen up in triumph;
the horse and his rider he has hurled into the sea.

EXODUS 12 : 37–42, 50–51; 13 : 1–3, 13–22; 14; 15 : 1–21

What does the Lord demand of the Israelites for leading them out of Egypt? In what way is it similar to, yet different from, the price he exacts from the Egyptians?

What signs accompany the Israelites on their journey?

The words *redeem*, *deliver*, and *ransom* are crucial to the Exodus story. Why?

Didn't Old Pharaoh
Get Lost?

1. I - saac, a ran-som while he lay up-on an al-tar
2. Jo - seph by his false breth-ren sold, God raised a-bove them
3. The Lord said un-to Mo - - ses, "Go un-to Pha-raoh

1. bound; Mo - ses, an in-fant cast a-way, by
2. all; to Han-nah's child the Lord fore-told how
3. now, for I have hard-ened Pha-raoh's heart; to

1. Pha - raoh's daugh-ter found:
2. E - li's house should fall: } Did not old Pha-raoh get
3. me he will not bow":

lost, get lost, get lost? Did not old Pha-raoh get lost in the Red Sea?

4. Then Moses and Aaron,
   To Pharaoh did go,
   "Thus says the God of Israel,
   Let my people go."
   CHORUS—Didn't, etc.

5. Old Pharaoh said, "Who is the Lord
   That I should obey him?"
   "His name it is Jehovah,
   For he hears his people pray."
   CHORUS—Didn't, etc.

6. Hark! hear the children murmur,
   They cry aloud for bread.
   Down came the hidden manna,
   The hungry soldiers fed.
   CHORUS—Didn't, etc.

7. Then Moses numbered Israel,
   Through all the land abroad,
   Saying, "Children, do not murmur,
   But hear the word of God."
   CHORUS—Didn't, etc.

8. Then Moses said to Israel,
   As they stood along the Shore,
   "Your enemies you see today,
   You'll never see no more."
   CHORUS—Didn't, etc.

9. Then down came raging Pharaoh,
   That you may plainly see,
   Old Pharaoh and his host
   Got lost in the Red Sea.
   CHORUS—Didn't, etc.

10. The men and women and children,
    To Moses they did flock;
    They cried aloud for water,
    And Moses smote the rock.
    CHORUS—Didn't, etc.

11. And the Lord spoke to Moses,
    From Sinai's smoking top,
    Saying, "Moses, lead the people,
    Till I shall bid you stop."
    CHORUS—Didn't, etc.

Knowing that this song is a Negro spiritual, can you tell what much later historical situation of an enslaved people is being used here as a correspondence to the Egyptian bondage? What other biblical correspondences occur in the song? What, then, does a "Pharaoh" symbolize?

Echod mi yodayeh

(variations on a song of the Passover Feast)

Who knows one?

    I, Moses, I! With my
    bush and my bulrush
    Nile-cradle, my black
    Midianite woman they despised, who made
    the golden calf; I, half
    meek, half red rage, a face
    lit once with Lordlight.
                       With my
    age, with my rod
    one man who found the way of the
    one God;

Who knows two?

    Ask the hills
    where the stone sleeps, the sand
    sifting in Babylonian gardens, the Hand
    that made the Tables;

Who knows three?

    I, dreaming among thickets in Ur
    called Abraham, a woolgatherer
    Godgathered; the arm of my crook
    first shaped the rivercrossed
    People of the Book;

    My father would have cut my throat
    for God's sake! but God found a goat
    go-between, and a skin
    of such a sacrificial animal served my
    son to commit sin;

Forget I cheated my brother
and my blind father. I
wrestled with the angel until
holy halfman, he crimped me in the groin and
marked me with the race, Israel;

Who knows four?

I, Sarai,
surnamed Princess
sister and bride
barren till pride
and veiled beauty withered
and my tongue knew the bitter:

                                    I conceived;
You know me with my pitcher by the well
in the last livid weather of the sun
a bearer of warring twins, the one
wife of Isaac and the happiest
woman in all that Chronicle;
shameless, I favored Jacob, so
loving the smooth of his neck I laid
goatskin upon it, that Isaac gave him
his blessing, blind;

Leah, a whisper in the night,
humbled, I yet pulled Jacob against me
hornhanded between furrow and evening light;

I, Rachel; patience. I
know fourteen better than four,
biting my tongue, bore
Joseph and the other
I would have named Ben-oni,
a child of sorrow, the bald
truth of everything, only he
over my dying breath called
him Benjamin;

Who knows five?

Genesis, Exodus, Leviticus
Numbers and Deuteronomy
blinking in black ink with bickering
dot and diamond, oxhead
Aleph and longtailed Lamed written
on scroll, wound on wood, bound
in velvet with silver stars and bars
blessing and burden borne on the rolled
shoulder of the Rabbi

safe now in the
sanctuary of living Zion;

Who knows six?

God knows who once cried
GIVE ME BACK MY LAW
being angry at Israel
and stood aghast how it came pouring in
scroll upon scroll gold
tassel and silver tag volume
and folio
            (remember this paper bulwark
for the drytongued
whispers of old men under the swordrack
curse and clatter of Roman legionaries):

of
the scatter of seed in
land and Mankind, hand-
washing sin-offering, the
rending of garment in repentance, oil
of unction festival of light
the right of the Prince and the choice
of the wise judge . . .
                        till He sat
weary among the cherubim having
at last the checkered pavements of Heaven
no place to lay His foot;

Who knows seven?

The maker of wine wax and braided
bread and the blackcapped cheder-boy who
sings the blessing with his father. I light
candles I hardly believe in, but I
hate to see them gutter and blink out;

Who knows eight?

Father, husband and son marked
with Abraham's covenant accept
with the knife and the wine, skullcap
prayershawl and phylacteries sometimes
spittle and a yellow badge, bread
from the earth, rainbows, Leviathan
and all piebald qualities of Mankind;

Who knows nine?

I know nine. Between
conception and parturition I held
the life, first trembling then strangely
turbulent

till he broke from me through red
rings of pain and with a rumpsmacked yell
declared himself in the firmament

beside me, a stranger
unique in Creation;

Who knows ten?

Certainly Rabbi Hillel. Shammai perhaps who
when the would-be proselyte jeered:
Repeat to me the body of your Law
while I am standing on one foot and I will
worship your God—
sent him

in anger to the rival. Hillel only
replied: From Ten and Two
I give you One: *Howsoever you would have men do to you
do unto them.* That is the Law;
the rest is Commentary;

Who knows eleven?

I, Joseph, a rather sharp
but innocent young man (ask
Potiphar's wife), a go-getter and goat-
sitter in a patched coat
dreamer of sheaves and stars, uneasy
prison comfort of butler and
baker waiting for the head-
chopper, having offended Pharaoh
                                    —I don't know why
though Rashi says he found a fly
floating in his wine
and sawdust in his bread;

Who knows twelve?

Firstborn Reuben fickle
as water Simeon Priest-Levi
savage in sweat and beardcurl the lion
Judah a company
marked with faces of four mothers and heavenly
prophecy Zebulun at seahaven Issachar
burdened the serpent wisdom of Dan
Gad in the strength of a tough
soldier rough-hand oily-nose a clamor
hoarse-voiced at the bed of Jacob
Asher binding sheaves under the hart's leap
of Naphtali Joseph his son-tribes Ephraim and Manasseh

and Benjamin, the issue
of patience and old age,
a child of sorrow;

Who knows thirteen?

Moses Maimonides, a healer of men
declared the Lord the vast
unchanging first and last
Creator of all.
If he had known the spiral
nebula in Andromeda, perhaps
he would have composed a
blessing upon the sight of it; if
he had known the infinitesimal seed-
breaker, the maker of mushroom clouds, perhaps
he would have turned his face to the wall
but not away from God.

Thirteen are the attributes of Divinity
Twelve are the Tribes of Israel
Eleven are the stars of Joseph's dream
Ten are the Commandments
Nine are the months of pregnancy
Eight are the days of Circumcision
Seven are the days of Sabbath-count
Six are the Laws of the Mishnah
Five are the Books of the Torah
Four are the Mothers
Three are the Fathers
Two are the Tables of the Commandments
and
One is our God in Heaven and on Earth.

PHYLLIS GOTLIEB

The title of this poem translates from the Hebrew as "Who knows one?"

The following information may help you to reread this poem with greater understanding. This is a poem that repays reading many times. The first five books of the Bible, the Pentateuch, make up the books of the Torah which are carefully kept in the Ark in every Jewish synagogue. Aleph and Lamed are letters of the Hebrew alphabet. Mishnah means tradition. At first the Mishnah was passed on orally but by the second century A.D. it was written down. The German Nazis made Jews wear a yellow Star of David during World War II.

What event does this poem celebrate? How has the poet used numbers in her celebration? Why does Rachel know fourteen better than four?

What are some of the "piebald qualities of mankind" that this poem celebrates?

How did Rabbi Hillel reduce the ten commandments on the two tablets to one law?

How does this author characterize the twelve tribes of Israel?

Moses Maimonides was a famous and learned Jewish scholar. What did he know? Who is the "maker of mushroom clouds"? What would Maimonides have done had he known of such things?

"I light candles I hardly believe in . . ." Discuss this statement in light of the poem as a whole.

I Will Rain Down
Bread from Heaven

The Israelites complained to Moses and Aaron in the wilderness and said, "If only we had died at the Lord's hand in Egypt, where we sat round the fleshpots and had plenty of bread to eat! But you have brought us out into this wilderness to let this whole assembly starve to death." The Lord said to Moses, "I will rain down bread from heaven for you. Each day the people shall go out and gather a day's supply, so that I can put them to the test and see whether they will follow my instructions or not. But on the sixth day, when they prepare what they bring in, it shall be twice as much as they have gathered on other days." Moses and Aaron then said to all the Israelites, "In the evening you will know that it was the Lord who brought you out of Egypt, and in the morning you will see the glory of the Lord, because he has heeded your complaints against him; it is not against us that you bring your complaints; we are nothing." "You shall know this," Moses said, "when the Lord, in answer to your complaints, gives you flesh to eat in the evening, and in the morning bread in plenty. What are we? It is against the Lord that you bring your complaints, and not against us."

Moses told Aaron to say to the whole community of Israel, "Come into the presence of the Lord, for he has heeded your complaints." While Aaron was speaking to the community of the Israelites, they looked toward the wilderness, and there was the glory of the Lord appearing in the cloud. The Lord spoke to Moses and said, "I have heard the complaints of the Israelites. Say to them, 'Between dusk and dark you will have flesh to eat and in the morning bread in plenty. You shall know that I the Lord am your God.' "

That evening a flock of quails flew in and settled all over the camp, and in the morning a fall of dew lay all around it. When the dew was gone, there in the wilderness, fine flakes appeared, fine as hoar frost on the ground. When the Israelites saw it, they said to one another, "What is that?" because they did not know what it was. Moses said to them, "That is the bread which the Lord has given you to eat. This is the command the Lord has given: 'Each of you is to gather as much as he can eat: let every man take an omer a head for every person in his tent.' " The Israelites did this, and they gathered, some more, some less, but when they measured it by the omer, those who had gathered more had not too much, and those who had gathered less had not too little. Each had just as much as he could eat. Moses said, "No one may keep any of it till morning." Some, however, did not listen to Moses; they kept part of it till morning, and it became full of maggots and stank, and Moses was angry with them. Each morning every man gathered as much as he could eat, and when the sun grew hot, it melted away. On the sixth day they gathered twice as much food, two omers each. All the chiefs of the community came and told Moses. "This," he answered, "is what the Lord has said: 'Tomorrow is a day of sacred rest, a sabbath holy to the Lord.' So bake what you want to bake now, and boil what you want to boil; put aside what remains over and keep it safe till morning." So they put it aside till morning as Moses had commanded, and it did not stink, nor did maggots appear in it. "Eat it today," said Moses, "because today is a sabbath of the Lord. Today you will find none outside. For six days you may gather it, but on the seventh day, the sabbath, there will be none."

Some of the people did go out to gather it on the seventh day, but they found none. The Lord said to Moses, "How long will you refuse to obey my commands and instructions? The Lord has given you the sabbath, and so he gives you two days' food every sixth day. Let each man stay where he is; no one may stir from his home on the seventh day." And the people kept the sabbath on the seventh day.

Israel called the food manna; it was white, like coriander seed, and it tasted like a wafer made with honey.

"This," said Moses, "is the command which the Lord has given: 'Take a full omer of it to be kept for future generations, so that they may see the bread with which I fed you in the wilderness when I brought you out of Egypt.' " So Moses said to Aaron, "Take a jar and fill it with an omer of manna, and store it in the presence of the Lord to be kept for future generations." Aaron did as the Lord had commanded Moses, and stored it before the Testimony for safe keeping. The Israelites ate the manna for forty years until they came to a land where they could settle; they ate it until they came to the border of Canaan. (An omer is one tenth of an ephah.)

The whole community of Israel set out from the wilderness of Sin and traveled by stages as the Lord told them. They encamped at

Rephidim, where there was no water for the people to drink, and a dispute arose between them and Moses. When they said, "Give us water to drink," Moses said, "Why do you dispute with me? Why do you challenge the Lord?" There the people became so thirsty that they raised an outcry against Moses: "Why have you brought us out of Egypt with our children and our herds to let us all die of thirst?" Moses cried to the Lord, "What shall I do with these people? In a moment they will be stoning me." The Lord answered, "Go forward ahead of the people; take with you some of the elders of Israel and the staff with which you struck the Nile, and go. You will find me waiting for you there, by a rock in Horeb. Strike the rock; water will pour out of it, and the people shall drink." Moses did this in the sight of the elders of Israel. He named the place Massah and Meribah, because the Israelites had disputed with him and challenged the Lord with their question, "Is the Lord in our midst or not?"

EXODUS 16 : 2–36; 17 : 1–7

What had rained down on three other groups earlier in the Bible narrative?

What new kind of correspondence is suggested here?

Where else has the number 40 had great significance? What is its meaning in this story?

For the biblical writers the "bread of heaven" and the water from the rock are symbols of God's mercy. What symbolic action do the Israelites perform with a token portion of manna?

WHO IS ON THE LORD'S SIDE?

You'll Be a Witness for the Lord

1. Mo - ses was a man of God; God called Mo - ses from the
2. "Mo - ses, Mo - ses, come and see; I'll tell you what you can
3. Mo - ses down in E - gypt Land sung and prayed___ for___

1. burn - ing bush: "Go on down___ in___ E - gypt's land and
2. do for me: I want you to let them i - dols a - lone and
3. wick - ed man. Hav - ing God___ at___ his right hand, he

1. bring my chil - dren out of Pha - raoh's hand. And
2. place my law _ up - on the ta - bles of stone. And
3. brought the chil - dren out of Pha - raoh's land. And

1. you'll be a wit - ness for the Lord; and you'll be a wit - ness
2. you'll be a wit - ness for the Lord; and you'll be a wit - ness
3. Mo - ses was a wit - ness for the Lord; and Mo - ses was a wit - ness

1. for the Lord; and you'll be a wit-ness for the Lord; and
2. for the Lord; and you'll be a wit-ness for the Lord; and
3. for the Lord; and Mo-ses was a wit-ness for the Lord; and

1. you'll be a wit - ness for the Lord!"
2. you'll be a wit - ness for the Lord!"
3. Mo-ses was a wit - ness for the Lord!

4. When my soul is burden' down,
   I ask the Lord to turn my life around.
   The Lord washed all my sins away;
   He taught me how to watch and pray.
   CHORUS—My soul was a witness for the Lord (etc.)

5. Just about the time I thought I was lost,
   My dungeon shook and my chains fell off;
   Yes, just about the time I thought I was lost,
   My dungeon shook and my chains fell off.
   CHORUS—My soul was a witness for the Lord (etc.)

Who are the two witnesses for the Lord in this song? Where, in Chapter One, did we meet the second one?

What is the connection between being "turned around" and having "chains fall off"?

Israel at
Mount Sinai

In the third month after Israel had left Egypt, they came to the wilderness of Sinai. They set out from Rephidim and entered the wilderness of Sinai, where they encamped, pitching their tents opposite the mountain. Moses went up the mountain of God, and the Lord called to him from the mountain and said, "Speak thus to the house of Jacob, and tell this to the sons of Israel: You have seen with your own eyes what I did to Egypt, and how I have carried you on eagles' wings and brought you here to me. If only you will now listen to me and keep my covenant, then out of all peoples you shall become my special possession; for the whole earth is mine. You shall be my kingdom of priests, my holy nation. These are the words you shall speak to the Israelites."

Moses came and summoned the elders of the people and set before them all these commands which the Lord had laid upon him. The people all answered together, "Whatever the Lord has said we will do." Moses brought this answer back to the Lord. The Lord said to Moses, "I am now coming to you in a thick cloud, so that I may speak to you in the hearing of the people, and their faith in you may never fail." Moses told the Lord what the people had said, and the Lord said to him, "Go to the people and hallow them today and tomorrow and make them wash their clothes. They must be ready by the third day, because on the third day the Lord will descend upon Mount Sinai in the sight of all the people. You must put barriers round the mountain and say, 'Take care not to go up the mountain or even to touch the edge of it.' Any man who touches the mountain must be put to death. No hand shall touch him; he shall be stoned or shot dead: neither man nor beast may live. But when the ram's horn sounds, they may go up the mountain." Moses came down from the mountain to the people. He hallowed them and they washed their clothes. He said to the people, "Be ready by the third day; do not go near a woman." On the third day, when morning came, there were peals of thunder and flashes of lightning, dense cloud on the mountain and a loud trumpet blast; the people in the camp were all terrified.

Moses brought the people out from the camp to meet God, and they took their stand at the foot of the mountain. Mount Sinai was all smoking because the Lord had come down upon it in fire; the smoke went up like the smoke of a kiln; all the people were terrified, and the sound of the trumpet grew ever louder. Whenever Moses spoke, God answered him in a peal of thunder. The Lord came down upon the top of Mount Sinai and summoned Moses to the mountaintop, and Moses went up. The Lord said to Moses, "Go down; warn the people solemnly that they must not force their way through to the Lord to see him, or many of them will perish. Even the priests, who have access to the Lord, must hallow themselves, for fear that the Lord may break out against them." Moses answered the Lord, "The people cannot come up Mount Sinai, because thou thyself didst solemnly warn us to set a barrier to the mountain and so to keep it holy." The Lord therefore said to him, "Go down; then come up and bring Aaron with you, but let neither priests nor people force their way up to the Lord, for fear that he may break out against them." So Moses went down to the people and spoke to them.

God spoke, and these were his words:

I am the Lord your God who brought you out of Egypt, out of the land of slavery.

You shall have no other god to set against me.

You shall not make a carved image for yourself nor the likeness of anything in the heavens above, or on the earth below, or in the waters under the earth.

You shall not bow down to them or worship them; for I, the Lord your God, am a jealous god. I punish the children for the sins of the fathers to the third and fourth generations of those who hate me. But I keep faith with thousands, with those who love me and keep my commandments.

You shall not make wrong use of the name of the Lord your God; the Lord will not leave unpunished the man who misuses his name.

Remember to keep the sabbath day holy. You have six days to labor and do all your work. But the seventh day is a sabbath of the Lord your God; that day you shall not do any work, you, your son or your daughter, your slave or your slave girl, your cattle or the alien within your gates; for in six days the Lord made heaven and earth, the sea, and all that is in them, and on the seventh day he rested. Therefore the Lord blessed the sabbath day and declared it holy.

Honor your father and your mother, that you may live long in the land which the Lord your God is giving you.

You shall not commit murder.

You shall not commit adultery.

You shall not steal.

You shall not give false evidence against your neighbor.

You shall not covet your neighbor's house; you shall not covet your neighbor's wife, his slave, his slave girl, his ox, his ass, or anything that belongs to him.

When all the people saw how it thundered and the lightning flashed, when they heard the trumpet sound and saw the mountain smoking, they trembled and stood at a distance. "Speak to us yourself," they said to Moses, "and we will listen; but if God speaks to us we shall die." Moses answered, "Do not be afraid. God has come only to test you, so that the fear of him may remain with you and keep you from sin." So the people stood at a distance, while Moses approached the dark cloud where God was.

Then [God] said to Moses, "Come up to the Lord, you and Aaron, Nadab and Abihu, and seventy of the elders of Israel. While you are still at a distance, you are to bow down; and then Moses shall approach the Lord by himself, but not the others. The people may not go up with him at all."

Moses came and told the people all the words of the Lord, all his laws. The whole people answered with one voice and said, "We will do all that the Lord has told us." Moses wrote down all the words of the Lord. He rose early in the morning and built an altar at the foot of the mountain, and put up twelve sacred pillars, one for each of the twelve tribes of Israel. He then sent the young men of Israel and they sacrificed bulls to the Lord as whole-offerings and shared-offerings. Moses took half the blood and put it in basins and the other half he flung against the altar. Then he took the book of the covenant and read it aloud for all the people to hear. They said, "We will obey, and do all that the Lord has said." Moses then took the blood and flung it over the people, saying, "This is the blood of the covenant which the Lord has made with you on the terms of this book."

Moses went up with Aaron, Nadab and Abihu, and seventy of the elders of Israel, and they saw the God of Israel. Under his feet there

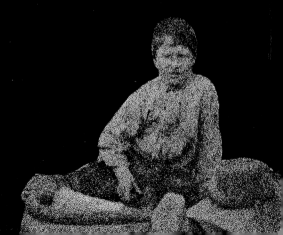

was, as it were, a pavement of sapphire, clear blue as the very heavens; but the Lord did not stretch out his hand toward the leaders of Israel. They stayed there before God; they ate and they drank. The Lord said to Moses, "Come up to me on the mountain, stay there and let me give you the tablets of stone, the law and the commandment, which I have written down that you may teach them." Moses arose with Joshua his assistant and went up the mountain of God; he said to the elders, "Wait for us here until we come back to you. You have Aaron and Hur; if anyone has a dispute, let him go to them." So Moses went up the mountain and a cloud covered it. The glory of the Lord rested upon Mount Sinai, and the cloud covered the mountain for six days; on the seventh day he called to Moses out of the cloud. The glory of the Lord looked to the Israelites like a devouring fire on the mountain-top. Moses entered the cloud and went up the mountain; there he stayed forty days and forty nights.

EXODUS 19; 20 : 1–21; 24

The word *Sinai* means "cliffs." Mount Sinai lies between the Gulfs of Suez and Akaba. It has three large peaks, one of which is called Horeb. How does the mountain play a part in the ceremony enacted there? What natural elements is the Lord identified with here?

Of the Ten Commandments which the Lord spoke to Moses, which seems to you the most important?

What sacrificial offering is made? Why?

When the elders of Israel "saw" God, what architectural image was very impressive to them? What symbol of paradise other than a garden is suggested by this image?

The Golden
Calf

When the people saw that Moses was so long in coming down from the mountain, they confronted Aaron and said to him, "Come, make us gods to go ahead of us. As for this fellow Moses, who brought us up from Egypt, we do not know what has become of him." Aaron answered them, "Strip the gold rings from the ears of your wives and daughters, and bring them to me." So all the people stripped themselves of their gold earrings and brought them to Aaron. He took them out of their hands, cast the metal in a mold, and made it into the image of a bull calf. "These," he said, "are your gods, O Israel, that brought you up from Egypt." Then Aaron was afraid and built an altar in front of it and issued this proclamation, "Tomorrow there is to be a pilgrim feast to the Lord." Next day the people rose early, offered whole-offerings, and brought shared-offerings. After this they sat down to eat and drink and then gave themselves up to revelry. But the Lord said to Moses, "Go down at once, for your people, the people you brought up from Egypt, have done a disgraceful thing; so quickly have they turned aside from the way I commanded them. They have made themselves an image of a bull calf, they have prostrated themselves before it, sacrificed to it and said, 'These are your gods, O Israel, that brought you up from Egypt.'" So the Lord said to Moses, "I have considered this people, and I see that they are a stubborn people. Now, let me alone to vent my anger upon them, so that I may put an end to them and make a great nation spring from you." But Moses set himself to placate the Lord his God: "O Lord," he said, "why shouldst thou vent thy anger upon thy people, whom thou didst bring out of Egypt with great power and a strong hand? Why let the Egyptians say, 'So he meant evil when he took them out, to kill them in the mountains and wipe them off the face of the earth'? Turn from thy anger, and think better of the evil thou dost intend against thy people. Remember Abraham, Isaac, and Israel, thy servants, to whom thou didst swear by thy own self: 'I will make your posterity countless as the stars in the sky, and all this land, of which I have spoken, I will give to them, and they shall possess it forever.'" So the Lord relented, and spared his people the evil with which he had threatened them.

Moses turned and went down the mountain with the two tablets of the Tokens in his hands, inscribed on both sides; on the front and on the back they were inscribed. The tablets were the handiwork of God, and the writing was God's writing, engraved on the tablets. Joshua, hearing the uproar the people were making, said to Moses, "Listen! There is fighting in the camp." Moses replied,

> "This is not the clamor of warriors,
> nor the clamor of a defeated people;
> it is the sound of singing that I hear."

As he approached the camp, Moses saw the bull calf and the dancing, and he was angry; he flung the tablets down, and they were shattered to pieces at the foot of the mountain. Then he took the calf they had made and burned it; he ground it to powder, sprinkled it on water, and made the Israelites drink it. He demanded of Aaron, "What did this people do to you that you should have brought such great guilt upon them?" Aaron replied, "Do not be angry, sir. The people were deeply troubled; that you well know. And they said to me, 'Make us gods to go ahead of us, because, as for this fellow Moses, who brought us up from Egypt, we do not know what has become of him.' So I said to them, 'Those of you who have any gold, strip it off.' They gave it to me, I threw it in the fire, and out came this bull calf." Moses saw that the people were out of control and that Aaron had laid them open to the secret malice of their enemies. He took his place at the gate of the camp and said, "Who is on the Lord's side? Come here to me"; and the Levites all rallied to him. Then he said to them, "These are the words of the Lord the God of Israel: 'Arm yourselves, each of you, with his sword. Go through the camp from gate to gate and back again. Each of you kill his brother, his friend, his neighbor.'" The Levites obeyed, and about three thousand of the people died that day. Moses then said, "Today you have consecrated yourselves to the Lord completely, because you have turned each against his own son and his own brother and so have this day brought a blessing upon yourselves."

The next day Moses said to the people, "You have committed a great sin. I shall now go up to the Lord; perhaps I may be able to secure pardon for your sin." So Moses returned to the Lord and said, "O hear me! This people has committed a great sin: they have made themselves gods of gold. If thou wilt forgive them, forgive. But if not, blot out my name, I pray, from thy book which thou hast written." The Lord answered Moses, "It is the man who has sinned against me that I will blot out from my book. But go now, lead the people to the place which I have told you of. My angel shall go ahead of you, but a day will come when I shall punish them for their sin." And the Lord smote the people for worshiping the bull calf which Aaron had made.

The Lord spoke to Moses: "Come, go up from here, you and the people you have brought up from Egypt, to the land which I swore to Abraham, Isaac, and Jacob that I would give to their posterity. I will send an angel ahead of you, and will drive out the Canaanites, the Amorites and the Hittites and the Perizzites, the Hivites and the Jebusites. I will bring you to a land flowing with milk and honey, but I will not journey in your company, for fear that I annihilate you on the way; for you are a stubborn people." When the people heard this harsh sentence they went about like mourners, and no man put on his ornaments. The Lord said to Moses, "Tell the Israelites, 'You are a stubborn people: at any moment, if I journey in your company, I may annihilate you. Put away your ornaments now, and I will determine what to do to you.'" And so the Israelites stripped off their ornaments, and wore them no more from Mount Horeb onward.

EXODUS 32; 33:1–6

Which of the Ten Commandments had Moses' "stubborn" people broken in his absence? How does Moses manage to soften God's anger? Of which earlier patriarch are you reminded?

Fear turned the Israelites to seek a different, older god, and in retaliation Moses ordered the Levites to turn against brother, friend, and neighbor, and kill. How can this killing be seen as a sacrifice? A vision of his people's destiny made Moses order such a holy war. What is Moses' vision? Is individual life often considered less valuable than the survival of a whole society?

The Fairy Goose

An old woman named Mary Wiggins got three goose eggs from a neighbor in order to hatch a clutch of goslings. She put an old clucking hen over the eggs in a wooden box with a straw bed. The hen proved to be a bad sitter. She was continually deserting the eggs, possibly because they were too big. The old woman then kept her shut up in the box. Either through weariness, want of air or simply pure devilment, the hen died on the eggs, two days before it was time for the shells to break.

The old woman shed tears of rage, both at the loss of her hen, of which she was particularly fond, and through fear of losing her goslings. She put the eggs near the fire in the kitchen, wrapped up in straw and old clothes. Two days afterward, one of the eggs broke and a tiny gosling put out its beak. The other two eggs proved not to be fertile. They were thrown away.

The little gosling was a scraggy thing, so small and so delicate that the old woman, out of pity for it, wanted to kill it. But her husband said: "Kill nothing that is born in your house, woman alive. It's against the law of God."

"It's a true saying, my honest fellow," said the old woman. "What comes into the world is sent by God. Praised be he."

For a long time it seemed certain that the gosling was on the point of death. It spent all the day on the hearth in the kitchen nestling among the peat ashes, either sleeping or making little tweeky noises. When it was offered food, it stretched out its beak and pecked without rising off its stomach. Gradually, however, it became hardier and went out of doors to sit in the sun, on a flat rock. When it was three months it was still a yellowish color with soft down, even though other goslings of that age in the village were already going to the pond with the flock and able to flap their wings and join in the cackle at evening time, when the setting sun was being saluted. The little gosling was not aware of the other geese, even though it saw them rise on windy days and fly with a great noise from their houses to the pond. It made no effort to become a goose, and at four months of age it still could not stand on one leg.

The old woman came to believe that it was a fairy. The village women agreed with her after some dispute. It was decided to tie pink and red ribbons around the gosling's neck and to sprinkle holy water on its wing feathers.

That was done and then the gosling became sacred in the village. No boy dare throw a stone at it, or pull a feather from its wing, as they were in the habit of doing with geese, in order to get masts for the pieces of cork they floated in the pond as ships. When it began to move about, every house gave it dainty things. All the human beings in the village paid more respect to it than they did to one another. The little gosling had contracted a great affection for Mary Wiggins and followed her round everywhere, so that Mary Wiggins also came to have the reputation of being a woman of wisdom. Dreams were brought to her for unraveling. She was asked to set the spell of the Big Periwinkle and to tie the Knot of the Snakes on the sides of sick cows. And when children were ill, the gosling was brought secretly at night and led three times around the house on a thin halter of horsehair.

When the gosling was a year old it had not yet become a goose. Its down was still slightly yellowish. It did not cackle, but made curious tweeky noises. Instead of stretching out its neck and hissing at strangers, after the manner of a proper goose, it put its head to one side and made funny noises like a duck. It meditated like a hen, was afraid of water, and cleansed itself by rolling on the grass. It fed on bread, fish, and potatoes. It drank milk and tea. It amused itself by collecting pieces of cloth, nails, small fish-bones, and the limpet-shells that are thrown in a heap beside dung hills. These pieces of refuse it placed in a pile to the left of Mary Wiggins's door. And when the pile was tall, it made a sort of nest in the middle of it and lay in the nest.

Old Mrs. Wiggins had by now realized that the goose was worth money to her. So she became firmly convinced that the goose was gifted with supernatural powers. She accepted, in return for setting spells, a yard of white frieze cloth for unraveling dreams, a pound of sugar for setting the spell of the Big Periwinkle and half a donkey's load of potatoes for tying the Knot of the Snakes on a sick cow's side. Hitherto a kindly, humorous woman, she took to wearing her shawl in triangular fashion, with the tip of it reaching to her heels. She talked to herself or to her goose as she went along the road. She took long steps like a goose and rolled her eyes occasionally. When she cast a spell she went into an ecstasy, during which she made inarticulate sounds, like "boum, roum, toum, kroum."

Soon it became known all over the countryside that there was a woman of wisdom and a fairy goose in the village, and pilgrims came secretly from afar, at the dead of night, on the first night of the new moon, or when the spring tide had begun to wane.

The men soon began to raise their hats passing old Mary Wiggins's house, for it was understood, owing to the cure of Dara Foddy's cow, that the goose was indeed a good fairy and not a malicious one. Such was the excitement in the village and all over the countryside, that what was kept secret so long at last reached the ears of the parish priest.

The story was brought to him by an old woman from a neighboring village to that in which the goose lived. Before the arrival of the goose, the other old woman had herself cast spells, not through her own merits but through those of her dead mother, who had a long time ago been the woman of wisdom in the district. The priest mounted his horse as soon as he heard the news and galloped at a breakneck speed toward Mary Wiggins's house, carrying his breviary and his stole. When he arrived in the village he dismounted at a distance from the house, gave his horse to a boy, and put his stole around his neck.

A number of the villagers gathered and some tried to warn Mary Wiggins by whistling at a distance, but conscious that they had all taken part in something forbidden by the sacred laws of orthodox religion, they were afraid to run ahead of the priest into the house. Mary Wiggins and her husband were within, making little ropes of brown horsehair which they sold as charms.

Outside the door, perched on her high nest, the little goose was sitting. There were pink and red ribbons around her neck and around her legs there were bands of black tape. She was quite small, a little more than half the size of a normal, healthy goose. But she had an elegant charm of manner, an air of civilization, and a consciousness of great dignity, which had grown out of the love and respect of the villagers.

When she saw the priest approach, she began to cackle gently, making the tweeky noise that was peculiar to her. She descended from her perch and waddled toward him, expecting some dainty gift. But instead of stretching out his hand to offer her something and saying, "Beadai, beadai, come here," as was customary, the priest halted and muttered something in a harsh, frightened voice. He became red in the face and he took off his hat.

Then for the first time in her life the little goose became terrified. She opened her beak, spread her wings and lowered her head. She began to hiss violently. Turning around, she waddled back to her nest, flapping her wings and raising a loud cackle, just like a goose, although she had never been heard to cackle loudly like a goose before. Clambering up on her high nest, she lay there, quite flat, trembling violently.

The bird, never having known fear of human beings, never having been treated with discourtesy, was so violently moved by the extraordinary phenomenon of a man wearing black clothes, scowling at her and muttering, that her animal nature was roused and showed itself with disgusting violence.

The people watching this scene were astonished. Some took off their caps and crossed themselves. For some reason it was made manifest to them that the goose was an evil spirit and not the good fairy which they had supposed her to be. Terrified of the priest's stole and of his breviary and of his scowling countenance, they were only too eager to attribute the goose's strange hissing and her still stranger cackle to supernatural forces of an evil nature. Some present even caught a faint rumble of thunder in the east, and although it was not noticed at the time, an old woman later asserted that she heard a great cackle of geese afar off, raised in answer to the fairy goose's cackle.

"It was," said the old woman, "certainly the whole army of devils offering her help to kill the holy priest."

The priest turned to the people and cried, raising his right hand in a threatening manner:

"I wonder the ground doesn't open up and swallow you all. Idolaters!"

"O father, blessed by the hand of God," cried an old woman, the one who later asserted she had heard the devilish cackle afar off. She threw herself on her knees in the road, crying: "Spare us, father."

Old Mrs. Wiggins, having heard the strange noises, rushed out into the yard with her triangular shawl trailing and her black hair loose. She began to make vague, mystic movements with her hands, as had recently become a habit with her. Lost in some sort of ecstasy, she did not see the priest at first. She began to chant something.

"You hag," cried the priest, rushing up the yard toward her menacingly.

The old woman caught sight of him and screamed. But she faced him boldly.

"Come no farther," she cried, still in an ecstasy, either affected, or the result of a firm belief in her own mystic powers.

Indeed, it is difficult to believe that she was not in earnest, for she used to be a kind, gentle woman.

Her husband rushed out, crying aloud. Seeing the priest, he dropped a piece of rope he had in his hand and fled around the corner of the house.

"Leave my way, you hag," cried the priest, raising his hand to strike her.

"Stand back," she cried. "Don't lay a hand on my goose."

"Leave my way," yelled the priest, "or I'll curse you."

"Curse, then," cried the unfortunate woman. "Curse!"

Instead, the priest gave her a blow under the ear, which felled her smartly. Then he strode up to the goose's nest and seized the goose. The goose, paralyzed with terror, was just able to open her beak and hiss at him. He stripped the ribbons off her neck and tore the tape off her feet. Then he threw her out of the nest. Seizing a spade that stood by the wall, he began to scatter the refuse of which the nest was composed.

The old woman, lying prostrate in the yard, raised her head and began to chant in the traditional fashion, used by the women of wisdom.

"I'll call on the winds of the east and of the west, I'll raise the winds of the sea. The lightning will flash in the sky and there'll be great sounds of giants warring in the heavens. Blight will fall on the earth and calves with fishes' tails will be born of cows . . . ."

The little goose, making tweeky noises, waddled over to the old woman and tried to hide herself under the long shawl. The people murmured at this, seeing in it fresh signs of devilry.

Then the priest threw down the spade and hauled the old woman to her feet, kicking aside the goose. The old woman, exhausted by her ecstasy and possibly seeking to gain popular support, either went into a faint or feigned one. Her hands and her feet hung limply. Again the people murmured. The priest, becoming embarrassed, put her sitting against the wall. Then he didn't know what to do, for his anger had exhausted his reason. He either became ashamed of having beaten an old woman, or he felt the situation was altogether ridiculous. So he raised his hand and addressed the people in a sorrowful voice.

"Let this be a warning," he said sadly. "This poor woman and . . . all of you, led astray by . . . foolish and . . . . Avarice is at the back of this," he cried suddenly in an angry voice, shaking his fist. "This woman has been preying on your credulity, in order to extort money from you by her pretended sorcery. That's all it is. Money is at the back of it. But I give you warning. If I hear another word about this, I'll . . . ."

He paused uncertainly, wondering what to threaten the poor people with. Then he added:

"I'll report it to the Archbishop of the diocese."

The people raised a loud murmur, asking forgiveness.

"Fear God," he added finally, "and love your neighbors."

Then, throwing a stone angrily at the goose, he strode out of the yard and left the village.

It was then the people began to curse violently and threaten to burn the old woman's house. The responsible people among them, however, chiefly those who had hitherto paid no respect to the superstition concerning the goose, restrained their violence. Finally the people went home and Mary Wiggins's husband, who had been hiding in a barn, came and brought his wife indoors. The little goose, uttering cries of amazement, began to collect the rubbish once more, piling it in a heap in order to rebuild her nest. That night, just after the moon had risen, a band of young men collected, approached Mary Wiggins's house and enticed the goose from her nest, by calling, "Beadai, beadai, come here, come here."

The little goose, delighted that people were again kind and respectful to her, waddled down to the gate, making happy noises.

The youths stoned her to death.

And the little goose never uttered a sound, so terrified and amazed was she at this treatment from people who had formerly loved her and whom she had never injured.

Next morning, when Mary Wiggins discovered the dead carcass of the goose, she went into a fit, during which she cursed the village, the priest, and all mankind.

And indeed it appeared that her blasphemous prayer took some effect at least. Although giants did not war in the heavens and though cows did not give birth to fishes, it is certain that from that day the natives of that village are quarrelsome drunkards, who fear God but do not love one another. And the old woman is again collecting followers from among the wives of the drunkards. These women maintain that the only time in the history of their generation that there was peace and harmony in the village was during the time when the fairy goose was loved by the people.

LIAM O'FLAHERTY

How are the Irish villagers in this short story, like the Israelites, "a stubborn people"? Is there a Moses figure in the story? What other actions and images connect with the Bible?

Wanderers in the Wilderness Forty Years

The Lord spoke to Moses and said, "Send men out to explore the land of Canaan which I am giving to the Israelites; from each of their fathers' tribes send one man, and let him be a man of high rank." So Moses sent them from the wilderness of Paran at the command of the Lord, all of them leading men among the Israelites. . . .

When Moses sent them to explore the land of Canaan, he said to them, "Make your way up by the Negeb, and go on into the hill country. See what the land is like, and whether the people who live there are strong or weak, few or many. See whether it is easy or difficult country in which they live, and whether the cities in which they live are weakly defended or well fortified; is the land fertile or barren, and does it grow trees or not? Go boldly in and take some of its fruit." It was the season when the first grapes were ripe.

They went up and explored the country from the wilderness of Zin as far as Rehob by Lebo-hamath. They went up by the Negeb and came to Hebron, where Ahiman, Sheshai, and Talmai, the descendants of Anak, were living. (Hebron was built seven years before Zoan in Egypt.) They came to the gorge of Eshcol, and there they cut a branch with a single bunch of grapes, and they carried it on a pole two at a time; they also picked pomegranates and figs. It was from the bunch of grapes which the Israelites cut there that the place was named the gorge of Eshcol. After forty days they returned from exploring the country, and came back to Moses and Aaron and the whole community of Israelites at Kadesh in the wilderness of Paran. They made their report to them and to the whole community, and showed them the fruit of the country. And this was the story they told Moses: "We made our way into the land to which you sent us. It is flowing with milk and honey, and here is the fruit it grows; but its inhabitants are sturdy, and the cities are very strongly fortified; indeed, we saw there the descendants of Anak. We also saw the Amalekites who live in the Negeb, Hittites, Jebusites, and Amorites who live in the hill country, and the Canaanites who live by the sea and along the Jordan."

Then Caleb called for silence before Moses and said, "Let us go up at once and occupy the country; we are well able to conquer it." But the men who had gone with him said, "No, we cannot attack these people; they are stronger than we are." Thus their report to the Israelites about the land which they had explored was discouraging: "The country we explored," they said, "will swallow up any who go to live in it. All the people we saw there are men of gigantic size. When we set eyes on the Nephilim (the sons of Anak belong to the Nephilim) we felt no bigger than grasshoppers; and that is how we looked to them."

Then the whole Israelite community cried out in dismay; all night long they wept. One and all they made complaints against Moses and Aaron: "If only we had died in Egypt or in the wilderness!" they said. "Far happier if we had! Why should the Lord bring us to this land, to die in battle and leave our wives and our dependents to become the spoils of war? To go back to Egypt would be better than this." And they began to talk of choosing someone to lead them back.

Then Moses and Aaron flung themselves on the ground before the assembled community of the Israelites, and two of those who had explored the land, Joshua son of Nun and Caleb son of Jephunneh, rent their clothes and addressed the whole community: "The country we penetrated and explored," they said, "is very good land indeed. If the Lord is pleased with us, he will bring us into this land which flows with milk and honey, and give it to us. But you must not rebel against the Lord. You need not fear the people of the land; for there we shall find food. They have lost the protection that they had: the Lord is with us. You have nothing to fear from them." But by way of answer the assembled Israelites threatened to stone them, when suddenly the glory of the Lord appeared to them all in the Tent of the Presence.

Then the Lord said to Moses, "How much longer will this people treat me with contempt? How much longer will they refuse to trust me in spite of all the signs I have shown among them? I will strike them with pestilence. I will deny them their heritage, and you and your descendants I will make into a nation greater and more numerous than they." But Moses answered the Lord, "What if the Egyptians hear of it? It was thou who didst bring this people out of Egypt by thy strength. What if they tell the inhabitants of this land? They too have heard of thee, Lord, that thou art with this people, and art seen face to face, that thy cloud stays over them, and thou goest before them in a pillar of cloud by day and in a pillar of fire by night. If then thou dost put them all to death at one blow, the nations who have heard these tales of thee will say, 'The Lord could not bring this people into the land which he promised them by oath; and so he destroyed them in the wilderness.'

"Now let the Lord's might be shown in its greatness, true to thy proclamation of thyself—'The Lord, long-suffering, ever constant, who forgives iniquity and rebellion, and punishes sons to the third and fourth generation for the iniquity of their fathers, though he does not sweep them clean away.' Thou hast borne with this people from Egypt all the way here; forgive their iniquity, I beseech thee, as befits thy great and constant love."

The Lord said, "Your prayer is answered; I pardon them. But as I live, in very truth the glory of the Lord shall fill the earth. Not one of all those who have seen my glory and the signs which I wrought in Egypt and in the wilderness shall see the country which I promised on oath to their fathers. Ten times they have challenged me and not obeyed my voice. None of those who have flouted me shall see this land. But my servant Caleb showed a different spirit: he followed me with his whole heart. Because of this, I will bring him into the land in which he has already set foot, the territory of the Amalekites and the Canaanites who dwell in the Vale, and put his descendants in possession of it. Tomorrow you must turn back and set out for the wilderness by way of the Red Sea."

The Lord spoke to Moses and Aaron and said, "How long must I tolerate the complaints of this wicked community? I have heard the Israelites making complaints against me. Tell them that this is the very word of the Lord: As I live, I will bring home to you the words I have heard you utter. Here in this wilderness your bones shall lie, every man of you on the register from twenty years old and upward, because you have made these complaints against me. Not one of you shall enter the land which I swore with uplifted hand should be your home, except only Caleb son of Jephunneh and Joshua son of Nun. As for your dependents, those dependents who, you said, would become the spoils of war, I will bring them in to the land you have rejected, and they shall enjoy it. But as for the rest of you, your bones shall lie in this wilderness; your sons shall be wanderers in the wilderness forty years, paying the penalty of your wanton disloyalty till the last man of you dies there. Forty days you spent exploring the country, and forty years you shall spend—a year for each day—paying the penalty of your iniquities. You shall know what it means to have me against you. I, the Lord, have spoken. This I swear to do to all this wicked community who have combined against me. There shall be an end of them here in this wilderness; here they shall die." But the men whom Moses had sent to explore the land, and who came back and by their report set all the community complaining against him, died of the plague before the Lord; they died of the plague because they had made a bad report. Of those who went to explore the land, Joshua son of Nun and Caleb son of Jephunneh alone remained alive.

When Moses reported the Lord's words to all the Israelites, the people were plunged in grief. They set out early next morning and made for the heights of the hill country, saying, "Look, we are on our way up to the place the Lord spoke of. We admit that we have been wrong." But Moses replied, "Must you persist in disobeying the Lord's command? No good will come of this. Go no further; you will not have the Lord with you, and your enemies will defeat you. For in front of you are the Amalekites and Canaanites, and you will die by the sword, because you have ceased to follow the Lord, and he will no longer be with you." But they went recklessly on their way toward the heights of the hill country, though neither the Ark of the Covenant of the Lord nor Moses moved with them out of the camp; and the Amalekites and Canaanites from those hills came down and fell upon them, and crushed them at Hormah.

NUMBERS 13 : 1–3, 17–33; 14

What more merciful definition of God does Moses suggest to God than we have seen prior to this stage in the biblical narrative? What less severe punishment does God give the Israelites because of this definition? What were God's previous punishments of man?

Why won't Moses' generation of Israelites ever find the garden? How is their fate like Cain's? Can you think of contemporary "wildernesses"?

What I Expected

What I expected was
Thunder, fighting,
Long struggles with men
And climbing.
After continual straining
I should grow strong;
Then the rocks would shake
And I should rest long.

What I had not foreseen
Was the gradual day
Weakening the will
Leaking the brightness away,
The lack of good to touch
The fading of body and soul
Like smoke before wind
Corrupt, unsubstantial.

The wearing of Time,
And the watching of cripples pass
With limbs shaped like questions
In their old twist,
The pulverous grief
Melting the bones with pity,
The sick falling from earth—
These, I could not foresee.

For I had expected always
Some brightness to hold in trust,
Some final innocence
To save from dust;
That, hanging solid,
Would dangle through all
Like the created poem
Or the dazzling crystal.

STEPHEN SPENDER

How does this poem help to explain the difficulty of constant steadfastness
in a situation of subtle conflict? Does it apply to the situation of the Israelites
in the wilderness?

One More River to Cross

CHORUS

Oh, wasn't that a wide riv-er, riv-er of Jor-dan, Lord?

Wide riv-er, there's one more riv-er to cross. 1. Old
2. I

riv-er Jor-dan is so wide, (one more riv-er to
have some friends be-fore me gone, (one more riv-er to

cross), I don't know how to get to the oth-er side;
cross), by grace of God I'll fol-low on;

(one more riv-er to cross).
(one more riv-er to cross).

How does this song suggest that the struggle engaged in by the Israelites still goes on?

The Approach to the Promised Land

In the first month the whole community of Israel reached the wilderness of Zin and stayed some time at Kadesh; there Miriam died and was buried.

There was no water for the community; so they gathered against Moses and Aaron. The people disputed with Moses and said, "If only we had perished when our brothers perished in the presence of the Lord! Why have you brought the assembly of the Lord into this wilderness for us and our beasts to die here? Why did you fetch us up from Egypt to bring us to this vile place, where nothing will grow, neither corn nor figs, vines nor pomegranates? There is not even any water to drink." Moses and Aaron came forward in front of the assembly to the entrance of the Tent of the Presence. There they fell prostrate, and the glory of the Lord appeared to them.

The Lord spoke to Moses and said, "Take a staff, and then with Aaron your brother assemble all the community, and, in front of them all, speak to the rock and it will yield its water. Thus you will produce water for the community out of the rock, for them and their beasts to drink." Moses left the presence of the Lord with the staff, as he had commanded him. Then he and Aaron gathered the assembly together in front of the rock, and he said to them, "Listen to me, you rebels. Must we get water out of this rock for you?" Moses raised his hand and struck the rock twice with his staff. Water gushed out in abundance and they all drank, men and beasts. But the Lord said to Moses and Aaron, "You did not trust me so far as to uphold my holiness in the sight of the Israelites; therefore you shall not lead this assembly into the land which I promised to give them." Such were the waters of Meribah, where the people disputed with the Lord and through which his holiness was upheld.

From Kadesh Moses sent envoys to the king of Edom: "This is a message from your brother Israel. You know all the hardships we have encountered, how our fathers went down to Egypt, and we lived there for many years. The Egyptians ill-treated us and our fathers before us, and we cried to the Lord for help. He listened to us and sent an angel, and he brought us out of Egypt; and now we are here at Kadesh, a town on your frontier. Grant us passage through your country. We will not trespass on field or vineyard, or drink from your wells. We will keep to the king's highway; we will not turn off to right or left until we have crossed your territory." But the Edomites answered, "You shall not cross our land. If you do, we will march out and attack you in force." The Israelites said, "But we will keep to the main road. If we and our flocks drink your water, we will pay you for it; we will simply cross your land on foot." But the Edomites said, "No, you shall not," and took the field against them with a large army in full strength. Thus the Edomites refused to allow Israel to cross their frontier, and Israel went a different way to avoid a conflict.

The whole community of Israel set out from Kadesh and came to Mount Hor. At Mount Hor, near the frontier of Edom, the Lord said to Moses and Aaron, "Aaron shall be gathered to his father's kin. He shall not enter the land which I promised to give the Israelites, because over the waters of Meribah you rebelled against my command. Take Aaron and his son Eleazar, and go up Mount Hor. Strip Aaron of his robes and invest Eleazar his son with them, for Aaron shall be taken from you: he shall die there." Moses did as the Lord had commanded him: they went up Mount Hor in sight of the whole community, and Moses stripped Aaron of his robes and invested his son Eleazar with them. There Aaron died on the mountaintop, and Moses and Eleazar came down from the mountain. So the whole community saw that Aaron had died, and all Israel mourned him for thirty days.

When the Canaanite king of Arad who lived in the Negeb heard that the Israelites were coming by way of Atharim, he attacked them and took some of them prisoners. Israel thereupon made a vow to the Lord and said, "If thou wilt deliver this people into my power, I will destroy their cities." The Lord listened to Israel and delivered the Canaanites into their power. Israel destroyed them and their cities and called the place Hormah.

Then they left Mount Hor by way of the Red Sea to march round the flank of Edom. But on the way they grew impatient and spoke against God and Moses. "Why have you brought us up from Egypt," they said, "to die in the desert where there is neither food nor water? We are heartily sick of this miserable fare." Then the Lord sent poisonous snakes among the people, and they bit the Israelites so that many of them died. The people came to Moses and said, "We sinned when we spoke against the Lord and you. Plead with the Lord to rid us of the snakes." Moses therefore pleaded with the Lord for the people; and the Lord told Moses to make a serpent of bronze and erect it as a standard, so that anyone who had been bitten could look at it and recover. So Moses made a bronze serpent and erected it as a standard, so that when a snake had bitten a man, he could look at the bronze serpent and recover.

NUMBERS 20; 21:1-9

How do water and snakes figure symbolically in this portion of the wilderness story?

Psalm 114

When Israel went out of Egypt,
The house of Jacob from a people of strange language,
Judah was his sanctuary,
And Israel his dominion.
The sea saw it, and fled;
Jordan was driven back;
The mountains skipped like rams,
And the little hills like lambs.
What ailed thee, O thou sea, that thou fleddest?
Thou Jordan, that thou wast driven back?
Ye mountains, that ye skipped like rams;
And ye little hills, like lambs?
Tremble, thou earth, at the presence of the Lord,
At the presence of the God of Jacob;
Which turned the rock into a standing water,
The flint into a fountain of waters.

Why should the earth tremble?

Try listing the people, places, and objects in this psalm according to their acceptance or rejection of God.

The Death
of Moses

Then Moses went up from the lowlands of Moab to Mount Nebo, to the top of Pisgah, eastward from Jericho, and the Lord showed him the whole land: Gilead as far as Dan; the whole of Naphtali; the territory of Ephraim and Manasseh, and all Judah as far as the western sea; the Negeb and the Plain; the valley of Jericho, the Vale of Palm Trees, as far as Zoar. The Lord said to him, "This is the land which I swore to Abraham, Isaac, and Jacob that I would give to their descendants. I have let you see it with your own eyes, but you shall not cross over into it."

There in the land of Moab Moses the servant of the Lord died, as the Lord had said. He was buried in a valley in Moab opposite Beth-peor, but to this day no one knows his burial place. Moses was a hundred and twenty years old when he died; his sight was not dimmed nor had his vigor failed. The Israelites wept for Moses in the lowlands of Moab for thirty days; then the time of mourning for Moses was ended. And Joshua son of Nun was filled with the spirit of wisdom, for Moses had laid his hands on him, and the Israelites listened to him and did what the Lord had commanded Moses.

There has never yet risen in Israel a prophet like Moses, whom the Lord knew face to face: remember all the signs and portents which the Lord sent him to show in Egypt to Pharaoh and all his servants and the whole land; remember the strong hand of Moses and the terrible deeds which he did in the sight of all Israel.

DEUTERONOMY 34

Who is to be Moses' successor and why? Why is Moses unique among the patriarchs of the Pentateuch?

Moses

He left us there, went up to Pisgah hill,
And saw the holiday land, the sabbath land,
The mild prophetic beasts, millennial herds,
The sacred lintel, over-arching tree,
The vineyards glittering on the southern slopes,
And in the midst the shining vein of water,
The river turning, turning toward its home.
Promised to us. The dream rose in his nostrils
With homely smell of wine and corn and cattle,
Byre, barn and stall, sweat-sanctified smell of peace.
He saw the tribes arrayed beside the river,
White robes and sabbath stillness, still light falling
On dark heads whitened by the desert wave,
The Sabbath of Sabbaths come and Canaan their home.
All this he saw in dreaming. But we who dream
Such common dreams and see so little saw
The battle for this land, the massacres,
The vineyards drenched in aboriginal blood,
The settlement, unsatisfactory order,
The petty wars and neighboring jealousies
And local troubles. But we did not see,
We did not see and Moses did not see,
The great disaster, exile, diaspora,
The holy bread of the land crumbled and broken
In Babylon, Caesarea, Alexandria
As on a splendid dish, or gnawed as offal.
Nor did we see, beyond, the ghetto rising,
Toledo, Cracow, Vienna, Budapesth,
Nor, had we seen, would we have known our people
In the wild disguises of fantastic time,
Packed in dense cities, wandering countless roads,
And not a road in the world to lead them home.
How could we have seen such things? How could we have seen
That plot of ground pledged by the God of Moses

Trampled by sequent tribes, seized and forgotten
As a child seizes and forgets a toy,
Strange languages, strange gods and customs borne
Over it and away with the light migrations,
Stirring each century ancestral dust.
All this was settled while we stood by Jordan
That first great day, could not be otherwise.
Moses saw that day only; we did not see it;
But now it stands becalmed in time for ever:
White robes and sabbath peace, the snow-white emblem.

EDWIN MUIR

What dream rose in Moses' nostrils as he looked out over the Promised Land? What do we dream? What do we see? What is it that neither Moses nor we ourselves could see?

How has the poet traced the story of mankind in terms of an original home, an exile, and a homecoming?

———————

A new relationship between brothers comes about in this chapter. What does this tell about Moses as compared to Abel, Shem and Japheth, Isaac, Jacob, and Joseph? How can the relationships of the six sets of brothers be seen as parallel to the developing relationship between God and man?

List the numbers which are used in this chapter and explain their significance. Where have some of them occurred earlier in the biblical story? Why do certain numbers keep recurring throughout?

What images of blood, water, and serpents or other demonic creatures are in this chapter? How do the biblical writers use them?

Here is another brief dictionary of some of the names in this chapter.

Aaron: enlightened, illumined
Eleazar: God my help
Jehovah: The Lord

Joshua: God saves
Miriam: fat, thick, strong
Moses: one who is drawn
out

What is the significance of each of these names in terms of what the characters *are* and *do* in their stories?

Typically a hero experiences a mysterious birth; goes through a withdrawal and initiation period; sees visions and hears voices; travels a perilous journey to undertake a quest where he takes part in a fierce struggle; dies; and is in some way reborn or memorialized. Can you see any or all of these stages of a hero's life in the stories of the patriarchal heroes of this book?

A VERY PRESENT HELP
IN TROUBLE

God is our refuge and strength,
A very present help in trouble.
Therefore will not we fear, though the earth be removed,
And though the mountains be carried into the midst of
    the sea;
Though the waters thereof roar and be troubled,
Though the mountains shake with the swelling thereof.
There is a river, the streams whereof shall make glad the
    city of God,
The holy place of the tabernacles of the most High.
God is in the midst of her; she shall not be moved:
God shall help her, and that right early.
The heathen raged, the kingdoms were moved;
He uttered his voice, the earth melted.
The Lord of hosts is with us;
The God of Jacob is our refuge.
Come, behold the works of the Lord,
What desolations he hath made in the earth.
He maketh wars to cease unto the end of the earth;
He breaketh the bow, and cutteth the spear in sunder;
He burneth the chariot in the fire.
"Be still, and know that I am God:
I will be exalted among the heathen,
I will be exalted in the earth."
The Lord of hosts is with us;
The God of Jacob is our refuge.

PSALM 46

The chapters of this book follow the overall story
pattern of the first five books of the Bible, known
as the Pentateuch (from the Greek, meaning "five
books"). The Pentateuch is most basically a narrative, whose framework presents the story of God's
people from the time of Creation until the point
at which, led by Joshua, they are ready to enter their
Promised Land.

The kernel of the Pentateuch narrative is Israel's

descent into Egypt and her return to the Promised Land. The "hero" of the story is both God and Israel as a whole. Individual champions act as God's representatives. The story is primarily a story of redemption: despite Israel's disobedience and lack of faith, the chosen leaders redeem her from her sufferings.

We have seen already, in the story of Jacob's ladder, how the constant attempt of Israel was to "climb over her enemies" and go directly to the source of all power, God. This fifth chapter makes the point even more strongly and clearly. The law of Moses was, for Israel, the law of God. In dealing with all things, human and natural, through the law, Israel was regarding everything that surrounded her as a means of reaching God. The law symbolizes the proper and harmonious order of things; through the law, Israel will achieve the strength to cope with the Egyptians and the alien Canaanite tribes, with the parched droughts of the desert and the rigorous demands of the shepherd's life. When she departs from the law, she is punished.

The effect of the law is to humanize. The Hebrews believed that the Promised Land was being given to them and taken away from the Canaanites because the Canaanites still practiced the cult of slaughter of their first-born. For the Jews, the first-born still belongs to God, but its blood could be redeemed by substituting the blood of an animal. The story of the sacrifice of Isaac was told to symbolize and preserve Israel's humane insight. Isaac's story therefore illustrates Israel's concern for human life and teaches that animals should be sacrificed, not children. While we study the story of Isaac for literary purposes, the work itself derives from religious, moral, and nationalistic elements as well. Literature is always *about* something. The story of Isaac is about a great leap taken by man's mind, the leap taken when a nation substitutes animal slaughter for human sacrifice.

The blood of the lamb became a hallmark of this crucial biblical insight, and the image has lived on in western literature ever since. In Egypt, the Hebrew found himself subjected to systematic, tyrannical slavery, and to the eventual death of his people as an independent nation. Moses escaped from Pharaoh's ritual murder of the first-born by being conveyed to safety in an ark (the watertight basket); after meeting with God on the mountaintop, he returned to lead his people to redemption. At the turning point of the story, the first-born of Egypt were all slain and the first-born of the Hebrews were spared because the doorways of their homes were smeared with the blood of the lamb. Thus the Exodus narrative also is a story of redemption from human sacrifice. The first-born still belongs to God, but the life of the lamb is offered instead, and the blood of the lamb becomes the symbol of redemption.

A simple diagram of the Pentateuch looks something like this:

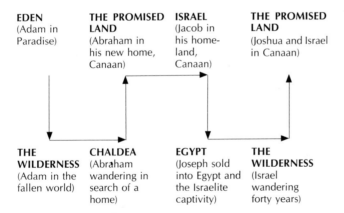

EDEN
(Adam in Paradise)

THE PROMISED LAND
(Abraham in his new home, Canaan)

ISRAEL
(Jacob in his home-land, Canaan)

THE PROMISED LAND
(Joshua and Israel in Canaan)

THE WILDERNESS
(Adam in the fallen world)

CHALDEA
(Abraham wandering in search of a home)

EGYPT
(Joseph sold into Egypt and the Israelite captivity)

THE WILDERNESS
(Israel wandering forty years)

In this chart, everything across the top line is metaphorically and symbolically the same; this is also true of everything across the bottom line. The top line is divine (the garden) and the bottom line is demonic (the wilderness) if we read the symbols as the biblical writers intended.

317

We have suggested that the most effective way of understanding biblical realities is to look inside our own minds, instead of starting with the notion that something "out there" is being studied. The realities of biblical literature are imaginative realities, visions in which what is expressed is an inseparable mixture of things as they *are* and things as they *could be*.

We also suggested that you can think of yourself as an ark, as a way of getting the whole world inside your own head so that you can imaginatively cope with it. You can also think of your mind as a wilderness or prison. Most people do feel, at least some of the time, as though they were in bondage, as though they were enslaved by all sorts of circumstances and feelings. It is by thinking of oneself in this way that the central thrust of biblical literature is felt most immediately and deeply. It is a literature which expresses a basic human effort, the effort toward liberation and redemption, freedom, peace, and justice. The writers of the Bible, as well as other writers, have liberated their minds and have been able, through their literature, to communicate something of that liberation to their readers. The basic narrative of a quest for a promised land will continue as long as literature lasts. In the mind of every man there is always one more mountain to climb, one more river to cross.

Index of Authors and Titles